GOD
Truths

Steven K. Dunn

THREE SKILLET

GOD TRUTHS, Dunn, Steven K.

First Edition

God Truths, Book 1
Collected and Edited by Steven K. Dunn

☗☗☗ THREE SKILLET

www.ThreeSkilletPublishing.com

Cover design by Farley L. Dunn

A Fresh Look

I did not write the devotions in this book.

I should have been so fortunate, for they speak masterfully to our modern-day lives, our days filled with stumbling blocks unknown to the Early Church. Each entry references Scripture in an easily under-standable way that rings true to the intent of the Holy Word.

This book acts as a spiritual loadstone that points to the Father as the Author of our faith, the Son as His Emissary to humanity, and the Holy Spirit as the Enabler of our salvation. Start reading at any point in the year, and by the time you've absorbed each edifying morsel, you will feel closer to God. You will sense a deeper understanding of the Word, and you will be better prepared to hear the whisper of the Master's voice when He speaks to you.

In a crisis, pull out this book. When the birds sing, open its pages. At prayer time, return to your favorite passages. Make notes, underline, mark up the margins. Make these devotions yours, and they will stay with you for the rest of your life.

Steven K. Dunn

— January —

January 1 – 6 Excuses for Tossing Out Your Old Life

AT THE START of the new year, we want to grasp the chance for a new start. It's all around us, and we don't want to miss out. The **old year out** and the **new year in**. We vow this one will be different. We can see the **end of winter**, and we look **forward to spring**. It's our promise of new life. We even experience this fresh start in our finances. Many businesses (and Uncle Sam!) conclude the fiscal year at the end of December. January is our opportunity to **strike out in a newly responsible direction**.

Here's what God's Word says about tossing out your old life when you come to Christ.

Isaiah 43:18-19 says we no longer must **worry about our past**. "Remember not the former things, nor consider the things of old. Behold, I am doing a new thing; now it springs forth, do you not perceive it? I will make a way in the wilderness and rivers in the desert."

Lamentations 3:22-23 assures us we will be continually **refreshed in Jesus**. "The steadfast love of the Lord never ceases; his mercies never come to an end; they are new every morning; great is your faithfulness."

Ezekiel 11:18-19 is our promise we will become **kinder, warmer people**. "And when they come there, they will remove from it all its detestable things and all its abominations. And I will give them one heart, and a new spirit I will put within them. I will remove the heart of stone from their flesh and give them a heart of flesh."

Romans 6:3-4 tells us we are following in the **footsteps of Jesus**. "Do you not know that all of us who have been baptized into Christ Jesus were baptized into his death? We were buried therefore with him by baptism into death, in order that, just as Christ was raised from the dead by the glory of the Father, we too might walk in newness of life."

2 Corinthians 5:17 says we are **made brand new** through our salvation. "Therefore, if anyone is in Christ, he is a new creation. The old has passed away; behold, the new has come."

Philippians 3:13-14 points to our goal, which is **Christ and our heavenly reward**. "Brothers, I do not consider that I have made it my own. But one thing I do: forgetting what lies behind and straining forward to what lies ahead, I press on toward the goal for the prize of the upward call of God in Christ Jesus."

Our **old life out** and our **new one in. We are different than before.** We can see the end of the disaster we were, and we **look forward to the promise** of new life. From our family and friends to our finances, there's no reason to keep what we were when we can become what Jesus wants us to be. There's no excuse. It's time to connect with Jesus today.

January 2 – Bringing Down the Curtain

VISIT A STAGE performance. From a distance, the backdrops, stage, and **all the trappings seem human-sized**. Yet, step to the curtain, and try to pull it aside, and you'll find it's a heavy thing, **often the height of a house**, and it blocks any attempts to see through to the other side. **Anything can be going on behind that curtain, and the viewers won't know.** The stage crew can be building a vast scene of backdrops and fakery, and we'll have no idea until the curtains are opened wide.

What are we hiding behind the curtains we present to the world? What are we constructing behind the curtains of our public persona that we want to **keep hidden from everyone else?**

Proverbs 26:12 says: "Do you see a man who is wise in his own eyes? There is more hope for a fool than for him."

We need to live a curtain-free life, theater-in-the-round. Every part of who we are **must be on display for everyone to see**. **It's proof of our calling in Christ.** It's how we prove to the world that we truly love him.

Let's toss our curtains aside and fully love the lost for Jesus.

January 3 – God's Dog Tags

WHAT'S THE USE of dog tags? Obvious, you say. Certainly, for our pets, but **what about the ones worn by humans? Yes, human dog tags.** The sort **soldiers wear**. What's the use of those dog tags?

It's to identify the soldier as belonging to the army of their choice. If they are injured or (God forbid) killed, **we want to know where to send them so they can receive their just reward.**

1 Corinthians 3:22-23 tells us this applies to the soldiers in God's army, also. "Whether Paul or Apollos or Cephas or the world or life or death or the present or the future—all are yours, and you are Christ's, and Christ is God's."

You've got your dog tags on! They are seen **in the life you live**, the **words you say**, and your **weekly church attendance**. Your prayers … **your trust in God** … your cool head when trouble comes your way. **Those are the dog tags you wear.** When you are injured in your work for the Lord, or it's time for you to travel home, **your dog tags are your ticket to your just reward**.

We boast of Jesus because he has claimed us for his own.

January 4 – God Awaits Your Return

AN ADORABLE four-panel, hand-drawn storyboard recently appeared on a social media site. A woman reaches her hand out to a dog. The dog barks, calling, "Welcome home."

The woman asks, "What did you do today?"

The dog sits on its haunches and barks, saying, "I waited for you."

The fourth and final panel is the most touching. The dog's red tongue appears, and he looks up at the woman, saying, **"You are all I have."**

We leave the house for the day, meet friends and coworkers, and we return. Our pet is a small part of our day.

We are every part of our pet's day. Their lives are all about us. **God's focus on us is just as powerful.**

Isaiah 51:11 tells us: "And the ransomed of the Lord shall return and come to Zion with singing; everlasting joy shall be upon their heads; they shall obtain gladness and joy, and sorrow and sighing shall flee away."

Some people read this verse to celebrate God's blessing when we return to him. **It's so much more.** This verse tells us how much God anticipates our arrival when we remember **how important we are to him**.

God looks at us and says, "I waited for you."

God blesses us because he loves us. We are his children, and that's **good enough reason for him**.

When God is our everything, the way we see life changes completely.

January 5 – 2 Ways to Foster Love

RAISING KIDS is tough. It's easy to let them **get under our skin**. Our last nerve gets bamboozled, and we want to react, and **not always in a good way**. God says, **"Hold on to your taters."**

You see, **God understands a better way**. Ephesians 6:4 tells us: "Fathers, do not provoke your children to anger, but bring them up in the discipline and instruction of the Lord."

Harsh words create resentment. Love eases our child's path to adulthood. Otherwise, we will foster a prickly personality that will hardly show God's love.

Our 1st Way to Foster Love: *We need to nurture.* Show kindness. **Be gentle.**

Our 2nd Way to Foster Love: *We must guide them to right living.* We do that with **our example that reflects the love of God**.

Our children will learn to love when they are shown kindness and concern.

January 6 – 3 Occasions Sickness Was Defeated

WE ARE HUMAN. We live in bodies of **flesh and bone.** We are born, gifted with a span of time, and come to our end.

That's the way of being human. That's who we are, and there's no way to take our journey another direction. **No one gets forever on the face of the earth**. It's not in the cards, nor would we want it to be. We must clear the way for the next generation to come to the forefront, just as our parents and grandparents before us.

Yet, the rough patches, **the days of sickness**, are unwelcome. They are sandpaper on exposed bone. No one looks forward to illness in any shape or form. God's Word gives us **3 Occasions Sickness Was Defeated** by the power of the almighty God. Let's look at these one at a time.

The 1st Occasion Sickness Was Defeated: Matthew 4:23-24 says Jesus healed **all manner of diseases**, including palsy and those of the mind. "… So his fame spread … and [Jesus] healed them."

The 2nd Occasion Sickness Was Defeated: Matthew 9:6-7 says the man confined to his bed was told to **get up and walk**, and he did, **healed by the power of Jesus**. "… Rise, pick up your bed and go home …"

The 3rd Occasion Sickness Was Defeated: Matthew 9:28-30 says the blind received their sight because they **believed on the power of the Master to heal them**. "… [Jesus] touched their eyes, saying, 'According to your faith be it done to you.' And their eyes were opened."

We won't live forever, but **God is with us on our journey**. He comforts us and offers healing to **those who ask in faith and trust**

10

in his name. Be like the man who couldn't walk or like those who couldn't see. Ask of Jesus and **place your faith in him as your healer** and your redeemer.

Jesus is our solace, and our journey is eased when our faith is rooted in him.

January 7 – A Good Reason to Hope in God

MUCKY BOOTS ARE part of being a Christian. It's a human thing. Gunk will be **everywhere we walk**, and as followers of Christ, our duty is to ensure **it's regularly washed away**.

We must be "washed white as snow" when we choose to walk with Jesus. Our "washing" comes by the **blood shed on the cross** and is symbolized **by the water baptism**. We go under as the old man (mucky boots) and come up new (white as snow).

That should be exciting. Here's how Romans 5:5 renders the scene: "And hope does not put us to shame, because God's love has been poured into our hearts through the Holy Spirit who has been given to us."

Let's reword this verse like this: "And hope **lets us stand proud**, because God's love has been poured into our hearts through the Holy Spirit who has been given to us."

Mucky boots gone! The gunk of the world down the drain! We've gone through the power wash, **the deep-clean cycle**, and we're coming up smelling like roses for the Lord. **That's a clean we want to share with the world.** The reason we can hope in God? As the verse says, "the Holy Spirit … has been given to us." Whoop, whoop! **Shout with joy! Our time to rejoice in Christ has come!**

Today's our day to have a good reason to hope in God.

January 8 – 9 Things About God, the Powerful and Great

SOME DOUBT THAT God exists. Others say he's **unknowable, incomprehensible, enigmatic**. We have an entire volume of books and letters dedicated to him, and yet he is described simply as the GREAT I AM. **Can we know the true nature of God?**

Exodus 34:6-7 gives us a good idea. "The Lord passed before him and proclaimed, 'The Lord, the Lord, a God merciful and gracious, slow to anger, and abounding in steadfast love and faithfulness, keeping steadfast love for thousands, forgiving iniquity and transgression and sin, but who will by no means clear the guilty, visiting the iniquity of the fathers on the children and the children's children, to the third and the fourth generation.' "

Here's what we learn about God: 1. He is merciful. *He forgives us when he doesn't have to.* 2. He is gracious. *He treats us in a kind manner, as a friend.* 3. He is slow to anger. *He puts up with our nonsense.* 4. He abounds in steadfast love. *He looks on us with adoring eyes.* 5. He also abounds in faithfulness. *He supports our efforts to live for him.* 6. He has steadfast love for thousands. *This is generations ... a thousand generations.* 7. He forgives iniquity, transgression and sin. *He only asks that we repent.*

We also learn of God's no-nonsense side: 8. He will not clear the guilty. *We must want his forgiveness to receive it.* 9. He visits our wrongdoing on our children and grandchildren. *He holds humanity accountable.*

Go ahead. **Say that God doesn't exist.** Say he's **unknowable, incomprehensible, and enigmatic. It won't change the truth.** God is the GREAT I AM, powerful and great, and **his nature is revealed in the Word of God**.

Look up to God. He's there, waiting on us to find him.

January 9 – **God's Giveaway Rule**

HERE'S A FUNNY quip we see on t-shirts and gag gifts: **The one who dies with the most toys wins.** That's funny, but it's not God's way. God says **the opposite is true.** Here's **God's Giveaway Rule** in Luke 6:38. "Give, and it will be given to you. Good measure, pressed down, shaken together, running over, will be put into your lap. For with the measure you use it will be measured back to you."

It's not the one that dies with the most toys that wins. It's the one that's **given the most toys away.** That pool you put in. **How many times did you encourage your Sunday school class to come use it?** Your new car. **Did you give anyone a ride to church ... and how often?** Your raise at work. **Did any of it go to missions? More than ten percent?**

God's giveaway rule says that **the more you give away, *the more God will give back to you.*** Your generosity will **nourish generosity in others. One good deed will precipitate a second.** Your brotherly love will spread with growth so vigorous that **not even the devil will be able to slow it down.**

God gives to us so that we can share our surplus with those around us. When we live generously, life is better for everyone.

January 10 – **Our Answer Through Prayer**

GOT A NEED and no answer? **Is your car on its last legs?** Have you charged your cards to the limit? **Are you ready to throw things out the window?** Here's something for you to try: **Prayer.**

There's a secret to prayer, though, one that's **vital for you to learn. Prayer is not magic. We can't pray and expect our answer to appear**. Let's look at Matthew 21:22: "And whatever you ask in prayer, you will receive, if you have faith."

Here's the key: **Believe. Again, not magic.** This is an **attitude … a viewpoint-changing behavior.**

Here's how it works: 1. We admit that we have a desire for our circumstances to change. 2. We commit that desire into prayer with God. 3. We resolve (believe) that from this moment forward, our change is starting. 4. We become aware of and open to opportunities to bring about our desired change. 5. We begin living out the new life promised us by God.

So, come on. **Give it a try. Prayer will work for you.** Give God a chance. He'll come through for you today.

January 11 – **4 Considerations for Respecting Others**

THE TEN COMMANDMENTS are straight from the Bible. God's rules. *The Almighty's guide for living a righteous life.* Yet, there's not much there about *how to treat those we live with each day.* Well, nothing, really. It's all not, not, not … apart from the fourth one, to honor your father and your mother. The rest, yah, it *sets up fences we're not to break through.*

The letters to the Thessalonians in the New Testament *diverge from that tradition* and *set our personal guidelines in order.* 1 Thessalonians 4:9 says: "Now concerning brotherly love you have no need for anyone to write to you, for you yourselves have been taught by God to love one another."

Wait, you cry. This doesn't teach us anything. It only says *it doesn't need to teach us*. Something's missing here, like the **instructions for respecting those around us**.

There's the flaw in your reasoning. See, we have the New Testament, an entire tome chock full of how to love (respect) one another. How did Jesus say it in Matthew 7:12? "So whatever you wish that others would do to you, do also to them, for this is the Law and the Prophets."

13

There, the New Testament and the Old summed up in one sentence, giving us *4 Considerations for Respecting Others*. **Consideration No. 1:** *Don't be partial.* (James 2:9) **Consideration No. 2:** *Pay what you owe.* (Romans 13:7) **Consideration No. 3:** *Mind the law of the land.* (Hebrews 13:17) **Consideration No. 4:** *Share the credit.* (Philippians 2:3)

There they are. The Bible is *chock full of more*. Get in there. Read it. Be the kind person God wants you to be. Respect is at the core of our Christian walk. Never compromise how you treat others.

January 12 – The Seesaw of Choice

CHOICE. IS IT CONSCIOUS, meaning, can we **change the probability of something happening**, or is our choice **determined by the very probability of us choosing** this thing or that? In other words, if we have a plate of candies, red, blue, and yellow, are we bound to **choose certain colors in a predictable pattern?** Probability says yes. A certain percentage of people will choose each color, regardless of their individual choices. **How does that apply to salvation?** Will a certain number of people ALWAYS travel the broad road to destruction, **no matter how urgently we spread the gospel of Christ?** Do our efforts make a difference? **Or does probability carry a heavier weight than choice?** Psalm 145:20 reveals why this question is so important. "The Lord preserves all who love him, but all the wicked he will destroy." **ALL.** The Lord preserves ALL who love him. Anyone who makes the choice for salvation … that's right, you … God will **preserve, keep safe, and welcome into his arms** when your time on Earth is done.

Everyone else, well, **read the verse again**. It's pretty clear. **We're all on the seesaw of choice.** Up or down, **Christ or the world. Choose now.** It's your time. **You can set probability aside when you invite Jesus to be part of your life.** Your Heavenly reservation is assured when you pick Jesus as your Savior and Lord.

January 13 – 3 Calls to Worship from Psalms

THE MODERN THING is to **Celebrate Us!** Cheer on the **Things We've Done Right!** Whoop! Whoop! Let's gather around for a party because **We're the Best We Can Be!**

All that's okay, but there's a fly in the ointment, something that **takes a little of the gleam off the chrome. We can't afford to forget that our success comes from God.** We find *3 Calls to*

14

Worship from Psalms.

Our 1st Call: Psalm 66:4 says we are **to recognize the Almighty as our source of strength**, our position of power, and our reason for redemption. "All the earth worships you and sings praises to you; they sing praises to your name." **Let's jump and cheer for our glorious King!**

Our 2nd Call: Psalm 95:6-7 tells us to **kneel before God**. Our place is under him, and we must concede his state of supremacy. "Oh come, let us worship and bow down; let us kneel before the Lord, our Maker! For he is our God, and we are the people of his pasture, and the sheep of his hand." **When we fall to our knees, God lifts us up to stand by him.**

Our 3rd Call: Psalm 99:9 is our call to **sing praises unto our Holy God**, for he is eternally deserving of our fervent worship. "Exalt the Lord our God, and worship at his holy mountain; for the Lord our God is holy!" **Join in a rousing hymn. Link arms with other believers. Let God hear your voice of praise.**

Our praise starts in our hearts, but if it's not seen on our face, it's doubtful it's there at all.

January 14 – Turning the Soil for Our Spring Garden

WINTER IS a time of rest for the landscape. Many types of trees lose their leaves, flowers no longer bloom (or even die back), and the grass **becomes brown and brittle**. That seems like a good thing for the gardener. A season of rest, maybe some relaxation, even a trip to a warmer clime to **take a break from our chores**.

That's well and good, but under that winter scene, weeds are doing what they do, germinating and preparing to burst forth at the first hint of spring's warmth. **If we don't turn the soil during winter, we won't be prepared for our spring garden.**

Spiritually we must be as the diligent gardener. Read in Mark 6:12 how we are to turn our spiritual soil. "So they went out and proclaimed that people should repent."

Sometimes we say that people have **turned over a new leaf**. Maybe our new saying needs to be, **"He just turned over a new clod of dirt."**

That's sounds comical, but for the gardener it makes perfect sense. When we turn the soil, we **upset the germination process**, and we **defeat the weeds before they can begin to grow**. When we give people the opportunity to change from their wrongdoing to a better way of living, we've **uprooted the sins already growing** in their lives and **interrupted the germination process of many more**.

One caution: *We don't dump herbicide on our garden to eliminate the weeds.* That will do it, certainly, but it **kills all the good plants**, too. We must be selective, adding our weed killer carefully, so we only remove the things that shouldn't be there.

Our call to repent should be the same. We must state our position judiciously. We can't risk driving people away by dousing them with sin-i-cide.

Jesus taught in kindness, with **welcoming words and good deeds**. Let's be like Jesus and draw the world unto him.

January 15 – Life as a Dandelion

TODAY'S TITLE is puzzling. Life as a dandelion? Aren't dandelions weeds? We certainly try to eradicate them from the garden.

Here's the thing about dandelions: 1. They are a good source of nutrition. 2. They spread willingly and rapidly. 3. Once they put down roots, they are difficult to disturb. They grow right back.

That's how we need to live as Christians. 1. We must feed the hungry with the good news of Christ. 2. We must be willing to minister to as many as God sends our way. 3. We must be firmly rooted in the Word and in the teachings of Christ.

Romans 5:15 speaks to our dandelion life with authority: "But the free gift is not like the trespass. For if many died through one man's trespass, much more have the grace of God and the free gift by the grace of that one man Jesus Christ abounded for many."

It's time to get rooted in God that *many may be gifted with the good gift of salvation.*

Christ isn't just for us. He's for all of us.

January 16 – God's Very Good Gift

WE LOVE the squeal of delight when we give a gift to a child. As parents, it warms us inside to know we've **given our child a moment of joy**. As a grandparent, the feeling is even better. We've formed a **deeper connection with someone we love**. The act of giving is as important as the receiving. **We get as much out of the gift as the child who receives it.**

Why would God not want to give us his good gifts? The Word says we are formed in his image. We are modeled after him, **our emotions, thoughts, the things that drive us forward. What gives**

us joy motivates God, also.

Luke 11:13 tells us: "If you then, who are evil, know how to give good gifts to your children, how much more will the heavenly Father give the Holy Spirit to those who ask him!"

Who's saying these words? Is it someone who knows, or is someone **shooting the breeze,** talking just to fill the time? In this verse, we find **Jesus sharing his heart.** He's taught the disciples the Lord's Prayer, and now he's presenting **important spiritual lessons to his followers.**

Are you seeing this? **God's Son is talking.** Jesus knows how his Father **feels, reacts, and views humanity. We are God's children, and the Father wants to give good gifts to us.** The very good gift from this verse is the Holy Spirit, **ready for those who ask.** Step out in faith. Ask for the Spirit to come into your life today. God's good gift is for you.

January 17 – 7 Ways to Honor Your Parents

THIS IS A SIMPLE instruction directly from the Word of God. There's no waffling about, no hem-hawing, *no way to get out of it if we want to claim to be a Christian.* Luke 18:20 spells it out. "You know the commandments: 'Do not commit adultery, Do not murder, Do not steal, Do not bear false witness, Honor your father and mother.' "

The first four of these are obvious. We wouldn't sleep around, not and keep a clear conscience. Murder? Theft? To blatantly mislead someone with lies? *Too horrible to contemplate. Yet, honoring our parents seems harder, less distinct, more difficult to pin a face on.*

How do we honor our parents? Here are 7 ways:

1. *Show them your gratitude with flowers once a month.*
2. Call them on the phone to chat. Every week. About nothing.
3. *Ask them their opinion and respect it. It may be fuddy-duddy, but it is theirs.*
4. Pray for their needs. Let them know you did and ask them how things turned out.
5. *Encourage them with cards, social media posts, and small gifts.*
6. Don't bring up old hurts. Forgive them. Start each day fresh.
7. *Speak of and about them positively, even in private. What better honor can you give?*

That's a good start, *7 Ways to Honor Your Parents*. Make a list. *Check them off*. Get started today. Honor your parents, and you'll find that God will honor you.

January 18 – You Are Not Forgotten

ARE YOU AFRAID to open your blinds? Is your mailbox **empty of anything that matters?** Do you even remember the last time your doorbell rang? **It seems life consists of losing things that we value.** Youth. Possessions. Friends. Financial security. We post on our social media account, "Anyone out there?" We feel the **richness of life**, the **joy of living**, the **companionship of friends and family** has evaporated. We are bankrupt in our heart.

Why bother crawling out of bed, we moan, as we turn the alarm off once again. God says, "Chin up! **I remember your name. I know who you are.** I am there for you **in the dark and the light**, in the **bad and the good**, in the times of lack and the times of plenty." Read of God's promise in Psalm 9:18: "For the needy shall not always be forgotten, and the hope of the poor shall not perish forever."

Has your joy account become drained? You are not forgotten. Have your investments in your friends gone topsy-turvy? God is your hope. Has your family depleted your emotional accounts? **You may be poor at the moment**, but God's investment in you will yield bountiful rewards. Look up, look up. **Your God is on the horizon**, and your turnabout is on the way. You are never without a friend when you walk with the Lord.

January 19 – You Are Given Perfection in God

WHO'S SPREADING rumors about you? **Let it go. You are given perfection in God.** Who called you names to bring you down? **They aren't worth your energy. You are given perfection in God.** Those circumstances you're caught up in? **They aren't who you are. You are given perfection in God.** That failed relationship? Your child, arrested again? **That's not you, says the Word of God. You are better than anything that can come against you. God created you to live in his perfection.** Deuteronomy 25:15 says: "A full and fair weight you shall have, a full and fair measure you shall have, that your days may be long in the land that the Lord your God is giving you."

The treasured King James Version of the Holy Bible says you

will have **"a perfect and just weight."** What is a perfect and just weight? **Everything you deserve.** Did you read that or just skim it? God's Word says **you will have everything you deserve.** If you're really taking this in, **you should be excited by now.** God is giving you everything you deserve and a long life to enjoy it. **That sounds like perfection in anyone's book.**

Let's move **out of our sad times and into our glad times.** Let's partner with the Lord. We are better with God than without him. He is our daily dose of perfection.

January 20 – 5 Marks of the True Christian

IT'S EASY TO say, "If … then." If you behave in this certain way, then I'll feel that way toward you. In other words, if you measure up, I'll give you my love. **That's not the Christian way.** Romans 12:9-10 tells us: "Let love be genuine. Abhor what is evil; hold fast to what is good. Love one another with brotherly affection. Outdo one another in showing honor." Let's go one step further. This passage is titled in the English Standard Version as **Marks of the True Christian.**

So, what are the marks of the true Christian? Let's list them. **1. Our love, concern, and interest in others must be genuine.** *2. We must genuinely hate and avoid evil.* **3. We must cling to good living like our life depends on it.** *4. We must have affection for our fellow believers.* **5. We must go out of our way to honor those who fellowship with us.**

If we're not doing these things, **how are we different from the world?** Let's show our true selves, and let's do it with love.

January 21 – Let's Talk About Spiritual Gifts

YOU KNOW about natural gifts in music, sports or the arts. **We refer to successful people as "talented or gifted in one or more areas in life."** One person might look under the hood of a car and **intuitively understand what to do,** while someone else might **effortlessly express themselves on paper.** Then there are chefs, financial wizards, and artists who excel without seeming to try.

Spiritual gifts are very different and expressed through your natural gifts (or talents). You **plant churches** using your natural gift of carpentry. You **serve as a church administrator** through your natural gift of leadership. You **guide people in understanding of the Word** through your natural teaching gifts or abilities.

19

Here are 8 ways to understand spiritual gifts.

1. There are at least 22 spiritual gifts listed in the Bible, with 6 identified as the Gifts of the Spirit in Isaiah 11:2-3 and 9 listed in 1 Corinthians 12:8-10.
2. Every believer has a gift. (1 Corinthians 12:6-7)
3. You receive your gift(s) when you accept Jesus as your savior. (2 Timothy 1:6)
4. Spiritual gifts can be lost, just like any natural talent that goes undeveloped. (Matthew 25:14-30)
5. Spiritual gifts can be used carelessly and decimate your walk with Christ. (1 Corinthians 14)
6. Some spiritual gifts are of higher value, but you can't allow pride to shadow your spiritual talents. (1 Corinthians 12:31)
7. You can't pick and choose your gifts. They are given at the discretion of the Holy Spirit. (1 Corinthians 12:7)
8. Your spiritual gifts will mature through practice and training. (Romans 12:4-6)

Here are 5 questions you can ask to discover your gifts from the Holy Spirit.

1. Have I prayed for direction in finding my gifts?
2. Where am I being successful in my Christian ministry?
3. What gifts do other people remark on (or see) in my life?
4. Which gifts jump out at me when I read the list in 1 Corinthians 12:8-10?
5. Do I enjoy practicing those gifts?

In 1 Timothy 4:14 in the New International Version of the Bible, Paul advises: "Do not neglect your gift, which was given you through prophecy when the body of elders laid their hands on you." Practicing your spiritual gifts will provide opportunities for the Holy Spirit to help you excel as the new person you've become. **God wants you to succeed. Recognizing your spiritual gifts is key to your success.**

January 22 – **God Notices You**

THERE ARE A lot of people on our planet. Earth teems with her billions, **nearly eight of them in 2020**. It's easy to get lost in the crowd. Amazon's publishing arm, Kindle Paperbacks and Kindle E-Books, releases **100,000 new and never before published titles** *each month*. New authors are like **minnows in a sea heaving with a vast moray of bigger fish. How can God keep track of us?**

Try finding your car in a mall parking lot. Or attend a sports venue with 50,000 other fans. Your much-loved mode of transportation becomes **lost in a field of glittering glass and rainbow paint**. There are more stars in the Universe than we can write without using cryptic mathematical terms. **2 x 10^{23} stars. It blows the thinking process.** Yet, **and here's the majesty of our God: W**e are noticed by the great Creator of the cosmos. Psalm 9:12 tells us: "For he who avenges blood is mindful of them; he does not forget the cry of the afflicted."

Life can beat us down, and **God sees our pain**. Our finances can crumble, and **God knows our exhaustion**. People can turn on us, and still ... still ... God steps to us and says, **"I hear your prayer of need."** *God notices you.* Let's repeat that. *God notices you.* You are special in his eyes, and **he loves you completely**.

Never give up on God, because he never gives up on you.

January 23 – God's Unbroken Embrace

LIVING IN A military neighborhood is tough. On one hand, being military, people's yards are **uncluttered and well-kept**. Neighbors are **sociable and tolerant of differences. Cookouts are neighborhood affairs.** On the other hand, deployments **leave loved ones behind**. Last minute hugs, that **final kiss before the plane** is boarded, the children **waving to the sky as long as they can see the contrail**. We feel abandoned by those we love, even if we know they have no choice but to do as the government commands.

God assures us his arms never leave us. He is there in every trial we face, every situation that threatens to consume us, and during the **lonely moments when we feel abandoned**. Jeremiah 31:3 says: "The Lord [says,] I have loved you with an everlasting love; therefore I have continued my faithfulness to you." Reread those four words: **"with an everlasting love."** Is your gizzard sparking with God's glory? Are you ready to shout God's love from the top of a radio tower? Do you feel you can hardly keep it in?

Let's say it again. God loves us with a love that is everlasting. It never ends, doesn't fade, will not go away, and is available 24/7. God assures us his faithfulness is for always, and will continue in an unbroken line until the end of existence. When we can't see past the moment, God looks at forever, and **his arms are still around us.**

We are eternally held in God's unbroken embrace.

January 24 – God Wants to Give You Wisdom

ARE YOU UNSURE of tomorrow? Do you need insight in how to move ahead? You're confused about **your relationships, your finances, and God's place in your life? You have a wisdom generator waiting on you.** God wants to give you **more wisdom than you think you can contain.** James 1:5-6 says: "If any of you lacks wisdom, let him ask God, who gives generously to all without reproach, and it will be given him. But let him ask in faith, with no doubting, for the one who doubts is like a wave of the sea that is driven and tossed by the wind."

You must break out your faith to kick your wisdom generator into action. You can't **waver or waffle.** You can't **believe today and backtrack tomorrow.** *First*, you simply "ask God, who gives generously to all," for direction in the choices you make. **Read your Bible to learn the nature of God.** Then be open to God's prompting. *Second*, you must "ask in faith, with no doubting." Otherwise you will be **tossed by the wind and never find your anchor of confidence.** Don't let Doubting Thomases and Second-guess Susies get you sidetracked. *Third*, move out **on the promises of God.** Step into your new direction. Trust in God's foresight to lead you into a better tomorrow.

God is lifting you up. Release what's holding you back and trust in the Lord.

January 25 – 2 Words of Grace

GRACE IS A learned thing. No one comes by it naturally. We see it in others, **experience it when we've stumbled,** and are grateful when we receive it. **Yet, it's harder to practice when it's our turn to show it.**

Merriam-Webster tells us grace is **unmerited divine assistance.** Here's the key word in Webster's definition. **Unmerited.** Webster's definition for unmerited is **not earned and not deserved.**

Whoa! That means grace is … **free?** For everyone? **Anytime?** If we can't earn it, and we don't deserve it, and yet we receive it anyway … **it's good to be on the receiving end.**

How do we learn to give out grace to those around us, people who **haven't earned our assistance and definitely don't deserve it?** Here are **2 Words of Grace from the Word of God.**

Our 1st Word of Grace: 2 Peter 1:5 says **our faith in God will lead us to the knowledge of grace.** "For this very reason, make every effort to supplement your faith with virtue, and virtue with knowledge."

Our 2nd Word of Grace: Job 17:9 tells us to **live according to the teachings of the Word.** "Yet the righteous holds to his way, and he who has clean hands grows stronger and stronger."

Showing grace can be a challenge. It's only grace when someone doesn't deserve it. Who can do that? **When we grow to become like Jesus, we can.** Let's model ourselves after Christ starting today. Jesus is our example, and grace comes through our likeness to him.

January 26 – What's This About Living Forever?

FOREVER IS A long time. **Eternal life, that's how we say it in the church. We will live forever and ever in the great by-and-by.** Why all this focus on living forever? Is it something we really want?

Arthur C. Clarke, in his book *The City and the Stars,* tells of the last two cities on Earth. They have diverged into one city where each individual is continually reborn, versus one that **still cycles through the pattern of birth and death.** The main character is forced to choose, this city or that, my home or yours. **He couldn't live in both.**

We are making that choice right now. 1 John 2:25 tells us: "And this is the promise that he made to us—eternal life." We will leave this world with its cycle of life and death behind and enter the great by-and-by. The very act of accepting Christ as our Savior and Lord **points us toward forever.** See, in Clarke's book, the main character could choose to stay in either world. **We don't have that choice. We will move on**.

What we receive once we leave this world **depends on the choice we make now.** Let's choose Christ. He is the only choice that makes sense.

January 27 – God's Treasured Possession

LET'S DISCUSS WHAT God loves most. *The tithe.* **Perhaps that's it.** It's an Old Testament tradition, but surely it equates to our love for the Lord.

Or maybe God loves *big church buildings* with lots of stained glass. Certainly, they **demonstrate our devotion to him**. *Obedience.* **Ah, that's it.** He loves obedience more than sacrifice. The scriptures tell us so.

Actually, none of those. Not our tithe, not the glorious edifices we build in his name, or the obedience we offer to him. Seriously. None of them are God's most treasured possession.

Read along in James 4:5: "Or do you suppose it is to no purpose that the Scripture says, 'He yearns jealously over the spirit that he has made to dwell in us'?" To catch the impact of this verse, we must look closely at one word: **yearns**. Merriam-Webster says **yearn** is **"to long persistently."**

What does God **long for persistently?** **"The spirit that he has made to dwell in us."** That's God's truest, most treasured possession. It's also why he takes delight in each sinner reborn into the kingdom. We see this confirmed in Luke 15:7: "Just so, I tell you, there will be more joy in heaven over one sinner who repents than over ninety-nine righteous persons who need no repentance."

We – **you and me** – are God's treasure. **He yearns for the spirit that sparks life in us, and *he holds out his hand to draw us home*.** God really does love you, more than anything else in creation.

January 28 – 2 Benefits from Trusting in God

FIRE-BREATHING ministers try to frighten us into salvation. We are bashed on the head with Paul's words of what's okay and not okay. "Accept Jesus today because you could die tonight" ... **maybe even on the way home from the prayer meeting.** We shiver in dread and look both ways before crossing the street.

God says to hold our horses. Scare tactics **aren't his way**. There's a better reason for choosing to serve him. Proverbs 3:24 gives us *2 Benefits from Trusting in God*. "If you lie down, you will not be afraid; when you lie down, your sleep will be sweet."

That's an improvement, wouldn't you say? Our benefits aren't freedom from the fires of hell or from worry about being hit by a stray car before we can repeat the sinner's prayer. Certainly, those are benefits, also, but the real benefits come when we form a spiritual connection with Christ.

Benefit No. 1: Fear is banished. Worry is thrown out the door. Nothing that matters can harm us any longer.

Benefit No. 2: We will get a good night's rest ... tonight ... tomorrow ... and every night when we trust in God.

God loves us. **He wants to shower his benefits on us**. When we place our trust in him, **the windows of heaven open to us.**

Hand-in-hand with Jesus is the only place to be.

January 29 – **You Will Love This!**

WE LIVE IN a romantic world. Well, certainly not all of it, but civilization absolutely **survives on romance**. Without it, the population of Earth would age out within 100 years, and there would be **nothing of humanity left. Why, oh why, then, does Paul say in 1 Corinthians 7:1 what he does?** "Now concerning the matters about which you wrote: 'It is good for a man not to have sexual relations with a woman.' "

That's Paul's answer, not the question. Paul says, to be precise and to quote him exactly, **"It is good for a man not to have sexual relations with a woman." Whoa!** Really? If so, it's the end of the world as we know it, to quote a more modern source of cryptic wisdom. **Does Paul really mean what he says?** Can this be true from the pen of one of **our most revered saints in the Bible?**

We must understand Paul's focus in life. He was consumed with the work of the Lord. The immediacy of Christ's return enthralled him, and **he wore blinders to everything else. Even so, in the next verse, Paul relents for the rest of us.** 1 Corinthians 7:2 says: "But because of the temptation to sexual immorality, each man should have his own wife and each woman her own husband."

Breathe a sigh of relief. We can move on. **Humanity isn't written off yet.** The real challenge is to love our spouse and ensure that we **allow time for the work of God, also.** We can't let one consume the other. They must both have a place in our life. God takes our needs into account, because he understands the children he created.

January 30 – **Our Good Blessings from Jesus**

MAKE A LIST. Pull out a sheet of paper and **grab a pencil. Number the lines 1-10.** That's enough to start. You can add to your list later. **Fill in the things that have happened to you today.** Add them all, **good and bad.** That sweet hug from your kid? Put it at **number one.** Did the dishwasher overflow? **Write it down. Don't leave anything out.** At the end of the day, you have your **list of good things the Lord is doing** in your life.

What!?! No way! **Not with bad things on my list. *Yes way*.** Read in Romans 8:28: "And we know that for those who love God all things work together for good, for those who are called according to his purpose."

This verse is clear. God's good plan for your life **isn't just the sugar cookies and the juicy steak**. All of it – **every bit** – is part of his plan. When we love God, follow the precepts outlined in the Word, and trust in the Son to be our guide, every single thing that happens to us is working out for our good. Every. Single. Thing. Are you seeing it, yet? Have you taken hold of this idea? **All of it.** For. Our. Good. The broken shoestring. The declined credit card. The red light that kept you from getting to work on time.

Here's the difference between disaster and deliverance. Did you let the lesson from that experience **change your behavior the next time?** Did you replace your shoestrings with a better-quality set? Have you begun monitoring your credit card balance? Do you leave earlier for work to **give yourself time** to **be on time?**

Remember, **all things** work together for good when we are called to do the work of the Lord. We step up to the plate. We change our behavior. We become better in our walk with God. Jesus wants us to grow in him, and that's a very good thing.

January 31 – **Your Hope in God**

WHERE IS God's hope to be found when the storms of life whip around us? Deluges of desperation threaten to drown us. Hailstones of hopelessness pummel us black and blue. We groan at the dark clouds rising around us and pray for a vision of blue skies and sunshine.

Our hope awaits us. Read in Colossians 1:3-5: "We always thank God [for] your faith in Christ Jesus and … because of the hope laid up for you in heaven."

How do we reveal this hope? Can we access it here on earth? God says, "Of course, my treasured child. My hope is for you now and always." Psalm 42:11 promises our hope through praise to the Father. 1 Peter 1:21 tells us our salvation is our hope in Jesus. 1 John 3:3 assures us our hope in God purifies us in the Lord. Proverbs 14:32 is our guarantee of hope through a God-filled life. Psalm 71:5 offers God as our hope from our youth.

The devil wants us to think the storm will last forever. NOT SO! From the beginning of time, God knew the situations we would face, and he prepared our hope and rescue. Jesus is the answer. The cross is the process. We are the reason.

Our hope in God flows to us when we hold out our hand to release Jesus from the cross.

— February —

February 1 – **Outmatched by a Good Man**

IT FEELS LIKE the deceitful politician or businessman gets ahead. If they can pull the wool over enough people's eyes, **all the good things are theirs for the taking.** Wipe your e-mail server? **Ache, appoint me Secretary of State.** Tweet incorrect facts? **Call it an alternate truth.** Advertise a product as reliable, ignoring the safety recalls? *I'm not the responsible party.* Advance in office by casting your supporters under the bus? *Hey, please focus on the good parts of my campaign.* **The bad stuff is fake news, anyway.**

What has happened to the good man we want in power over us? Profits don't stand up as a justification for our actions. Exodus 23:1 gives us good advice: "You shall not spread a false report. You shall not join hands with a wicked man to be a malicious witness." **God's not mincing his words here.** No hem and haw, not a mention of backfilling, **beating around the bush**, begging the question, or **giving us the shilly-shally**.

God says don't do it. As in, **stop!** No more false reports. If someone is known to tell untruths, **hands off, back away, take a hike, Mike. We can't equivocate when it comes to the truth. Passing the buck no longer works for the Christian.**

We must get off the fence and **proclaim the truth of the Father**. No more runarounds, weaseling, or **telling white lies**. It's over. It's done with. **If we blow hot and cold, God will cast us off and our salvation will be in peril. Live by God's standard. The Father will lift us up before all men.**

God's truth is never underrated.

February 2 – **You Are God's Gift to the Needy**

FINDING SUCCESS in the world is sometimes an impossible task. *It simply can't be done.* Poverty. Grow up in a financially desperate situation, and you are *unaware how to claw your way out.*

Get a job, we say. *How, when you don't have presentable clothes?*

Get an education. With no money? *When you are unaware that you can receive financial aid, it's useless to you.*

What about contacts? *You have none.* Family support for when you are getting started? *They can barely survive themselves.*

See it the way Proverbs 13:23 tells it: "The fallow ground of the poor would yield much food, but it is swept away through injustice."

Fallow means unplanted, unused. Fallow also means *the lives of the poor are full of unrealized possibilities.* They can do so very much with their lives *if someone will help them by planting the seed.* **That's where we come into play.** God sends us to help those who literally can't help themselves.

Training. *We can provide that.* **Clothing.** *Let's go shopping.* **Contacts? Financial support?** *Let's get it done.* This is God's way. He has blessed us so that *we might provide opportunities to those in greater need.* **We are God's gift to the needy.** Let's unwrap our opportunities and spread them around.

God has a plan for us. Let's get to it.

February 3 – **5 Keys to Sarah's Faith**

SARAH, ABRAHAM'S WIFE, is forever remembered as the mother of her people, the ancestress of the twelve tribes of Israel. She is the mother of Isaac, whose sons would one day fall out with one another over a bowl of stew. God established Sarah's faith as he took her hand and set her on a path that would change the world forever.

Here are **5 Keys to Sarah's Faith** in God.

Key No. 1: God renamed Sarah (from Sarai) to signify she would bear a son in her old age. Genesis 17:15 says: "And God said to Abraham, 'As for Sarai your wife, you shall not call her name Sarai, but Sarah shall be her name.' "

Key No. 2: Sarah was ninety when she conceived Isaac. Genesis 17:19 tells us: "God said, '... Sarah your wife shall bear you a son, and you shall call his name Isaac. I will establish my covenant with him as an everlasting covenant for his offspring after him.' "

Key No. 3: Sarah entertained the Lord, who was able to read her thoughts. Genesis 18:12-13 tells the story: "So Sarah laughed to herself, saying, 'After I am worn out, and my lord is old, shall I have pleasure?' The Lord said to Abraham, 'Why did Sarah laugh and say, "Shall I indeed bear a child, now that I am old?"' "

Key No. 4: God rescued Sarah from becoming the forced bride of the king of Gerar. Genesis 20:14 relates: "Then Abimelech took sheep and oxen, and male servants and female servants, and gave them to Abraham, and returned Sarah his wife to him."

Key No. 5: God blessed Sarah with joy in her old age. Genesis

28

21:6-7 reveals the cause: "And Sarah said, 'God has made laughter for me; everyone who hears will laugh over me.' And she said, 'Who would have said to Abraham that Sarah would nurse children? Yet I have borne him a son in his old age.' "

The life of Sarah is a testament to what God can do for one person. **You are equally special to God.** He wants to build your faith as he did for Sarah. God is watching out for you, and **he will be there when you need him**.

God is faithful and will protect us in every situation.

February 4 – 3 Honors Your Parents Deserve

OLD HOLLYWOOD was a glamorous place. Rising stars were pampered and petted. Fancy clothes, flashy cars, and elegant houses flowed from the studios like *an oasis in the desert*. The best of the crew received special recognition. They were honored in *three special ways*.

- They received *top billing on the theater's marquee*. Their name came first, and that was an honor.
- They were *honored with an Oscar*. The first Academy Awards ceremony took place in May of 1929.
- They earned a star on the *Hollywood Walk of Fame*, the first (in 1960) honoring director Stanley Kramer.

How do you show your parents that they are the best out there? *How do you honor the people who gave you life?*

The 1st Honor Your Parents Deserve: Proverbs 23:15-16 says speaking with wisdom, *thinking before you respond,* offers your parents top billing on the list of people you respect. "My son, if your heart is wise, my heart too will be glad. My inmost being will exult when your lips speak what is right."

The 2nd Honor Your Parents Deserve: Proverbs 23:22 tells you that *spending time with your parents* as they age is an honor greater than the Academy Awards. "Listen to your father who gave you life, and do not despise your mother when she is old."

The 3rd Honor Your Parents Deserve: Proverbs 23:24-26 says that to *live by the laws of the Lord* is to give your parents a Star on the Walk of Their Life. "The father of the righteous will greatly rejoice; he who fathers a wise son will be glad in him. Let your father and mother be glad; let her who bore you rejoice. My son, give me your heart, and let your eyes observe my ways."

It's all about the love. The world loved Old Hollywood, and they honored them in multiple ways. 1 Corinthians 13:13 reflects the foundation of the *honor you should show your parents*. "So now faith, hope, and love abide, these three; but the greatest of these is love."

Give your parents a call. *Take them out for lunch.* Spend time with them. **Make sure they know you care.** When you honor your parents, God will honor you.

February 5 – God Gives You Power Over Your Abuser

WHAT'S DEFLATED your balloon? What's got your coattails dragging in the mud, and you **can't seem to hitch them up?** What has you feeling like your life's alarm is broken, and you'll **always be late for every good thing?**

Some people have a valid reason for hanging their chin on their chest, for constantly having red eyes, and for holding out their hand hoping for a little help from a kind person. They were violated as a child. Poverty was their childhood companion. Divorce. Illness. Bankruptcy. A cruel boss who torments them endlessly.

Here's the thing. Those circumstances don't determine your outlook on life **unless you let them**. They only have the power over you that **you choose to give them**.

God offers you a way out. Matthew 11:28 reveals God's hand **out and supporting you**. "Come to me, all who labor and are heavy laden, and I will give you rest." God can allow you to move past that violation. When it returns to torment you, your **time in prayer and in reflection on the goodness of God** will be your steady rock of assurance.

Your childhood lack can become your motivation to **vault yourself into your future success**. God will guide you along the way. God has a **better spouse waiting for you**. There are good people out there. Find one who will read the Bible with you and hold your hands in prayer. Illness can't be allowed to steal the joy of the Father. This is an opportunity to **bond together in prayer** with those of your church family. A fresh financial start can be a chance to rethink your priorities. **Put God first** and let material possessions take second place to the things of the spirit. Kindness is Christ's way. A soft answer turns away wrath. Finding small ways to make your situation better is Jesus' path to a **successful business relationship**.

Go ahead, **air up that balloon**. Send your coat **to the cleaners**.

Reset life's alarm, and you will **get the good things** you desire. God is your plan. His redemption is your goal. **Living for Jesus is your way to move forward.**

Focus on the future and Jesus will take you there.

February 6 – **God Is Our Rest**

LIFE ISN'T GOOD for everyone. The past – *we can't undo that.* Things that happened to us as children remain embedded in our thoughts. Illness – *the chronic kind.* It comes back again and again, even when we claim healing. Relationships – *we sabotage them repeatedly.* We can never get it right.

God wraps his arms around us and tells us everything will be okay. The past is our past, and he doesn't wipe it from our memory, *but it will be okay, anyway.* Isaiah 14:3 is our consolation. "… The Lord shall give you rest from your sorrow, and from your fear, and from the hard bondage wherein you were made to serve."

Your sorrow, *it can't bring you distress any longer.* Fear is from yesterday. *You are delivered today.* Whatever your hard bondage was – abuse, drugs, a financial wasteland, relationships – *God releases you.* **God wants to be our comfort and our rest.** *He wants to be the peace that gets us through every storm.*

Reach out to God. **Give him your troubles.** *His shoulders are broad, and he can carry each one.* God is the peace that smooths every rough path we cross.

February 7 – **2 Death Defying Triumphs from God**

COMING TO AN end is the way of the world. Mountains that rise today will become **the future's sand washing up on the beach**. Clouds billow and hide the sun, and equally fast, they **tumble to the ground as rain and disappear**. Cars, houses, investments, all **run their course and come to an end**.

Relationships rarely last a lifetime. **They are special when they do**. Living creatures are the same. **Here, then gone**. Even knowing what's coming, we find the transition jarring. It's difficult to give up what we love. Often, it **breaks our heart**, especially when we **lose someone we love**.

God's Word gives us hope. In fact, it does better than that. Isaiah 25:8 gives us **2 Death Defying Triumphs from God**. "He will swallow up death forever; and the Lord God will wipe away tears from all faces, and the reproach of his people he will take away from

31

all the earth, for the Lord has spoken."

Death Defying Triumph No. 1: This verse tells us our loss is temporary. Our loved ones are not gone forever. **Christ came to banish the sting of death and replace it with victory.**

Death Defying Triumph No. 2: God will remove our sorrow and replace it with hope. We will (and should) miss our loved ones, but we can rejoice that **they are with the Father, and their pain is no more**.

We can't stop the cycle of beginning and ending. **It's the way of God's creation.** We can find hope in the victory that God gave us **through the sacrifice of Jesus on the cross**. We find new life in our Lord, and death is our passage to eternity with him.

February 8 – 5 Conditions for Prosperity

SO, YOU WANT God to prosper you. You want **God's good things to come your way**. You've rounded up the promise verses in the Word, and you're ready for God to **bring them to fruition in your life**. God says, "Now it's your turn. What are you willing to do to gain my prosperity?" 2 Chronicles 31:21 tells us: "And every work that he undertook in the service of the house of God and in accordance with the law and the commandments, seeking his God, he did with all his heart, and prospered." Here are the **5 Conditions We Must Satisfy for God to Prosper Us**.

Our 1st Condition: *"... in the service of the house of God ..."* Prosperity comes to us when we are in God's service. We don't receive prosperity for our own benefit. God's prosperity is to further his kingdom.

Our 2nd Condition: *"... in accordance with the law ..."* We must align ourselves with the legal guidelines governing our situation. No shady income. No tax evasion. No concealed assets.

Our 3rd Condition: *"... in accordance with the commandments ..."* We have eleven, ten from Moses and another from Jesus. Follow them. Do what they say. If we don't, God has no call to fill up our bank accounts.

Our 4th Condition: *"... seeking his God ..."* Where is God in your plans? Leave him out, and the rest falls apart. Our prosperity comes to us hand in hand with our connection to God.

Our 5th Condition: *"... he did with all his heart ..."* No waffling allowed. We must jump in with both feet, all in. Give your business efforts every opportunity to be successful. If God is in what you're doing, you and your business will come out on top.

God does want to prosper you. **He does want good things to come your way.** His promise verses are for you. **Now it's your turn. Go all in.** We will prosper in God when we choose to follow his plan.

February 9 – **Keeping Ourselves All Christian**

LET'S START OFF with a term used in the field of medicine. **Adulteration.** Merriam-Webster says it's *a process*. It's something that happens to a pure substance that *changes it and makes it worse*. Take olive oil. One of its benefits is the ability to use it on high heat without it smoking. Yet, *mix in old olives* to the preparation, and we get low-grade olive oil. It will have a *low smoke point*. **It's less than the best.** Or online pharmacies. Profit trumps purity, and the goods we receive *don't contain what we expect*. By *adding chalk or other inert substances* to our medicines, the unhealthy results raise the profits of unscrupulous businesses. **People die in the process.**

Now let's look at the Biblical use of our word. Let's use Exodus 20:14. "You shall not commit adultery." As Christians, we know what this verse means. *Keep the marriage bed pure.* Don't let the physical urges of reproduction control us until we *step over the lines of propriety* and good judgment.

Let's apply the medicinal definition of this term to our lives. What happens when we let our roving eyes *take us down the road of adultery?* We take something pure, our relationship with Christ, and *make it worse.* We mix in poor judgment, make bad decisions, and create an offense to our spouse, to gain something that *gratifies our carnal nature.* We go for fun rather than purity. We add something worthless to our salvation, and *people die in the process*. They die through sexual disease. They die through emotional devastation. They die through divorce. They die through our insensitivity to the divine nature of our Christian witness. They see our actions and run from the cross.

Our standard is Jesus. The rules in the Bible are there for a reason. *When we keep ourselves all Christian, every part of us, we remain a profound witness to draw others to Jesus.* Purity in Christ is a treasure. Let's not mess it up.

February 10 – **Washed by God's Rain**

WE LOVE THE ocean. The image of tumbling mountain streams

carries away our imaginations. Who doesn't see a tropical water-fall and **wish we were there?** No one much likes a downpour to unsettle their day's plans. Yet, the water we enjoy must come from somewhere. Without the rain that washes out our Saturday baseball game, crops wouldn't grow and rivers would run dry.

There's something else the rain does for us. It washes every-thing clean. Dust is a part of life. It stirs into the air from car tires, takes flight at the touch of farmers' plows, and soars in the wind. It can't help getting all over us and the things we own. The rain – a good, heavy shower – **carries it all away**.

We must allow God to be the rain for us. Galatians 5:24 says: "And those who belong to Christ Jesus have crucified the flesh with its passions and desires."

Here's the thing about a rain shower. Living things are **attached by the roots**. They remain **after the rain is gone**. Dead leaves and other debris are carried away in the gutters, dispersed by the flowing water. Our worldly passions and desires are washed away by God's cleansing rain of righteousness **only if we have first crucified them**. If we nourish them in secret, they will remain rooted in us. God's cleansing rain will have no effect on them. **We must be changed in God. We must become purified in him.** We must allow him to **clear away every dead branch and evil thing so that we can become like him**. We become pure in Christ when we desire only him.

February 11 – 4 Opportunities to Offer Submission

HERE'S THE QUESTION: Is God in control of your life? Bam! **Did that hit you in the face? Like,** where did that come from? That doesn't change the question. **Have you turned over control of your life to your Father in Heaven?** Let's look at **4 Opportunities to Offer Submission** from Ephesians 5:22-23: "Wives, submit to your own husbands, as to the Lord. For the husband is the head of the wife even as Christ is the head of the church, his body, and is himself its Savior." Let's look at each of these separately.

Our 1st Opportunity to Offer Submission: "Wives, submit to your own husbands." Take this portion of this passage the way you want, but if we're **headstrong and determined to have our own way**, we're out of the will of God.

Our 2nd Opportunity to Offer Submission: "For the husband is the head of the wife." It's time to step up to responsibility. **We**

can't always have things our way.

Our 3rd Opportunity to Offer Submission: "Christ is the head of the church." We come in second place. **God is always at the top of the power chain.**

Our 4th Opportunity to Offer Submission: "Christ ... is himself its Savior." We take three steps to salvation. **First, believe. Then, repent. Finally, receive.**

Christ is the head of the church. Everyone else comes under him.

February 12 – How to Get God's Joy

SET A GLASS of water in the freezer. Leave it there for a few hours, long enough to **coat the top with a solid layer of ice**. Then take a drink. **You can't, can you?** The water's still in there, liquid and tasty, fresh and waiting on you. There's a problem, though. There's a layer of ice on the top and it's **in the way of what you need on the other side**.

You can still drink the water ... **if you can get to it**. The question is how. **That's where God's Word comes in.** That water is the Joy of the Lord, and the ice is the spiritual distance between you and the Father of all creation. Psalm 89:15-16 says: "Blessed are the people who know the festal shout, who walk, O Lord, in the light of your face, who exult in your name all the day and in your righteousness are exalted."

You need to **shake it up**, punch a hole in the ice, and **get access to what God has on tap for you**. Psalm 118:15 tells how it's done. "Glad songs of salvation are in the tents of the righteous: The right hand of the Lord does valiantly." We get God's joy by **jumping up and shouting for him**. In the church, **shout amen!** At the breakfast table, **call out, "Praise the Lord!"** In your car, sing hallelujah at **the top of your lungs.** In your office, punch your hand into the air with a silent, **"Glory!"** On the way home, let your feet **dance in exuberant praise**.

You're seeing it, now. You're getting it. You can break through the ice to get to the joy of the Lord by **exalting him in every situation**. When we get Jesus inside of us, we begin to feel really, really good through and through.

February 13 – Our Call to Holiness

WHAT MAKES US holy? That's a God-thing, isn't it? **How can humanity reach such an exalted state?** Surely it's a goal, the

carrot on the stick, the thing we strive toward, **even when we know it's impossible this side of glory**.

Pope Paul, on November 1, 2019, said otherwise. He noted that the Apostles, the early saints in the Bible, **did, indeed, achieve holiness. They just didn't manage it alone.** They "lived with their feet on the ground" and achieved holiness by "the fruit of the grace of God and of [their] free response to it."

Pope Paul is saying the Apostles had a choice, and **they chose Jesus.**

We choose holiness by our response to the call of Christ. Here's one way it works from the New Testament.

1 Thessalonians 4:6-7 says: "That no one transgress and wrong his brother in this matter, because **the Lord is an avenger in all these things**, as we told you beforehand and solemnly warned you. For God has not called us for impurity, but in holiness."

The underlining isn't in the original, but essentially, payback is not ours. We must leave others' offenses against us in God's hands. When we can release our revenge into the care of God, we've taken **two steps up the holiness ladder**.

God is calling us to an exalted state. Salvation is our foot on the bottom rung. **It's time for us to climb.** Take the hand of Jesus and step up to holiness today.

We can do this, become like Christ, when we let him have control.

February 14 – **2 Seeds of God's Glory**

WHAT'S GOOD ENOUGH to convince you the garden you planted in spring will bear a harvest in September? You plow, plant seeds, weed, fertilize, and water, and for months, you get little more than **stumpy green plants breaking through the soil**.

Planting grapes is worse. **Three years.** You plant this year, and you must wait two more **before the first harvest.** Let's not get off on olive trees. Many don't produce **until they are twelve years old**. Who would plant olive trees as an investment? **Longleaf pine trees take upwards of 50 years to be usable as utility poles.**

Our hope in Christ has been maturing for 2,000 years. It's ripe for the harvest. 1 Peter 1:21 says: "Who through him are believers in God, who raised him from the dead and gave him glory, so that your faith and hope are in God." Jesus' sacrifice on the cross planted **2 Seeds of God's Glory**.

Our 1st Seed: Jesus was raised from the dead after three days, establishing our faith in him.

Our 2nd Seed: God covered him with divine glory, and his mortal flesh became immortal, establishing our hope in our resurrection.

When a longleaf pine breaks through the soil, it looks like grass for up to three years. It's not growing on the surface, but the **roots are establishing a foothold**. When growth begins above ground, it can **shoot up at the rate of two feet per year. Imagine a 4,000-foot-tall tree. That's where our faith and hope in Jesus are. It's time for the harvest. Let's move into it today.**

Jesus is fully prepared. He tells us now is our time.

February 15 – 2 Analogies for a Better Marriage

WEDDING PHOTOS are beautiful. Two people in love. Stars in their eyes. Tomorrow is a bright future, and *nothing will prevent them from achieving their anticipated goals*: a cozy home; much loved children; friends and a place in the community; retiring together, hand-in-hand.

Then, bo—nk! It all goes sideways. One small indiscretion. A sideways glance. That weekend in Vegas … *that never stays in Vegas.*

Proverbs 6:25-29 gives us **2 Analogies for a Better Marriage:** "Do not desire her beauty in your heart, and do not let her capture you with her eyelashes; for the price of a prostitute is only a loaf of bread, but a married woman hunts down a precious life. *Can a man carry fire next to his chest and his clothes not be burned?* Or can one *walk on hot coals and his feet not be scorched?* So is he who goes in to his neighbor's wife; none who touches her will go unpunished."

The emphasis isn't in the original, but that's the focus today. Let's pull out and look at each of these two analogies separately.

Analogy No. 1: *"Can a man carry fire next to his chest and his clothes not be burned?"* The passion of our illicit involvement outside of marriage isn't hidden. It burns into every part of us and is visible to everyone.

Analogy No. 2: *"Or can one walk on hot coals and his feet not be scorched?"* Not only can others see the damage we've done, our misdeed affects us, also. We become damaged through our affair.

Here's the key. **Don't even look.** As the passage says, *"Do not desire her beauty in your heart."*

Follow the marriage advice in the Word, and your relationship will be strengthened by the trust you find in each other.

February 16 – God's Comeback Answer

WHEN'S THE LAST time someone cut you off in traffic? How did you feel? Gracious, or not so loving? How about the gossip in the office? The one that makes up juicy tidbits to round out their salacious tales? Does your blood boil when you see them in the break room?

Think how God must feel when humanity ignores his precepts and rules in the Word and goes their own way. "Arrrgh," God cries. "Will you never get it right?"

Scrrrratch! *That's not what God says.* Read in Hosea 14:4. "I will heal their apostasy; I will love them freely, for my anger has turned from them."

Apostasy is the abandonment of a religious belief. Umm. That sounds like much of the modern world. Secularism, atheism, and even the denigration of Christian morality. The church has been cut off in traffic. We are being gossiped about with salacious tales of wrongdoing behind the church doors.

"Arrrgh! Get off our backs! We are following God's way, and it's the best way!" *God says, "I will love them freely, for my anger has turned from them."*

That's what God expects of us, also. We are to release our love and understanding and let it touch everyone we meet. God's answer is always love. Ours must be, too.

February 17 – 3 Gears We Need to Shift

DRIVING A MANUAL transmission on a track is a special feeling. We become a piece of the car, **an integral part of the process**. Our car's not getting up to speed unless we tell it what to do. We must shift the gears to get our speed machine out on the tarmac.

Some of us are stuck in first gear.

We wind out our spiritual transmission, and we can't seem to go any faster. We hit our stall speed, and our **Christian witness lugs along like we are back in the world**. God says there's **3 Gears We Need to Shift**. Read in Proverbs 21:4 in the New Living Translation: "Haughty eyes, a proud heart, and evil actions are all sin."

Our First Gear: Haughty eyes … **are you looking down on others as less than you?** Stop it. It's time to shift into the gear of respect. **Our Second Gear:** A proud heart ... **do you give yourself credit for what life has given you?** You're about to stall. Shift into gratefulness to God. **Our Third Gear:** Evil actions ... **and you think this is still okay?** You're about to burn out your transmission. Shift into obedience to the laws of the Lord.

God wants you on the winner's podium. He's showing you how it's done. It's time to shift gears into a better relationship with the Father and get your spiritual life up to speed.

February 18 – **Wanted, Dead or Alive**

TODAY'S TITLE IS wrong. That's right, misstated, misleading, and **misunderstood**. See, God wants us **dead AND alive**.

What?!? How can that be? We can't be dead and alive. **Can we?** Let's read in Romans 6:11: "So you also must consider yourselves dead to sin and alive to God in Christ Jesus."

Woo-hoo! That's us, redeemed in God and dead to the world! We have died in our worldly man and come alive in the power and authority of Christ. **Drunkenness and orgies, DEAD and in the grave! New life in Christ, gifted by the blood of the cross! Anger and a mean spirit, STOMPED UNDERFOOT and crushed forever! A kind spirit and generous heart, our right by association with the King! Gossip and lies, banished to the darkness where they belong! Forgiveness and faithfulness, ours in the Name of Jehovah Jireh!**

See, we are dead when we ask Jesus to rule in our lives. Our old self goes down into the cleansing waters, and when we come up, we are **filled with the new life of the forgiving Lord**. We are new, and there is **nothing of the old self to be found**. We walk in the new life of Christ and his love for us, and we don't look back. Nuh-uh, nuh-uh. **We look ahead to a better life with Jesus.**

Jesus wants us at his side, the old man dead and the new one fully alive.

February 19 – **Adam Takes a Detour**

GPS IS WONDERFUL when it works correctly. We punch in our destination, and we are **routed down this road**, along that street, and **past the worst obstructions**. We're even given the option of **choosing a quicker route if one becomes available**.

Adam let his GPS lead him astray. He took a detour in the Garden of Eden, and **God had to set him back on the right track**.

First, the Bible reveals that Adam was God's original human. Genesis 2:7 tells us: "Then the Lord God formed the man of dust from the ground and breathed into his nostrils the breath of life, and the man became a living creature."

Next, we learn that Adam had a job to do. He wasn't there to play. Even so, **something was missing.** Genesis 2:22 tells us: "And the rib that the Lord God had taken from the man he made into a woman and brought her to the man."

When push came to shove, Adam chose **lust over love for his Creator.** Eve became **more important to him than God.** Genesis 3:6 tells us: "… [Eve] took of its fruit and ate, and she also gave some to her husband who was with her, and he ate."

Here's what we need to see. We like to insinuate that Eve tricked Adam into transgressing God's rules, but **Adam was at her side.** He knew **exactly what he was doing.** He chose to let his physical attraction for Eve take precedence over his loyalty to the Lord. **God had one unbreakable rule, and Adam couldn't stay on course.** He thought he could **take a quicker route to his destination.** Instead, God's detour took him **into the fields to labor for his food** with the sweat of his brow.

Genesis 2:23 tells us: "Therefore the Lord God sent him out from the garden of Eden to work the ground from which he was taken."

That must have been a hard lesson for Adam to learn. Did he reach his destination? Did he manage to get back on track? We're here, aren't we? Adam lived another 900 years and fathered sons and daughters. **His detour legacy remains with us today.**

When God gives us directions, going the way he points us leads to a better end.

February 20 – **God's View of Time**

TAKE A FOUR-YEAR-OLD and listen to her words. This week she says, "I love apples." **The next week she won't touch them.** A small boy's favorite toy is forgotten as soon as he ages past the interest it held for him. He may remember having treasured the toy, but **he no longer adores it.**

Is God that way with us? His promises are yea and amen **as long as we're interesting to him? Not on your life!** Read in Isaiah 59:21: " 'And as for me, this is my covenant with them,' says the Lord: 'My Spirit that is upon you, and my words that I have put in your mouth, shall not depart out of your mouth, or out of the mouth of your offspring, or out of the mouth of your children's offspring,' says the Lord, 'from this time forth and forevermore.' "

God says his truth is still truth. His promises to us are still in effect. The agreements God entered into and recorded in the Word two thousand years ago **are still yea and amen to us today. Get a promise Bible. Read it from cover to cover**. Every promise you unearth between the covers is **still valid for you today**.

To a four-year-old, four years is the length of eternity. All of time has existed in four short years. To God, **time is immeasurable**. When he says forevermore, he **means what he says**.

Don't be afraid to trust in God. He hasn't changed his mind about loving you.

February 21 – **Two Energy Shots from God**

LIFE CAN TAKE our strength from us. We become exhausted by the chatter of daily problems, our bills begin to overwhelm us, and *the creaking of old age shatters our dreams of an active retirement*. It's like a day without caffeine, an enforced restriction that plans to stick around for the rest of our life.

God says NO WAY. You don't have to be that old, worn-out hulk. *God has a gift of better life to offer you.* Psalm 71:9 gives us our *Two Energy Shots from God*: "Do not cast me off in the time of old age; forsake me not when my strength is spent." This verse is phrased as a plea, but it's the answer that should excite us.

Our 1st Energy Shot from God: Do not cast me off in the time of old age. God is there as we mature into our future. He gifts us with his power. **He is our shot in the arm, our energy bump to carry us forward.**

Our 2nd Energy Shot from God: Forsake me not when my strength is spent. Our strength is limited by our youth, our bones, and our muscles. **God's strength is divine, and it has no limit or end.**

Our energy shots come from our faith in our Holy God. Turn to him today.

February 22 – **5 Promises Concerning John the Baptist**

JOHN THE BAPTIST was the cousin of Jesus. Only the book of Luke gives us the details of his birth. John's parents, Zechariah and Elizabeth, were both from the tribe of Aaron, who was the brother of Moses. Here are **5 Promises Concerning John the Baptist:**

41

The 1st Promise: *John's birth was foretold by an angel, despite his parents' advanced age.* Luke 1:13 tells us: "The angel said to him, 'Do not be afraid, Zechariah, for your prayer has been heard, and your wife Elizabeth will bear you a son, and you shall call his name John.' "

The 2nd Promise: *John's name was given him by his mother, validating the angel's command.* Luke 1:59-60 says: "And they would have called him Zechariah after his father, but his mother answered, 'No; he shall be called John.' "

The 3rd Promise: *John announced the coming of the Messiah, as foretold by Isaiah.* Mark 1:1-3 reveals his mission: "Behold, I send my messenger before your face, who will prepare your way, the voice of one crying in the wilderness: 'Prepare the way of the Lord, make his paths straight.' "

The 4th Promise: *John consented to baptize Jesus, releasing the power of the Holy Spirit over Jesus' life.* Matthew 3:15-16 unwinds the events: "But Jesus answered him, 'Let it be so now, for thus it is fitting for us to fulfill all righteousness.' Then [John] consented. And when Jesus was baptized, ... the Spirit of God descended like a dove coming to rest on him."

The 5th Promise: *John was the greatest man born, next to his cousin, Jesus.* Matthew 11:11 gives us the words of Christ: "Truly, I say to you, among those born of women there has arisen no one greater than John the Baptist."

John became a martyr of the early church. **His role was pivotal in bringing Jesus to the forefront of his ministry.** Thank God John was the man he was, that he **"prepared the way of the Lord and made his paths straight."** When we need a superhero to hold up as an example for our children, open the Bible. They are everywhere within the pages of the Book.

February 23 – 4 Impacts Rufus Made on Paul's Life

RUFUS MEANS, literally, "red." William II, a king of England, was nicknamed Rufus because of the color of his hair. The ancient Romans regularly gave the name Rufus to red-haired babies. We meet our Biblical Rufus in the scriptures on two occasions, once in Mark and another time in Romans. As far as we can tell, *both reference the same man.*

"And they compelled a passerby, Simon of Cyrene, who was coming in from the country, the father of Alexander and Rufus, to carry his cross." Mark 15:21.

"Greet Rufus, chosen in the Lord; also his mother, who has been a mother to me as well." Romans 16:13.

Here's what we know about Rufus and the *4 Impacts Rufus Made on Paul's Life.*

First, Rufus was the son of Simon of Cyrene. This is important because Simon carried the cross of Jesus down the Via Dolorosa, or the street Jesus walked in his final hours.

Second, Rufus was chosen by the Lord. Paul thinks highly enough of Rufus to single out Rufus for this honorable distinction among all Christians who are "chosen to follow in the faith."

Third, Rufus' mother treated Paul like her own son, and Paul seemed to consider Rufus his brother.

Fourth, Rufus' family was Paul's extended family. They essentially adopted the apostle after he became a Christian.

We don't know the difference we will make in other people's lives. Could Rufus have foreseen he was befriending the man who would pen definitive tomes that would *one day form a significant portion of the Church's Bible?* God places people in our path not only to benefit us, *but for us to benefit the future in the way we treat those in our care.*

Our impact on others lasts for generations, so let's treat them with love.

February 24 – Upholding God's Standard

HAVING A GOOD life is largely about maintaining standards. Personal care – **whether we've washed our hair and put on clean clothes.** Community involvement – **working to ensure our library and parks are maintained.** Neighborhood pride – **keeping our yard and house maintained with a degree of care.** If we let these things slip, things soon slide into disrepair, disuse, and disgrace. It's vital that **each of us participates if we want our lives to be the best they can be.**

God has pegged a standard by which we must live. Read in 1 Peter 2:24: "He himself bore our sins in his body on the tree, that we might die to sin and live to righteousness. By his wounds you have been healed."

Here's the standard set by this verse: **Jesus saw the most important thing on this planet as you and me. He felt we were worth dying for.** He let nothing, not even his desire to avoid the cross, get in the way of maintaining his standard of selfless love for humanity. Our half of this equation is what we must put into it, **to die to sin and live to righteousness**.

How can we do that? Jump into the Word of God, learn the example of Jesus, and **live by his moral benchmark**. Jesus summed up what he expects from us in Matthew 7:12: "So whatever you wish that others would do to you, do also to them, for this is the Law and the Prophets."

We're on board, now, prepared to live a good life in Jesus.

February 25 – 7 Inspiring Proclamations from Hosea

HOSEA WAS A MAN of mystery. We don't have any information about him outside of his book of prophecy. He married a prostitute, divorced her, and remarried the same woman. He was so attuned to God that he named his children according to God's revealed prophecies. One thing is certain: **Hosea excelled at delivering inspiring proclamations from God**.

Inspiring Proclamation No. 1: Hosea 6:1 says **God can bind up our hurts and wounds**. "Come, let us return to the Lord ... that he may heal us ... and he will bind us up."

Inspiring Proclamation No. 2: Hosea 6:3 assures us **God will shower us with his blessings**. "Let us know; let us press on to know the Lord; his going out is sure as the dawn; he will come to us as the showers, as the spring rains that water the earth."

Inspiring Proclamation No. 3: Hosea 10:12 promises **God's reward when we adhere to his standards.** "Sow for yourselves righteousness; reap steadfast love; break up your fallow ground, for it is the time to seek the Lord, that he may come and rain righteousness upon you."

Inspiring Proclamation No. 4: Hosea 13:4 reveals **God's foretelling of our Savior, Jesus.** "But I am the Lord your God from the land of Egypt; you know no God but me, and besides me there is no savior."

Inspiring Proclamation No. 5: Hosea 14:4 is our guarantee of **God's forgiveness when we turn to him.** "... I will love them freely, for my anger has turned from them."

Inspiring Proclamation No. 6: Hosea 14:6 says **God desires to prosper us in all that we do.** "His shoots shall spread out; his beauty shall be like the olive, and his fragrance like Lebanon."

Inspiring Proclamation No. 7: Hosea 14:9 tells us **we walk in**

wisdom when we follow God's plan. "Whoever is wise, let him understand these things ... for the ways of the Lord are right, and the upright walk in them ..."

We may not know where Hosea lived or exactly how long he preached, but *his words are ones we can treasure.* Hosea revealed the truth of God, and his words inspire us today.

February 26 – 3 Opportunities to Be Glad

LET'S TURN THAT frown upside down. Let's take that sad face and make it into a happy one. Today's your day to change your *growl to a cheer*, lift your *feet from the mud* that's keeping you back, and turn your *face into the sun.* **There's no time to be unhappy.** *We can't waste a moment on grousing and complaining.* Good times are on the way, and it's up to us to *prepare to receive them.*

Here are *3 Opportunities to Be Glad* from the book of Psalms.

Opportunity No. 1: We will find the peace of God in our hearts, for *he is the satisfaction of our souls.* Psalm 63:5 tells us: "My soul will be satisfied as with fat and rich food, and my mouth will praise you with joyful lips."

Opportunity No. 2: Our high standards for personal integrity earn us *joyous praise from God.* Psalm 64:10 tells us: "Let the righteous one rejoice in the Lord and take refuge in him! Let all the upright in heart exult!"

Opportunity No. 3: We will find happiness and rejoice with gladness when we *stand before God* having lived a clean life. Psalm 68:3 tells us: "But the righteous shall be glad; they shall exult before God; they shall be jubilant with joy!"

Our happiness is up to us. *Our joy flows from our honest and clean lifestyle.* We will be glad in the Lord when we *find our purpose in living* for him. Satisfaction in the world is temporary. Our gladness in God endures.

February 27 – 4 Signs Eleazar Was Blessed by God

ELEAZAR IN THE Old Testament was the nephew of Moses, the original High Priest of the Jewish nation. Eleazar was also Aaron's third son and was given charge of the entire tabernacle, including the holy objects inside dedicated to the worship of God. How did the third son of Aaron **take the primary position of power in the early years of the Jewish state?** Eleazar was blessed by God and lifted into his position of power by the hand of the Lord. Here are **4 Signs**

Eleazar Was Blessed by God.

The 1st Sign: Leviticus 10:1-2 reveals Eleazar's older brothers flouting the authority of God. "Now Nadab and Abihu, the sons of Aaron, each took his censer and put fire in it and laid incense on it and offered unauthorized fire before the Lord, which he had not commanded them. And fire came out from before the Lord and consumed them, and they died before the Lord." Eleazar was a **man after God's heart**, and he was lifted in their stead and **becomes Aaron's eldest son and God's choice for High Priest**.

The 2nd Sign: Numbers 19:3 shows us God's redemption through Eleazar. "And you shall give [the red heifer] to Eleazar the priest, and it shall be taken outside the camp and slaughtered before him." Eleazar was granted the authority to **purify the nation's wrongdoing through the archetypal sacrifice of the red heifer**.

The 3rd Sign: Numbers 20:25-26 tells us Eleazar received the priestly garments by God's command. "Take Aaron and Eleazar his son and bring them up to Mount Hor. And strip Aaron of his garments and put them on Eleazar his son. And Aaron shall be gathered to his people and shall die there." Eleazar served as the **High Priest of Israel for the next 20 years.**

The 4th Sign: Numbers 27:18-21 says Joshua consulted with Eleazar in the presence of God about the successor for Moses. "So the Lord said to Moses … 'Make him stand before Eleazar the priest … who shall inquire for him … before the Lord …' " God channeled his authority **through Eleazar, the High Priest of the Temple.**

God wants to bless each of us. When we see the signs, **let's lift our voices in praise to the Father.** God lifts us up when we place our faith in him.

February 28 – **Jesus and the Peace Flag**

COOPERATION. UNDERSTANDING. Getting along with people even when we disagree. **Those sound pretty good, like they are things we should do.** A good way to live. **Taking the high road and letting other people be as important as we are**. They remind us of Jesus' words in Matthew 7:12: "Whatever you wish that others would do to you, do also to them."

If we want people to work with us, we must choose to **work with them**. We can't argue and demand our way. If we want people to accept our viewpoint and let us live our lives, we must choose to **accept their viewpoint**, also. We can't bully them into being like us.

If we want … oh, this one's harder. If we want to get along with people even when we disagree, **that takes God**.

We need a peace flag. James 3:16 warns us: "For where jealousy and selfish ambition exist, there will be disorder and every vile practice." It's vital to understand the meaning of this verse. People are driven by jealousy and selfish ambition. That's easy. **What's hard is turning loose of what we want** and putting other people's needs and desires first.

Start with the easy things. Here are a few: Let someone cut in line and smile when they do. Greet the visitor in the strange clothes. Make them welcome. Let someone else decide where to eat for lunch. Then make a point to enjoy yourself. That's enough to start. Jesus will wave his peace flag over you, and you will become more like him with every kind choice you make.

Conflict cannot survive in the committed life of the Christian.

(February 29) – **Your Failure Is Not Final**

SO, YOUR LIFE has collapsed, and you're ready to throw in the towel. Others have invested in the stock market and gotten rich, and *your picks continually go belly up*. Your car died *just as the warranty expired*. Even your spouse left you, claiming you were a worthless waste of space.

Whoa! *God says to back up there.* Psalm 37:24 makes God's position clear: "Though he fall, he shall not be cast headlong, for the Lord upholds his hand."

God's got your back in this. The bad things that have happened to you *are not your future*. Your failure is not final, and *you can't afford to think that way*. You have tomorrow, and the next day, and the next, all the way to the end of your life. *You can make your future into just what you want it to be, no matter how many times you've flubbed up in the past.*

Here's how you can make a change for the better.

1. Find a different investment strategy. *Consult the experts.* What you pay them will come back to you in increased profits.
2. Try an extended warranty. *Purchase a car that's less than you can afford.* You may even get better gas mileage and cut your travel expense.
3. You are never a waste of space. *You have strong points.* Live up to them.

Your future improvements start today. Begin with God. *He will direct your path the way you need to go.*

God is our relief in the darkness that tries to steal our soul.

— March —

March 1 – 2 Spiritual Guides in the Night

TRY DRIVING HOME with no headlights. It's a risky thing to do. We chance one of two outcomes, either we are **stopped and given a ticket**, or we **crash head on into a car** that didn't know we were coming.

It happens more often than you think.

A TV motoring show decided to test the survivability of crashing **head on at sixty miles per hour**. Only the car with airbags showed **any chance of surviving**. Then they did the same test at 120 MPH (Crazy!) into a concrete barrier, and **the car was compacted**. We need headlights, sensors, and warning lights to keep us safe when driving at night.

We can also crash spiritually without God's guidance. Psalm 16:7 says God gives us **2 Spiritual Guides in the Night**. "I bless the Lord who gives me counsel; in the night also my heart instructs me."

We don't have to **strike out blindly in our journey with Jesus**. Our Christian walk isn't completed **by feel or touch**. We don't need to make our **best guess on how to live**. We have the hand of the Lord guiding us along the way.

Our 1st Spiritual Guide: *God is our GPS signal.* He tells us to turn here, avoid that, and beware, accident ahead. We know just where to head when we're guided by God.

Our 2nd Spiritual Guide: *God gives us a conscience for a reason.* It's our automatic warning system, our adaptive cruise control. It slows us down when our situation gets dicey and warns us of incoming danger.

We are safer when we're traveling with God. He is at our side to help us navigate every curve, mountain road, pothole, and engine problem along the way.

God lights our path when we place our full confidence in him.

March 2 – Our Final Lunge for God

LIFE IS A SERIES of stages. At the beginning, *everyone else is in control*. Kids are powerless in the shadow of their parents and teachers. Suddenly, we tower over our peers, and the adults that once awed us? We become *their equal in stature and authority*.

Then, life begins to steal our thunder. Six cars, three houses, and two grandchildren later, we realize we *can't walk up the stairs without getting winded.* Keeping the flowerbeds weeded becomes a chore almost not worth doing, and painting the gables on the house? *The ladder has grown too tall.* It's time to move on, to lie back, to let someone else do the work.

That doesn't pass the muster in our Christian walk. Our gray hairs don't matter. *God has business for us to attend.* Psalm 71:17-18 says we must declare the power of the almighty God: "O God, from my youth you have taught me, and I still proclaim your wondrous deeds. So even to old age and gray hairs, O God, do not forsake me, until I proclaim your might to another generation, your power to all those to come."

We are to teach the upcoming generation of the power of God. The precepts of the Bible, the way of righteous living, the standards of the saints, *we are the banner that announces the way of the Lord.* Our flowerbeds might become someone else's responsibility, but our legacy comes through our own hands. **Our final lunge for Christ must be to teach the truths in the Word.**

We arm the next leaders of the church by sharing the wondrous deeds God did in our youth.

March 3 – 5 Acts Revealing Judith's Courage

JUDITH IS NOT found in the Protestant Bible. Yet, her story, canonical in Roman Catholic texts, reveals a woman who took a courageous stand for God. Here are **5 Acts Revealing Judith's Courage.**

Courageous Act No. 1: *Judith takes command in a time of desperation.* The Assyrians have the Jews under siege, and the town magistrates are ready to surrender **until Judith steps up**.

Courageous Act No. 2: *Judith prays for direction from God.* She raises three prayers before God: **1. before her adventure 2. for strength to behead the enemy leader 3. to celebrate victory over the Assyrians.**

Courageous Act No. 3: *Judith knows her strengths and uses them.* As a beautiful woman, Judith uses sensuality to worm her way into the Assyrian camp, promising to **guide them to victory over Israel.**

Courageous Act No. 4: *Judith becomes weak to gain power over her enemy.* She throws a party for Holofernes, the Assyrian leader, and **flatters the general with platitudes to his vanity**.

Courageous Act No. 5: *Judith strikes when God gives her the opportunity.* Judith beheads the drunken Holofernes with two blows from his own sword, wraps the head in a jeweled bed canopy, and **carries it out of the camp**.

We find a similar fate meted out to Sisera, a commander of the Canaanite army of King Jabin of Hazor, in Judges 4:21: "But Jael the wife of Heber took a tent peg, and took a hammer in her hand. Then she went softly to [Sisera] and drove the peg into his temple until it went down into the ground while he was lying fast asleep from weariness. So he died."

The women in the Bible are **unparalleled in courage and in the power of the Living God**. We are stronger when we learn from them.

God empowers us to victory when we trust in him.

March 4 – **Our Proof of God**

WE'RE ALWAYS old to our children. The taller they grow, the older we get. They can never catch up to us. They can hardly imagine we were once their age, we liked swing sets, and we did daring things that no one would believe.

We recall our glory days as though they were yesterday, but our little ones think, "Yeah. Tall stories. That's all it is." We need to pull out our proof that we were as wonderful as we remember. Photos. Certificates. Awards. Maybe even show them a few scars.

The same is true of the miracles God has performed for us. Exodus 13:8 says: "You shall tell your son on that day, 'It is because of what the Lord did for me when I came out of Egypt.' "

What was your Egypt? Partying? Wild living? Nights on the town? Record the date of your salvation. Celebrate the change in your life from "all about me" to "all about Jesus." Tell the tales of what the Lord has done in your life so your children will never forget. Your proof of God is what will convince your children to follow in your spiritual footsteps.

March 5 – **God's Call for Healing**

A HACKING COUGH is no laughing matter. That sinus drip? **We want it gone**. Then there's an ache in our back and scratchy eyes; and soon we know the flu is here to stay.

Maybe it's worse, something that affects us in a **drastic way**.

Our appendix is inflamed, our tonsils need removed, or we hear the dreaded word ... tumor. We go into panic mode. We feel the floor **fall from under our feet**, and we are **adrift in despair**.

   God says, "Not so! You're not alone. I'm by your side."

   James 5:14-16 tells us what to do when **sickness rolls over us** and we're certain there's **no cure for us**. "Is anyone among you sick? Let him call for the elders of the church, and let them pray over him, anointing him with oil in the name of the Lord. And the prayer of faith will save the one who is sick, and the Lord will raise him up. And if he has committed sins, he will be forgiven. Therefore, confess your sins to one another and pray for one another, that you may be healed. The prayer of a righteous person has great power as it is working."

   We learn **three major things in this passage**. First, we get through this together. It's a joint effort. With God as our center, we are surrounded by the love of the Body. Second, our physical healing is directly connected to our spiritual healing. Our prayer of faith will not only ease our sickness, it will clear our slate of wrong deeds. Third, this only works if we are living righteously. How? We read the Bible and do what it says. That's direct from Harold Herring, the president of The Debt Free Army and an anointed teacher of God's Word.

   Let's step out on faith, place our trust in the Father, and band together as a team. **It's in striving together that we make our lives better.**

   God calls us to be healed. Let's accept all of it.

March 6 – **God Takes Our Case**

PUBLIC DEFENDER NO. 1. What does that mean to us? What's a public defender, anyway? First, a public defender is a lawyer, *fully qualified and prepared to use the law to our advantage*. The court respects the authority of a public defender. Second, a public defender doesn't cost us anything. The court recognizes that *we don't have the means or ability to defend ourselves*. We need the best help possible, hence, our public defender.

   Here's where this applies to us. *The world happens to us whether we like it or not.* Our health fails, *the economy stumbles*, even our relationships begin to fray no matter how hard we try to keep everything on an even keel. *We don't know how to fight back as our life slips out of control.*

That's when God steps in, *briefcase in hand*, and says, "I'm here, now. Your worries are over. I'll take your case." Read in Isaiah 62:8: "The Lord has sworn by his right hand and by his mighty arm: 'I will not again give your grain to be food for your enemies, and foreigners shall not drink your wine for which you have labored.' "

God has taken our case as our authority in the court of life. Your health? *Granted, by the stripes of Christ.* Your finances? *Approved, funded by the God of Creation.* Your relationships? *Rock solid and founded on the foundation of Jesus.*

Our part is to turn our case over to God, trust him, and *do what he suggests.* He's the expert, not us, and we want the highest authority on the job. Jesus can reinstate our life when we turn it over to him.

March 7 – Looking for God Nearby

PEOPLE AROUND the world travel great distances looking for God. Rome, the **great center of the Catholic Church**. Mecca, **for another faith**. How about Salt Lake City? People of three faiths **travel to the Holy Land** to make a connection with God.

There's nothing wrong with that, but if we think those are the **only places we can find God**, we are off the mark. Acts 17:27 says: "That they should seek God, and perhaps feel their way toward him and find him. Yet he is actually not far from each one of us."

Not far? **What does that mean?** It's so simple. **God is as far as (or as close) as our knees.** When we choose to approach him in prayer, we open a link between us and him, and we discover **he's been at our side all along**.

Go ahead, travel to Rome. You find God there **without a doubt**. He's in Mecca, in Salt Lake City, and you can **hardly miss God in the ancient sites of the Holy Land. He's also at your side right now.** Turn to him. **Trust in him**. He reaches out to you today.

God is where we find him, and he's never far away.

March 8 – 2 Ways of Taking Down the Devil

SLASH AND BURN. That's our mantra. We can't let evil remain in our lives if we want to live for our Lord. Parry, thrust, and cut deep. **We must slice away every wicked thing that keeps us from going all in for Jesus.** Hebrews 4:12 tells us: "For the word of God is living and active, sharper than any two-edged sword, piercing to the division of soul and of spirit, of joints and of marrow, and discerning the thoughts and intentions of the heart." **The Bible is our sword.** The words inside are the **cutting edge of our blade**. It flashes in our grasp when we stand over the challenges we face. **We need have no fear when we brandish the flaming sword of God.** This verse tells us **2 Ways of Taking Down the Devil** with the Word of God.

Our **1st Way of Taking Down the Devil:** The Word pierces to the division of soul and of spirit. The truths in the Bible **divide our physical impulses from the directives of the Father**. When we lift the Word, and it cuts to the core of who we are, only then can we see our choices clearly and make the right one. **We kick the devil out the door and walk wholly with Jesus.**

Our **2nd Way of Taking Down the Devil:** The Word discerns the thoughts and intentions of the heart. We learn between **desire and need, want and necessity, man's way and God's way**. The devil will try to distract us. The Bible gives us clarity, allowing us to find the right path carved through the obstacles along the way. **We put the devil to the sword when we live by the Word.**

Our success is found in God, and his Word is our sword of victory.

March 9 – God's Plan for Your Good

EVERYONE STARTS somewhere, and we usually start small. Who begins a YouTube channel with a full production facility and ten crew? It's usually one camera, one microphone, and **a person going it alone**. It's only when we have 100,000 subscribers that we can elevate our production facilities, hire help, and **call ourselves successful**.

A successful lawn company usually starts with one truck, one mower, and **one person doing one yard at a time**. Then, one day, they expand to multiple mowers, then to **a crew that can trim several yards at the same time**.

Why do we expect God to give us the lottery, and not just the $500 pot, but the $50 million one?

God is helping us, one subscriber, one lawn, one level of improvement at a time. Deuteronomy 30:9 says: "The Lord your God will make you abundantly prosperous in all the work of your hand, in the fruit of your womb and in the fruit of your cattle and in the fruit of your ground. For the Lord will again take delight in prospering you, as he took delight in your fathers."

Abundantly prosperous. Did you read that? **Abundantly pros-**

perous! We will be blessed in four ways:

No. 1: The work of our hand. That's our job, whatever we put our effort into.

No. 2: The fruit of our womb. This is our family, our children. They will turn out fine.

No. 3: The fruit of our cattle. Our investments, the return we sink into stocks and bonds.

No. 4: The fruit of our ground. Our future plans, initiated now, to come to harvest many years down life's road.

God not only has us covered, he takes delight in doing so. Today is your day. Take your first step forward in God.

March 10 – God's Not Picking On You

WHAT'S IT with the small stuff, we ask. You know what I mean, going slightly over the speed limit, snacking on the grapes before we put them on the scale, or the wink at our coworker when our spouse is at home. Small stuff. Little things, **ones that don't matter. Why does God care about that?**

Our weekend out with the boys. The girls' night out once a month. Like they say, **what happens in Vegas stays in Vegas.** We all need to let off a little steam, right? Let loose for a bit? Let down our hair and **ride the cutting edge** of the high life? If we stumble a bit, we **pay the bill** and go on. Our slate is cleared, and we **go back to our good life**. It doesn't make us bad people … does it?

Here's the thing. **Small stuff is what we call a "gateway drug."** It opens the door to bigger infractions, and **that's dangerous ground**. 1 Corinthians 11:32 reminds us that we will have a **final invoice to pay** when we reach life's end. "But when we are judged by the Lord, we are disciplined so that we may not be condemned along with the world."

God works to tug us back into line before the tally of our deeds **sinks us into addiction** or something worse. Yes, addiction. Do you think the speedster tearing up the highway started off at 100 mph? **Even the tickets he's received can't slow him down.** That's addiction, to keep doing something **even when the penalties overwhelm us**. God wants to stop the behaviors **before they get out of hand.** We don't want to be **arrested for stealing**, even if we manage to get away with it the first or second time … or **destroy our marriage** because we let that wink get out of control. Our stumble might take innocent people down with us. **God's not picking on you.** He wants to help you be the **best person you can be**. God is rooting for your success, and he is with you all along the way.

March 11 – 3 Lessons About Honesty

GEORGE WASHINGTON is our standard. How does that story go? **"I cannot lie, Father. I am the one who cut down the cherry tree."**

It's generally accepted now that the cherry tree incident never really happened, but **it exemplifies a truth we want our children to understand**. Even when it's tough, there's **no way to go except with the truth**. Leviticus 19:11 teaches us **3 Lessons About Honesty**. "You shall not steal; you shall not deal falsely; you shall not lie to one another."

The word Leviticus literally means "The Law." This verse is from the laws set up to help the children of Israel learn to **navigate their new world of independence**. For hundreds of years, they had been ruled over (read that as enslaved) by the leaders of Egypt. The pharaoh determined what the Israelites could and couldn't do. **Now they had to learn to go it on their own.** Let's look at the three lessons this verse teaches.

Lesson No. 1: You shall not steal. This one's easy. **Don't take something that's not yours**. It also means to return extra change, pay proper wages to your employees, and don't cheat on your taxes.

Lesson No. 2: You shall not deal falsely. This is about misrepresentation. Are you selling a car? Don't forget the warning light that only comes on when it's cold. **It's called honesty.**

Lesson No. 3: You shall not lie to one another. This can't be any clearer. Don't lie. Don't fudge. **Not even a little bit.** Say it like it is (with kindness, please). These lessons still apply to us today. We live better because of them. They are so important that **they are woven into the laws of our land.**

The Bible is our standard. Let's hold it high for everyone to see.

March 12 – Living as a Being of Light

IT'S TOUCHING to think of our loved ones as stars in the heavens. They are living in the sky, watching over us, their love shining down on us day to day. They are never lost to us when we can look up and see them every night. **God says we can have that right now.** We don't need to wait until we die. We can **blaze with the light of God's power** starting today. Colossians 2:13 tells us of God's quickening power: "And you, who were dead in your trespasses and the uncircumcision of your flesh, God made alive together with him, having forgiven us all our trespasses."

Bam! All darkness gone! <u>We are living in the light</u>. We were dead in our spirit, **and now we're beings of brilliantly shining light**. We are alive in God, for **he has forgiven us all our sins.**

Why wait until we die? **God wants to make us shine with his salvation right now**. Take the next step. **Become more than human**. Take your place in God's firmament. Become a shining star for the glory of his name. God is your uplifter and the glory of your face. You are wonderfully made in him.

March 13 – Enjoying Our Gifts from God

WHAT GOOD things have come your way recently? Has good news flooded your inbox? **A message from an old friend?** Maybe "good things" means financial gain for you. Has your credit card limit been raised? If so, that's a pat on your back for **managing your finances well**. How about your home? Is your yard green, your central air functioning properly, and your garage door operational? Did your kids make it to the bus this morning? No one suspended this year?

What are our gifts from God? If we pay attention to a few key mega-evangelists, we should be luxuriating in a **king-size home** with a **king-size bed** and two **king-size cars** in the **king-size garage**.

THAT'S NOT WHAT GOD'S WORD PROMISES US. Let's find the truth regarding God's gifts in Ecclesiastes 5:18-19. "Behold, what I have seen to be good and fitting is to eat and drink and find enjoyment in all the toil with which one toils under the sun the few days of his life that God has given him, for this is his lot. Everyone also to whom God has given wealth and possessions and power to enjoy them, and to accept his lot and rejoice in his toil—this is the gift of God."

Now that we've opened God's Word, let's break it down to see what it tells us. First, our enjoyment comes from **the work we do**. That's right. We are to "eat and drink and find enjoyment in [our] toil." **We can't sit on the sofa and expect to have God's blessing flow to us like a benefit check.** Second, we get to enjoy our king-size lifestyle **if God chooses to bless us with it**. It's not ours by right just because we accept the salvation of the cross. Our good gift from God is **the life he's given us to live**, whether one of hard work or prosperous ease.

57

If we want wealth, well, the Bible tells us how to achieve that also. By hard work and the sweat of our brow. Let's change our way of thinking. Let's begin to think like God.

March 14 – 3 Motivations from Zerubbabel

THERE ARE two types of people, those who like the safety of the status quo and those who refuse to be tied to the past. God wants us to leap into his future, **to take advantage of what he has to offer**, and to **move ahead in him**. And still, we have the mortgage payment, our health insurance, and the kid's new shoes to buy. How can we leap forward for God when we are tied to the real world all around us? Let's look at **3 motivations we can take from Zerubbabel** and apply them to our lives.

Motivation No. 1: Zerubbabel was a captive. He started in life's lowest state. He had nowhere to look but up, and there, **he found his motivation in God**. Ezra 3:2, 8 gives us Zerubbabel's backstory. "Then … Zerubbabel … built the altar of the God of Israel, to offer burnt offerings on it, [and] Zerubbabel … made a beginning, together with … all who had come to Jerusalem from the captivity."

Motivation No. 2: Zerubbabel found **motivation in his call from God**. He took God's charge on his life as a personal responsibility. Ezra 4:3 reveals Zerubbabel's strength of purpose. "But Zerubbabel, Jeshua, and the rest … said to them, 'You have nothing to do with us in building a house to our God; but we alone will build to the Lord, the God of Israel, as King Cyrus the king of Persia has commanded us.' "

Motivation No. 3: Zerubbabel chose **obedience over personal gain**. His motivation was to please God and do his divine will. Haggai 1:12 shows the result. "Then Zerubbabel … obeyed the voice of the Lord … as the Lord their God had sent him. And the people feared the Lord."

Let's apply these to how we must live today:

First, our starting place doesn't determine where God is able to take us. Second, our Christian walk depends on us, not those around us. Third, God must take first place in every decision we make.

Our total focus on God is our benchmark for our success in him.

March 15 – 3 Apollos Principles for Today

WE LEARN about the ministry of Apollos in the book of Acts. Paul goes on to reference Apollos in his first letter to the church at

Corinth. Apollos returns to us a final time in the book of Titus. Yet, many of us have never heard Apollos preached in today's churches, *despite Apollos being on par with Paul in the early expansion of the Christian movement.* Here are *3 Apollos Principles We Can Apply to Our Christian Walk Today.*

Apollos Principle No. 1: *Apollos learned the scriptures in detail.* Acts 18:24 tells us: "Now a Jew named Apollos, a native of Alexandria, came to Ephesus. He was an eloquent man, competent in the Scriptures." Apollos was an educated Alexandrian. Alexandria had a library with over 500,000 scrolls. *Apollos knew his stuff.*

Apollos Principle No. 2: *Apollos didn't hesitate to share what he knew of God.* Acts 18:26 tells us: "He began to speak boldly in the synagogue, but when Priscilla and Aquila heard him, they took him aside and explained to him the way of God more accurately." Here's the important part. Apollos was teachable. *He wanted to know more about the person of Jesus.*

Apollos Principle No. 3: *Apollos did what he could to spread the message of Christ.* Acts 18:27 tells us: "And when he wished to cross to Achaia, the brothers encouraged him and wrote to the disciples to welcome him. When he arrived, he greatly helped those who through grace had believed." Apollos' help was immediate and useful. He used the skills God had given him *in the way that best suited the occasion.*

Paul goes on to say in 1 Corinthians 3:6: "I planted, Apollos watered, but God gave the growth." Perhaps, if Apollos had been the letter writer we have in Paul, his words might have become part of today's Bible. Who knows? What we do know is that *Apollos lived his life by principles we can respect and emulate.*

Let's be like Apollos. Let's do what we can to further the kingdom of God.

March 16 – **Releasing the Lion Inside of Us**

LIONS ARE fearsome predators. They can take down prey *many times their size.* Not only can they work in tandem with other lions, the strength in their paws can *snap necks and bring instant death.*

God has given us the strength to be lions in the face of oppression. When bad things come our way, we can *roar in defiance, gather our partners in prayer, and take down our enemy.* 2 Kings 6:16 is our bastion of encouragement. "He said, 'Do not be afraid, for those who are with us are more than those who are with

59

them.' "

How big is your enemy? **Is your entire family plotting your downfall?** *Those who are with us are more than those who are with them.* **Are bill collectors knocking at your door?** *Those who are with us are more than those who are with them.* **Is your home fracturing at the seams?** *Those who are with us are more than those who are with them.* **Are your investments skittering away like marbles on a downhill slope?** *Those who are with us are more than those who are with them.* **Is your health report worse than a thunderstorm on a moonless night?** *Those who are with us are more than those who are with them.*

With Jesus at your side, you become fearsome in the face of the world. **God wants to release the lion inside of you.** He desires you to understand *you have the ability to take down prey many times your size.* **You can destroy those who rise against you and be victorious in the name of our Lord.** So, roar in defiance, *gather your partners in prayer*, and take down the enemy that has arisen against you. **Your time is now.** God is your strength, and you will be *successful when you trust in him.*

Step out on the Word of God. You cannot fail when Jesus is with you.

March 17 – 4 Proverbs for a Child's Solid Foundation

A SIXTH GRADE Texas teacher sat in a parent conference one spring, hoping to resolve several behavioral issues a boy had exhibited over the course of the year. Letters home hadn't made a difference. Phone calls had been likewise fruitless. Over the months of repeated interaction, the student's mother had agreed that her son needed to change his behavior, while the father repeatedly defended him.

The student's mother also taught in the district, and she was the teacher's usual home contact. At the principal's request, the father also attended the final meeting of the year. As the conference progressed, the boy's teacher watched the child's father repeatedly shift position in his chair, interrupt others, and drum a pencil on the tabletop without realizing he was doing any of those things. It was a revelation that **the nut hadn't fallen far from the tree.**

It's our job as parents to **rein in the nut,** to ensure that our children produce fruit that **helps them be successful** in their lives. Here are **4 Proverbs for a Good Foundation for Children.**

Proverb No. 1: Proverbs 13:1 says **discussing our expectations** is a good start. "A wise son hears his father's instruction, but a scoffer does not listen to rebuke."

Proverb No. 2: Proverbs 1:10 admonishes us to avoid people who **influence us to do wrong.** "My son, if sinners entice you, do not consent."

Proverb No. 3: Proverbs 15:5 tells us we must pay attention to the **instructions of our elders.** "A fool despises his father's instruction, but whoever heeds reproof is prudent."

Proverb No. 4: Proverbs 20:11 says the outcome of our life is **our responsibility.** "Even a child makes himself known by his acts, by whether his conduct is pure and upright."

No two children are the same. If we understand ourselves (as adults), we can help our children **mature into responsible people.**

God has a plan, and our children have a special part to play.

March 18 – 5 Ways Hezekiah Showcased Good Leadership

HEZEKIAH INHERITED the throne of Judah, the Southern Kingdom of Israel when he was 25 years old. He was a friend of the **prophet Isaiah** and grandson of the **prophet Zechariah.** Hezekiah, as a newly crowned king, made changes immediately, **starting a series of triumphs that would cement his name in the records forever as a truly great leader of Judah.**

Hezekiah's 1st Leadership Triumph: *Hezekiah reopened the Temple gates, once again giving the people access to God.* 2 Chronicles 29:3 tells us: "In the first year of his reign, in the first month, he opened the doors of the house of the LORD and repaired them."

Hezekiah's 2nd Leadership Triumph: *Hezekiah restored proper sacrifice and worship, overturning years of disrespect for God by previous kings.* 2 Chronicles 29:24 says: "And the priests slaughtered them and made a sin offering with their blood on the altar, to make atonement for all Israel. For the king commanded that the burnt offering and the sin offering should be made for all Israel."

Hezekiah's 3rd Leadership Triumph: *Hezekiah broke into pieces the brazen serpent Moses had made, forcing the people to turn from superstition back to God.* 2 Kings 18:4 relates: "He removed the high places and broke the pillars and cut down the Asherah. And he broke in pieces the bronze serpent that Moses had made, for until those days the people of Israel had made offerings to it."

Hezekiah's 4th Leadership Triumph: *Hezekiah trusted in God to defeat the attacking Assyrians.* 2 Kings 19:35 says: "And that night the angel of the LORD went out and struck down 185,000 in the camp of the Assyrians. And when people arose early in the morning, behold, these were all dead bodies."

Hezekiah's 5th Leadership Triumph: *Hezekiah asked God for a sign he would recover from a severe illness, and the sun stood still for part of a day. Hezekiah ruled for another 15 years.* Isaiah 38:8 tells us: " 'Behold, I will make the shadow cast by the declining sun on the dial of Ahaz turn back ten steps.' So the sun turned back on the dial the ten steps by which it had declined."

Hezekiah wasn't a perfect man. He had weaknesses. When he focused on the Lord, **God used Hezekiah to lead his people with courage, wisdom, and foresight.**

Our weaknesses are of little account when our strength comes from God.

March 19 – Relegating Shame to the Trash Heap

WHAT IS SHAME? Something *heaped on us* by someone in a more powerful position? Let's look at the definition of shame from Merriam-Webster: *"a painful emotion caused by ... guilt, short-coming, or impropriety"*

To feel shame, according to Webster's, we must have *one of three things happen.* **First might be guilt.** If we've done something wrong, broken a law, or *gone behind someone's back*, we might be a candidate for shame. **Second, we might have a shortcoming.** We can't do as well as expected of us. We fail the test, burn the toast, or *don't get into the best school.* **Third is impropriety.** We've stepped outside society's boundaries. We've worn the wrong clothes, *behaved awkwardly*, or broken an unstated (or stated) rule.

The Bible in Romans 10:11 tells us: "For the Scripture says, 'Everyone who believes in him will not be put to shame.' " Guilt is cast away. *It no longer applies to us.* We've been washed by the blood. Our shortcomings are now in God's care. He lifts us up to achieve success *through the power of his name.*

Impropriety in the world is a thing of our past. Our new boundaries *come from God and God alone. God says we will be mighty warriors in him.* We will stand tall in his name. When we speak, the demons will have to flee.

Are people putting you down for your faith? *Cast them off.* Are you nervous about sharing Jesus? *Your backbone is Christ.* Do you have regrets from your previous life? Jesus says you are forgiven, and *those things no longer apply to you.*

Toss out shame. *It belongs on the trash heap.* You are now a child of the holy God. Our relationship with the Savior is the only one that matters.

March 20 – 7 Truths Nahum Reveals About God

NAHUM IS best known for his prophesies against Nineveh, a prosperous city of Nahum's day. Nahum was much more than a **one-hit-wonder. He was a man tuned in to God, and his words reveal much about our Maker.** Here are **7 Truths Nahum Reveals About God.**

Truth No. 1: *God has an angry side.* **Don't rile him.** Nahum 1:2 says: "The Lord is a jealous and avenging God; the Lord is avenging and wrathful; the Lord takes vengeance on his adversaries and keeps wrath for his enemies."

Truth No. 2: *God protects those whom he loves.* **He is a refuge to his children.** Nahum 1:7 assures us: "The Lord is good, a stronghold in the day of trouble; he knows those who take refuge in him."

Truth No. 3: *The power of God manifests in acts of nature.* **God feels, and nature responds.** Nahum 1:3 reveals: "The Lord is slow to anger and great in power, and the Lord will by no means clear the guilty. His way is in whirlwind and storm, and the clouds are the dust of his feet."

Truth No. 4: *No one can plot successfully against God.* **God will intervene.** Nahum 1:9 points out: "What do you plot against the Lord? He will make a complete end; trouble will not rise up a second time."

Truth No. 5: *God wants us to celebrate him.* **His righteousness is our message of triumph.** Nahum 1:15 encourages us: "Behold, upon the mountains, the feet of him who brings good news, who publishes peace! Keep your feasts, O Judah; fulfill your vows, for never again shall the worthless pass through you; he is utterly cut off."

Truth No. 6: *God frees us from every problem.* **Our victory comes through him.** Nahum 1:13 is exciting: "And now I will break his yoke from off you and will burst your bonds apart."

Truth No. 7: *God restores his faithful with his majesty.* **There is no depth from which he will not deliver us.** Nahum 2:2 is a shouting verse: "For the Lord is restoring the majesty of Jacob as the majesty of Israel, for plunderers have plundered them and ruined their branches."

The next time the devil tries to beat you down, return to the words of Nahum. His prophesies will **lift you back into God's glory**, and you will be **renewed once more**. We can be bold in the Lord when we learn to trust in him.

March 21 – **Released from Despair**

PEOPLE CAN pick. They are like woodpeckers outside our window boring into a tree, pick, pick, pick, pick. Our thoughts ring with the oppression as they come against us, accusing us of things we didn't do, and *holding us to a benchmark not even they can reach.*

It's like the song *Charlie Brown* by The Coasters: "Why's everybody always pickin' on me?" We feel like a clown, always at the bottom of the pile, and *never able to break free of people's opinions of us.*

Psalm 57:3 says *we have a rescue on its way.* "He will send from heaven and save me; he will put to shame him who tramples on me. Selah. God will send out his steadfast love and his faithfulness!"

The word Selah is important in this verse, because it adds a tone to the sentences before and after that we must pay attention to. Selah is to *lift up, to exalt.* It also means *to continue forever.* Not only is the Lord on the way with help for our situation, *he will lift us up and exalt us on high.* He is our champion forever, and we will *never again be slandered or subject to reproach.*

It's time to get our excited boots on. *We are released from despair.* The world has no power over a child of the King. Today is our moment of victory. Let's cheer for our Jesus, our rescue and salvation.

March 22 – **3 Stages of God's Everlasting Love**

HOW MUCH do I love thee? Let me count the ways. That's from Elizabeth Barrett Browning, Sonnet No. 43. In her sonnet, Ms. Browning tells us the depths of her love, how it affects her daily thoughts, and that her love will continue after death, if God wills.

Let's change Ms. Browning's question a bit. **How much does God love us?** We can find the answer to that in Ephesians 2:4-7. "But God, being rich in mercy, because of the great love with which he loved us, **even when we were dead in our trespasses**, made us alive together with Christ—by grace you have been saved— and raised us up with him and **seated us with him in the heavenly places in Christ Jesus, so that in the coming ages he might show the immeasurable riches of his grace** in kindness toward us in Christ Jesus."

God's love for us grows richer as this passage continues. The bold text isn't in the original, but it shows that our God desires to do exceeding good things to reveal his eternal and unbounding love for his creation. God's love flows to us in **three stages of everlasting compassion and love**.

The 1st Stage of God's Everlasting Love: God loved us when we were **caked with sin**. " … even when we were dead in our trespasses …"

The 2nd Stage of God's Everlasting Love: God gives us a place **at the side of Jesus**. "… seated us with him in the heavenly places in Christ Jesus …"

The 3rd Stage of God's Everlasting Love: God's love flows our direction through the **eternal ages to come**. "… so that in the coming ages he might show us the immeasurable riches of his grace …"

Elizabeth Barrett Browning expressed eight ways her love flowed from her unto her beloved. God says there's **no end to the love** he showers over his children when they call him Father. God is rich in mercy and love, and he wants to share it with us.

March 23 – 3 Reasons to Get Out of the Sun

TRY SUMMER in Texas. Or South Florida or Arizona. The sun will fry your scalp. Stay out too long, and you'll boil your blood. Your body won't be able to cool off fast enough, and you'll risk **heat-stroke and possible death**.

That's a good reason to get out of the sun.

Anger can make us feel the same way. We sense our blood about to boil. We are ready to blow our top, and heaven help anyone who's around when we do. **We need to get in the shade.** Find a place out of anger's blaring sun. Slow down and let the **sweetness of peace** cool us inside. The book of Proverbs gives us **3 Reasons to Get Out of the Sun**.

Our 1st Reason: Proverbs 22:24-25 says angry people can **give us a sunburn**. "Make no friendship with a man given to anger, nor go with a wrathful man, lest you learn his ways and entangle yourself in a snare." We need to leave them outside and find our respite in the shade of a peaceful friend.

Our 2nd Reason: Proverbs 19:11 tells us overlooking others' flaws is **like a drink of cool water**. "Good sense makes one slow to anger, and it is his glory to overlook an offense." We can find the shady path if we look for it. It's up to us where we walk.

Our 3rd Reason: Proverbs 21:19 says we can easily **burn others with our anger**. "It is better to live in a desert land than with a quarrelsome and fretful woman." The Texas sun in a white-hot sky pales with the scorching we get from an angry person.

God says to get out of the sun. Run from angry people. They will drag us into the fire of their emotional maelstrom. God is our shade. He is our peace. We find our cooling solace in him.

March 24 – **What's the Point of Truth?**

SO, YOU WANT me to be honest. Truly? In everything? Like … about the color of your new living room curtains? And the way you keep your lawn? Or the turkey you prepared last Christmas, the one that was slightly burnt? (A partial lie. It was really burnt and tasted like it.)

How honest do you want me to be? I thought kindness, politeness, and all that stuff was the required oil to keep relationships running smoothly. And don't get me off on positive thinking. I'm supposed to say this will be my best day ever when I've already broken a shoelace and locked my keys in the car? And I haven't even clocked in at work?

Let's look at three scriptures on honesty to see what the Bible says.

Scripture No. 1: Leviticus 19:12 says it's not about politeness. Honesty is about standing up for the truth. "You shall not swear by my name falsely, and so profane the name of your God: I am the Lord." What we can't do is tell someone, "I promise, God's honest truth," when we know differently.

Scripture No. 2: Proverbs 14:5 says we must support honest dealing with other people. "A faithful witness does not lie, but a false witness breathes out lies." What we can't do is tell a false version of events for any reason, not even if we feel it's justified.

Scripture No. 3: James 3:14 says we must be honest about ourselves. "But if you have bitter jealousy and selfish ambition in your hearts, do not boast and be false to the truth." What we can't do is present ourselves as better than we are. No Photoshopping allowed. We must be as we appear to be.

So, go ahead. Be polite. Say the nice things. God certainly expects honesty, but we are to show kindness in everything we say. Jesus could cut to the chase, but he spoke with the heart of his Father in every word. We're most like Jesus when we live his truth before the world.

March 25 – **Recovering the Ball**

WE ALL FUMBLE now and again. We say the wrong word and hurt **feelings or an argument** ensues. We misplace a zero, and the **next three checks** bounce. We don't hear our alarm, and we get **another demerit** at work. God says to **quit focusing on our shortcomings**. He's got something better on the way.

Psalm 34:18 says **our broken heart calls out to him**. "The Lord is near to the brokenhearted and saves the crushed in spirit."

Psalm 147:3 promises our **hurts and failures are remedied by him**. "He heals the brokenhearted and binds up their wounds."

Acts 3:19 assures **we will be refreshed in his presence**. "Repent therefore, and turn back, that your sins may be blotted out."

Ezekiel 18:21-22 tells us **all our old slip-ups are wiped from the slate**. "But if a wicked person turns away from all his sins that he has committed and keeps all my statutes and does what is just and right, he shall surely live; he shall not die. None of the transgressions that he has committed shall be remembered against him; for the righteousness that he has done he shall live."

Matthew 9:13 is our guarantee that **Christ chooses us**. "Go and learn what this means: 'I desire mercy, and not sacrifice.' For I came not to call the righteous, but sinners."

Now's our time. Jesus came to set us back on our feet again. *Arguments resolved.* Financial mistakes cancelled. Job issues coming up roses. **We become changed when we choose to follow in the footsteps of Jesus.** We want to walk taller than we did before. Jesus ensures we will be better than we thought possible.

March 26 – **Our Lost Salvation**

WE CAN LOSE our keys, misplace our glasses, and even forget where we've put our wallet. A woman posted on social media that she misplaced her tablet for three weeks. She searched everywhere only to find it sitting in the passenger's seat beside her all along. The black case blended into her black upholstery, and it became invisible to her.

It was lost to her even as it was at her side all along.

Ah, that it should be so simple with our salvation. We search and search, trying to find the answers to life, and we don't realize God is holding it out to us all the time. We've lost our salvation through self-help programs, psychotherapy, and religions that promise no rules, no penalties, and everyone goes to heaven.

Psalm 3:8 tells it like it is: "Salvation belongs to the Lord; your blessing be on your people!" God is at our side offering us his salvation. It's up to us to open our eyes and take advantage of his offering. 1. Believe on Jesus as God. 2. Accept his authority over your life. 3. Change to become like him.

God's salvation is the blessing we can all have. Let's accept it today.

March 27 – **Escape Hatch Christianity**

STORM SITUATIONS are a fact of life in coastal communities. The worst of those occur in low-lying areas that can't drain heavy rainfall quickly enough. Then let an offshore wind drive the high tide to unprecedented levels, and *the water can become deadly.*

Survival experts warn people not to climb into their attics to escape rising water. There's no escape hatch to open air. Without an ax to pummel our way through the roof, *we are trapped in an impossible situation.* **It's vital to keep a way of escape in mind,** to have a *back door exit available,* to always consider alternative routes we can use.

The Bible tells us God has thought through an escape from every spiritual temptation we might face. 1 Corinthians 10:13 says: "No temptation has overtaken you that is not common to man. God is faithful, and he will not let you be tempted beyond your ability, but with the temptation he will also provide the way of escape, that you may be able to endure it." God will not let you be tempted beyond what you can withstand. He *provides the ax to make your escape hatch.*

Here are some ways to cut through the roof when the waters are rising higher than you dreamed possible.

- Leave the bar. Don't take that second drink.
- Turn off your computer. That website isn't for you.
- Stop listening. Gossip doesn't fit your Christian witness.

- Hang up the phone. That person isn't your spouse.
- Cut up the credit card. You can't afford the payments.
- Make a date with your kids. They need your attention.
- File your tax return on time. Keep your finances in order.
- Call your parents. You can resolve any conflict.

Cut your way out of your situation. *God has provided you a way.* It's up to you to take the first swing. *He will be there to pull you free.*

Break the bonds of temptation. Your strong arm comes from the redeeming power of Christ.

March 28 – 7 Steps to Giving a Good Jesus Report

WINGING IT is not a good style for a news reporter. If a reporter goes off script, they can seem *disorganized*, unsubstantiated, and *out of touch*. Perhaps their facts are all there, but no one will listen. They must follow a plan *to make their news shine.*

As Christians, our witness is the same. We can't evangelize the world with unregulated bursts of enthusiasm, no matter how well intentioned. Here are *7 Steps to Giving a Good Jesus Report.*

Step No. 1: *Write a Headline.* Your opening should be attention grabbing but true. Matthew 4:19 says Jesus "will show you how to fish for people!"

Step No. 2: *Write a Byline.* Identify who you are and your qualifications. 2 Corinthians 5:20 says "we are ambassadors for Christ."

Step No. 3: *Use a Hard News Lead.* Trim your opening statement to two sentences, never more. Names and details can come later. Mark 16-15-16 says that "he that believeth and is baptized shall be saved."

Step No. 4: *Tell the Whole Story.* Here's where you flesh out your lead. Give information, not your opinion. Mark 16:20 says they "went everywhere and preached, and the Lord worked through them, confirming what they said by many miraculous signs."

Step No. 5: *Add Quotes.* Support your story with the words of real people. Include first and last names. John 3:3 says that "Jesus answered and said ... except a man be born again, he cannot see the kingdom of God."

Step No. 6: *Attribute the Experts.* Tell where you got your information. Be specific. Acts 1:8 says you "will receive power when the Holy Spirit comes upon you."

Step No. 7: *Keep Your Report Terse and On-track.* Stick to the facts. No flowery language. Use strong verbs. Luke 12:12 says "the Holy Spirit shall teach you what to say."

Follow these steps, and you'll come across *as the expert you are.* Get out there. **Be bold.** *Stick to the facts, and you will lead people to Christ.*

The truth of God is powerful, and we need to share it regularly.

March 29 – 7 Levels of Andrew's Faithfulness

MANLY. BRAVE. *Filled with valor.* Andrew is a Greek name that means all of these, and Andrew the Apostle lived up to each one.

Although the name Andrew was in common use in the first century, it's notable that there's no equivalent name in either Hebrew or Arabic. To be named Brave was a foretaste of Andrew's future faithfulness to the burgeoning ministry of Jesus.

Here are *7 Levels of Andrew's Faithfulness* that fulfill his name's symbolic meaning.

Level No. 1: Andrew was the first disciple called by Jesus. The Master saw something in Andrew that was vital to his future ministry. Mark 1:17 gives us the Master's words, *"Follow me."*

Level No. 2: Andrew was Simon Peter's brother. Dedication and commitment to the ministry of Jesus ran in the family. Mark 1:16 reveals their family ties, *"Simon and Andrew [were] casting a net into the sea."*

Level No. 3: Andrew introduced Jesus to his brother, Simon Peter. He instinctively shared the Good News with those he cared about most. John 1:41 shows Andrew's priority, *"He first found his own brother Simon."*

Level No. 4: Andrew was the first disciple to see through the world's hype and uncover the truth of Jesus as the Messiah. John 1:41 also reveals Andrew's revelation, *"We have found the Messiah."*

Level No. 5: Andrew brought the boy with the two fishes to Jesus, allowing the Master to feed the Five Thousand. John 6:9 gives us Andrew's announcement, *"There is a boy here who has five barley loaves and two fish."*

Level No. 6: Andrew repeatedly brought people to Jesus, becoming an archetype of the modern evangelist. John 12:20-22 shows Andrew in action, *"Some Greeks ... asked him, 'Sir, we wish to see Jesus.' ... Andrew and Philip went and told Jesus."*

Level No. 7: Andrew exemplified the phrase "fishers of men," at the end of his life embracing crucifixion for his faith. Matthew 4:19 gives us Jesus' invitation, *"And [Jesus] said to them, 'Follow me, and I will make you fishers of men.' "*

Andrew stands the test of time. He is a man who wholly embraced the teachings of Jesus. He provides an example we can follow.

Our faithfulness to the Word is what leads others to Christ.

March 30 – God's Take on Marriage

YOU'VE DECIDED to tie the knot. Or maybe the knot's become frayed, and you want a way out. Maybe you're the one that's found a way to stay married, but yours doesn't follow the rules. You are relieved no one looks deeper than the surface. Let's crack the Good Book and **see what it has to say** about keeping our relationships in good working order.

God's 1st Take on Marriage: Paul's take in Colossians 3:18-19 is well known and often **quoted by proponents of strict biblical ideology**. "Wives, submit to your husbands, as is fitting in the Lord. Husbands, love your wives, and do not be harsh with them."

Speakers love to quote the "wives, submit to your husbands" part, but they often leave out the phrase "as is fitting in the Lord" that follows. **Marriage puts us on an equal footing**. One spouse does not get all the power.

God's 2nd Take on Marriage: 1 Peter 3:7 reveals the foundation for a loving relationship, but **there's one thing we need to clarify**. "Likewise, husbands, live with your wives in an understanding way, showing honor to the woman as the weaker vessel, since they are heirs with you of the grace of life, so that your prayers may not be hindered."

Let's look at the phrase "as a weaker vessel." At the time this was written, strength, size, and literal muscle ruled the world. Women's strength is in their cooperative nature and forceful determination. They are the **equal of any man**. We should focus on the next phrase, "they are heirs with you," instead.

God's 3rd Take on Marriage: In the book of Titus, we discover the **powerhouse of the marriage union**. Let's look at Verse 2:3-5. "Older women likewise are to … train the young women to love their husbands and children, to be self-controlled, pure, working at home, kind, and submissive to their own husbands, that the word of

God may not be reviled."

He who teaches, rules the world. She who instructs her daughters is the master of the household. Men, respect your wife's position in your marriage. **She is equal to you and deserves your very best**. Women, you are more powerful than you know. **Take your husband's hand and walk proudly at his side**. Marriage is a team effort. We succeed when both partners win.

March 31 – **Our Invisible Lifeline**

WE REMEMBER the gameshow *Who Wants to Be a Millionaire?* for the lifelines contestants could use when they didn't know the answer. One was to call a friend, *get a second opinion*, and hopefully move on to the next round. The real question for the contestant became, *did they trust their lifeline?* Did they believe their lifeline was *offering them valid aid?*

Were they more likely to win with or without the help of their lifeline?

John 20:29 reveals the lifeline Thomas used to secure his relationship with the Lord. "Jesus said to him, 'Have you believed because you have seen me? Blessed are those who have not seen and yet have believed.' "

Thomas believed because he *touched the hands of the Master* and knew the scars were from the cross. Thomas had his lifeline on speed dial, and *Jesus showed up just in time.*

What about the rest of us? Jesus isn't just "showing up" at our prayer meetings, arriving in the flesh, and offering us his hands so we can inspect his scars. *Where's our lifeline?* This verse says we are blessed more than Thomas when we believe in Christ *despite never having touched the palms of his hands.*

The contestants on the gameshow could dial up their lifeline on the phone. *We dial up Jesus through prayer, often on our knees.* He responds to us when we do, with *advice, love, and compassion* for the troubles we go through.

Let's find our lifeline in God. We become a millionaire in him when we do.

— April —

April 1 – Improving Your Self-Image

WE CHECK the mirror each morning to see if our collar lies flat, our hair is orderly, and the colors of our outfit match. We want to look our best when we exit the front door. It makes a difference, you see, in how people treat us. *When we look the part of a successful business owner or an affluent shopper, we elevate the treatment we receive from others.*

How can we improve the way we treat ourselves? We find the answer in Psalm 119:6. "Then I shall not be put to shame, having my eyes fixed on all your commandments." This is more than a spiritual quip, an empty platitude that we spout to appear in touch with our "God" side. *There's fact and real-life advice in this verse.*

Let's start with the last half, "… having my eyes fixed on all your commandments." **This works in every area of life.**

Drive the speed limit. You won't worry when you see a patrol car. *Respect the marriage bed. Unexpected texts won't worry you.* Don't cheat on taxes. Letters from the IRS will be good news. *Treat employees well. They will benefit your company.* Don't gossip. Your friends won't wonder if you can be trusted. *Don't lie. You won't have to keep track of what you've said.* Don't steal. You'll avoid jail time.

It also works in the spiritual realm. *Study God's Word. You'll understand the nature of the Father.* Attend church. Your children will respect God's place in your life. *Spend time in prayer. You'll become attuned to God's direction for you.*

Already you're feeling better about yourself. **Shame is no longer part of who you are.** You are what you appear to others, and *that's a very good thing.*

Align yourself with God, and he will become your biggest fan.

April 2 – Reaching Out for God's Blessing

HAVE YOU ever been around someone who feels entitled? By that I mean that they think good things should come to them *just because they deserve them.* No work involved. They say, "I'm owed this. It's mine by default, automatically, and without having to fight for it."

It goes against our work ethic, one that says we get good things

73

when we put in enough effort. Spend the time, earn the dime. That's the way it should be. We *work our 9-to-5*, and we *get our paycheck* at the end of the week.

What's our 9-to-5 in God's scheme of things? We read about it in Luke 14:13-14. "But when you give a feast, invite the poor, the crippled, the lame, the blind, and you will be blessed, because they cannot repay you. For you will be repaid at the resurrection of the just."

There are *four groups of people* we must include in our plans if we want God to bless us, or as we think of it in today's world, to *give us a paycheck for the hard work we've put in.*

Our 1st Group: The poor. These are people who've faced the gauntlet of life and financial success is outside their skillset. They will continue to suffer unless someone gives them a hand up.

Our 2nd Group: The crippled. This group was successful at one time, but life has cut them at the knees. It has also taken away their resolve for trying again. They've given up.

Our 3rd Group: The lame. Life is against this group from the onset. They never have a chance. Whether health or circumstances, they are doomed from the onset.

Our 4th Group: The blind. Call them nearsighted, on the cusp of trendy things, or just pig-headed, the blind among us can't see spiritual truth when it knocks them on the head.

It's easy as Christians to hunker in our churches and *clasp hands with the faithful.* **That's not what God wants us to do.** It's the poor, the crippled, the lame, and the blind who have nothing to offer us in return. *That's when God's blessings begin to kick in.* **That's when our paycheck becomes our due.**

When we give God our time, the Lord repays us every time.

April 3 – **Your Planting Season Is Today**

SEEDS HAVE a season. Some seeds need to be planted in the warmth of the sun. Others need to overwinter to begin the germination process. God says that *now is the time to plant your spiritual seed* so that your harvest can begin to mature. Hosea 10:12 tells our planting process: "Sow for yourselves righteousness; reap steadfast love; break up your fallow ground, for it is the time to seek the Lord, that he may come and rain righteousness upon you."

Our life lived by God's laws are the seeds that will begin to grow in the Lord. When we pay our bills. Our honest words. Being there for our children. Reading the Bible and *doing what it says.* These are what we need to do, in addition to *showing kindness, consideration, and love to those we meet.* Add to that **generosity and a welcoming hand**, and our field is coming along.

Our verse says fallow ground (unused opportunities) cannot be left unplowed. Look for the good you can do for others, and *your reward will expand beyond your imagination.*

Now is your season. Today is your time. The work of God needs you.

April 4 – **Your Morning Is About to Dawn**

THE TURNING of the earth is accepted fact. The sun drops below the horizon each evening, and darkness sweeps over the land. The night is vital to the workings of the land. Our crops, the weather, even us. We require sleep to *renew ourselves for the upcoming day.*

God is there for us to find in each new day. **His power sweeps over his children with the rising of the sun.** Just as your body washes the toxins of living from you each night, so God *renews you during the dark times that seem to overwhelm you.*

Psalm 30:5 is our *word of encouragement when we feel abandoned by God.* "For his anger is but for a moment, and his favor is for a lifetime. Weeping may tarry for the night, but joy comes with the morning."

Anger happens and is gone, a flash of light that disappears as soon as it happens. God wants us to *step back into his favor* with the rising of the morning sun. Tears may flood our eyes, but that's not who we are. **God is our joy**, and in him, we *release his peace and understanding* in every situation.

Earth turns. We don't question it. We accept the night as part of the process. Bad things happen. **That's part of life.** *Then God steps in, and our tears are wiped away.* **Trust in God.** *He is on the way.* **Better things are in store for you.**

Wait on it … wait on it … wait on it … *God is the lifter of your soul, and your morning is about to dawn in him.*

When our faith is rooted in God, we will bloom in the light of his grace.

April 5 – **3 Rescues for Children**

WE COME into the world as blank slates. We are pure clouds of emerging beauty floating in a clear sky.

We become what we encounter. **Our life molds us into the shape that will define our characters from then on**. We can become a gentle rain that enriches the lives of others or a thundering downpour that destroys everything in its path.

As parents, our duty is to be the mold that will ensure our child's growth toward the Lord. We equip our children **when we train them to love doing good** for others. We rescue them from the raging waters of life.

Proverbs 10:1 gives us our first rescue, the gift of wisdom. "A wise son makes a glad father, but a foolish son is a sorrow to his mother." Children can learn to make good choices. As parents, it's our joy to teach them by our good examples.

Proverbs 28:7 is our second rescue, the gift of rules. "The one who keeps the law is a son with understanding, but a companion of gluttons shames his father." Society is structured to provide safety and opportunity. When we follow the law, our children will benefit from our example.

Proverbs 8:32-22 lays out our third rescue, the gift of God. "And now, O sons, listen to me: blessed are those who keep my ways." Without God, all else is a broken string, good for nothing of importance. Our life lived for Jesus will rub off on our children.

No father, no mother wants their children to come to a bad end, to find their pleasure in drugs, gambling, or **activities that abuse others**. We set the example. **We are their guiding hand.** When we introduce our children to God, we get them started on the road to a good life.

April 6 – **Our Roots that Nourish Us**

ROOT-BOUND PLANTS can seem healthy at first glance. Their leaves are green, and we can polish them to a gleaming gloss. Here's the thing. They begin to choke, *they won't grow*, and their leaves will eventually yellow and fall off.

Plant a shade-loving shrub in full sun, and it may do well for a while. Soon, however, the soil will dry, and *the plant will be starved for moisture*. It will weaken, its growth will slow, and it will never reach its potential.

We need fertile soil and a good water source for the best growth. No matter how much attention we give the visible part of the plant, if the roots suffer, *the entire plant will soon die*. Jeremiah 17:8 tells us: "He is like a tree planted by water, that sends out its roots by the stream, and does not fear when heat comes, for its leaves remain green, and is not anxious in the year of drought, for it does not cease to bear fruit."

What's our water source, our stream that never dries up? What keeps our roots nourished even when the drought of financial hardship and emotional devastation batter us? Jesus is our river of life, *the source of our sustenance*, and the cooling respite in the heat of summer.

When we plant our roots in Jesus, we can weather every storm.

April 7 – **12 Words for Healing**

DOCTORS PLAY guesswork with our bodies. Don't believe that? Ask any doctor. It is why medicine is called a practice. Some prescriptions are easier to guess, but **it remains hit or miss when it comes to medicine**. Doctors give it their best shot, and if it doesn't work, they keep trying other things until they hit on the right one. Who's to say the right medicine isn't **found in the Bible?** Here's **12 Words for Healing from God's Holy Word**.

Exodus 15:26 says: "For I am the Lord, **your healer**."

Psalm 147:3 tells us: "He heals the brokenhearted and **binds up their wounds**."

Jeremiah 17:14 says: "**Heal me**, O Lord, and I shall be healed; save me, and I shall be saved, for you are my praise."

Acts 10:38 says: "He went about doing good and **healing all who were oppressed** by the devil, for God was with him."

1 Peter 2:24 tells us: "By his wounds **you have been healed**."

Isaiah 53:5 assures us: "But he was pierced for our transgressions; he was crushed for our iniquities; upon him was the chastisement that brought us peace, and **with his wounds we are healed**."

Psalm 103:2-3 says: "[He] forgives all your iniquity, who **heals all your diseases**."

Proverbs 3:7-8 tells us: "Fear the Lord, and turn away from evil. It will be **healing to your flesh** and refreshment to your bones."

Jeremiah 30:17 promises: "For I will restore health to you, and **your wounds I will heal**, declares the Lord."

Psalm 41:3 says: "The Lord sustains him on his sickbed; in his illness you **restore him to full health**."

Matthew 14:36 tells us: "And as many as touched [Jesus' garment] **were made well**."

James 5:15 is our promise of healing: "And the prayer of faith will save the one who is sick, and the **Lord will raise him up**."

You can't lose when you give God first shot. Hit or miss. **Jesus is our healer.** Christ wants you to come to him today.

April 8 – **The Sun Arises Each Morning**

NIGHTS CAN grow dark. In the Far North, the sun is shadowed by the earth for months at a time. When life goes awry, it seems like the lights have gone out completely. Our bills will never be paid. Our health will pull us down.

We will never find that perfect woman … or man. Yet. Let me repeat that. Yet, *yet*, **yet**, God says things are not over. There is light on the other side of the darkness. The sun will rise again, and you will bask in the *warmth of his glory*. 1 Peter 1:13 encourages you to **never give up hope**. "Therefore, preparing your minds for action, and being sober-minded, set your hope fully on the grace that will be brought to you at the revelation of Jesus Christ."

Do these things during the darkness: *Prepare for action. Stay focused on God's plan. Keep your hopes high.* How can you do these when the blackness threatens to overwhelm you? Here are three ways. 1. Spend time with other believers. 2. Join a Bible study (and participate). 3. Thank God daily for what he's promised to do for you.

You are going to make it through. *God is your strength.* **Jesus is at your side through every hour.** Your morning is coming. God says it's already on the way.

April 9 – **Susanna Chooses God**

SUSANNA COMES to us from the book of Daniel. Susanna was a godly woman, *trained in the Law of Moses*, and married to an influential man. The judges of Israel regularly met with her husband in his home. Susanna walked regularly in her walled garden, *in what she considered ultimate privacy.* The judges caught glimpses of her beauty and desired her.

While bathing in her garden, the judges connived their way into her private walled garden and accosted her, *threatening to debase her honor with lies* if she refused their advances. Daniel 13:22 says: "Susanna sighed deeply, and said, 'I am hemmed in on every side. … I choose not to do it … rather than to sin in the sight of the Lord.' "

Susanna was accused of vile things in court and *condemned to death* on the word of the wicked judges. Daniel 13:44 tells us: "And as she was being led away to be put to death, God aroused the holy spirit of a young lad named Daniel."

Yes, the same Daniel from the story of the lion's den. Daniel entered the picture, *called the people fools* (Yes, it's in the Bible.), and exposed the lies of the two judges with their conflicting testimony against Susanna. Susanna was saved, and the two judges *received the fate intended for the innocent woman of God.*

Susanna could have taken the easy way out, allowed the judges to have their way, and no one would have been the wiser. Except she didn't. *She took the higher road, even though it almost cost her life.* God used Susanna's integrity to establish Daniel's reputation among the people of Israel.

When God is our strength, we can endure whatever the devil throws our way.

April 10 – 3 Infusions of God's Love

INFUSION IS A cooking term. We can mix eggs and milk, stir sugar into our coffee, even scramble hamburger meat for spaghetti. **None of those does what an infusion does.** An infusion permeates **every part of whatever it touches**.

Infuse those brownies with dark chocolate, and the flavor **bursts from every bite**. Infuse your roast with cloves, and the aroma will **saturate your senses** with tasty goodness. When we infuse a spice or flavor into our food, it becomes **as much a part of the food** as the food itself. Here are **3 Infusions of God's Love** from Psalms.

Infusion No. 1: "For he has not despised or abhorred the affliction of the afflicted, and he has not hidden his face from him, but has heard, when he cried to him." Psalm 22:24. When we hurt, God surrounds us, fills our situation with his presence, and changes everything. His presence **permeates every part of our pain**.

Infusion No. 2: "Many are the afflictions of the righteous, but the Lord delivers him out of them all." Psalm 34:19. When trouble comes against us, the presence of God **bursts forth in every situation**. His power flows from us, and the bad things are turned around to our good.

Infusion No. 3: "Though I walk in the midst of trouble, you preserve my life; you stretch out your hand against the wrath of my enemies, and your right hand delivers me." Psalm 138:7. **God saturates us with his protecting power**. Every bad thing that comes our way is turned to tasty goodness by the power of the Lord.

We can't mix God into our lives one day a week. It's no good to stir him into our mealtime prayers. We can't even scramble him into our family time. **We must infuse God into every part of who we are for our lives to make a difference for him.** God wants to be our everything. He wants as much of us as we'll give him.

April 11 – God on the Line

A MAN SAID he realized he was old when his grandson asked why he always said to "hang up the phone." **Smart phones simply disconnect.** Another youth visited a friend's cabin in the mountains and couldn't get a signal with his smart phone. He didn't use the land line because he thought the phones were out of order. **He was hearing a dial tone for the first time.**

God says he is connected to you. There's no handset, no cell signal, no dial tone needed. John 14:13-14 tells how our call gets through. "Whatever you ask in my name, this I will do, that the Father may be glorified in the Son. If you ask me anything in my name, I will do it."

What's our phone? Prayer. How do we connect? On our knees. What do we ask? ANYTHING IN THE NAME OF JESUS. Why does this work **every time?** *So that the Father may be glorified in the Son.* Go on. Get connected. God is on the line, and he's waiting for your call today.

April 12 – 2 Times Joseph's Blessing Benefited Others

WHY DOES God shower his blessing on us? Why does the Father answer our prayers when we ask in faith and believe for the answer? If the answer is for us to feel good or have our need met, that's correct as far as it goes, **but it's only part of the answer. God showers more than enough on us so that it can spill over onto those around us.** Let's look at two times God blessed Joseph and the blessing Joseph received overflowed onto the people around him.

The 1st Overflowing Blessing: Genesis 39:1-23 describes events after Joseph was sold into slavery in the house of Potiphar, one of Pharaoh's officers. Potiphar saw God's hand on Joseph's life and made him overseer of his house and all that he had. Verse 5 tells us **"the Lord blessed the Egyptian's house for Joseph's sake."** Not only was Joseph blessed with reward for his faith in God, his Egyptian master increased in favor and wealth because of Joseph.

The 2nd Overflowing Blessing: Genesis 41:37-46 underscores Joseph's rise to the top of the Egyptian power chain. After spending time in prison, Joseph interpreted Pharaoh's dream, and as a reward, Pharaoh placed Joseph as the second highest authority in the kingdom. Verse 40 gives us Pharaoh's words: **"All my people shall order themselves as you command."** Joseph's new position of power blessed the entire nation with enough food to survive the upcoming famine.

Joseph was enslaved, then wrongly accused of sexual assault by his master's wife. He languished behind bars, forgotten by those who had offered to help him. Joseph must have felt abandoned by God and that his future was too dark to endure. **Not so. God was preparing Joseph for a mighty future.** Through his continual dependence on the Lord, **Joseph became a blessing to others when he refused to give up on his faith in God**.

Your faith in Jesus benefits more than just you. Your faithful walk with God showers blessings on those who share your life.

April 13 – 3 Revelations of Forgiveness

WE KNOW forgiveness is difficult. **That's not what this is about**. We're moving past that. We're accepting that we've **already decided to forgive** the bad guy, the one who's done us wrong, who's stepped on our toes and caused us pain.

We're starting off our forgiveness in the book of Mark. Mark 11:24-26 tells us: "Therefore I tell you, whatever you ask in prayer, believe that you have received it, and it will be yours. And whenever you stand praying, forgive, if you have anything against anyone, so that your Father also who is in heaven may forgive you your trespasses." **Our 1st Revelation of Forgiveness** reveals that unforgiven wrongs others have done to us will get in the way of God forgiving our sins. Ouch, and ouch, again. That makes forgiving others a **vital part of our relationship** with the Father.

Next we're moving to forgiveness in the book of Matthew. Matthew 6:14 tells us: "For if you forgive others their trespasses, your heavenly Father will also forgive you." **Our 2nd Revelation of Forgiveness** says we commit God to our cause when we offer forgiveness to those who have wronged us. God becomes our ally. **He teams up with us**. He gets on our side.

Now let's look at forgiveness in the book of Romans. Romans 12:20 tells us: "… If your enemy is hungry, feed him; if he is thirsty, give him something to drink; for by so doing you will heap burning coals on his head." **Our 3rd Revelation of Forgiveness** takes us to a new level. We must do good things for the person we have forgiven. That's right, even if we don't like them. Forgiving is the first step. We must **honor them**, also.

Forgiveness is a choice. It's easier when Jesus walks at our side.

April 14 – **Living as a Columbus**

SO, WHAT'S with Christopher Columbus? Why's he so highly touted in the annals of history? What did he do that thousands of others hadn't already done? And to top it off, was he the only one on the three ships that sailed from Spain to bump into the New World?

Here's Columbus' stand-out calling card. *He risked everything on a belief that no one could prove and wasn't accepted by much of the world.* The scientific community of Columbus' day generally thought the earth was flat … and that *we were at the center of the Universe.* Yes, the sun revolved around the earth (or so many people thought) as did Mars, Jupiter, and the stars. Giant turtles held up the earth, and all around the known land masses, the *oceans tumbled into the depths in ginormous, thundering waterfalls.* Few people expected the Nina, the Pinta, and the Santa Maria to return from their foray into the wild unknown.

That's how we need to live as Christians. *Take a risk.* Go where God tells us, *even if no one expects us to survive.* Proverbs 3:5 tells us: "Trust in the Lord with all your heart, and do not lean on your own understanding."

Columbus knew what his heart was telling him to do. He didn't need to have the route *mapped out on his smart phone*, or a Google app *showing him the way.* He just went, *discovered something he didn't expect*, and changed the world forever. **That's God's plan for us.** We may not end up where we thought we were headed, but we'll be *exactly where God wants us to be.*

God is our guide, and he will never lead us astray.

April 15 – **2 Steps to Perfection in Christ**

IT TAKES about 2,000 steps to walk a mile.

You can design a car in 7 steps, but it takes about 400 to build it. We can **step up to a task**, meaning to take responsibility, and we can **step aside** when we're in the way.

Vincent Van Gogh, artist, once said, "Great things are not done by impulse, but by a series of small things brought together." Helen Keller, author and activist, said, "I long to accomplish a great and noble task; but it is my chief duty to accomplish small tasks as if there were great and noble."

Every step we take to better ourselves is **vital to the next one** we take. No one wakes up one morning, and with no preparation, steps on the moon. That first happened in 1969, and it took years of concerted cooperation by hundreds of people and multiple rockets fired into space. Mark Twain, American author, once quipped, "The secret of getting ahead is getting started." Here are **2 steps to get you started toward your perfection in Christ**.

Step No. 1: Romans 2:13 says we are to **study and follow the precepts** set forth in the Word of God. "For it is not the hearers of the law who are righteous before God, but the doers of the law who will be justified."

Step No. 2: Matthew 12:50 tells us we become one with Christ when we are **one with God's will** for our life. "For whoever does the will of my Father in heaven is my brother and sister and mother."

Your perfection won't happen overnight. **It's a series of small steps**. **Reading the Bible** and **doing what it says** is the best way to start. Your new life in Christ begins with one step toward him.

April 16 – **The Jesus Portal**

LET'S START BY defining portal. Merriam-Webster says it's a **door or an entrance**, especially one that is grand or imposing. Then, Webster's goes on to say it can be an **approach to a bridge or a tunnel**. So, a portal guides us through a doorway to a distant place we cannot see. **Jesus is that for humanity.** He is our guide, our approach to the perfection of an afterlife he offers everyone. The book of Psalms gives us **three encouraging depictions of our Jesus portal**.

Our 1st Depiction: Psalm 48:14 tells us we have a **guide to our everlasting home**. "[For] this is God, our God forever and ever. He will guide us forever."

Our 2nd Depiction: Psalm 49:15 assures us the **grave is not our destination**. "But God will ransom my soul from the power of Sheol, for he will receive me."

Our 3rd Depiction: Psalm 73:26 gives us confidence in the **redeeming power of Jesus**. "My flesh and my heart may fail, but God is the strength of my heart and my portion forever."

Jesus is the door, and **we come to God through him**. He is our portal to new life in God. Here's how it works: 1. Accept that Jesus is the Son of God. 2. Choose to give Jesus control of your life. 3. Model your new life after Jesus in the Bible.

You can become a child of God today. You can walk through that door. **Jesus welcomes you on the other side**. Life flows from God. When we choose to walk with him, he blesses us daily.

April 17 – **Our Compass Points to Jesus**

WE DON'T HAVE to question a compass. We don't ask it, "Where do you want me to go today?" There's no intent in a compass' needle. We can't *influence the direction it points by our will or desire*. The needle will always point the same direction, north. We don't have to understand the compass. It works, and *that's all we need to know for it to lead us home*.

Proverbs 3:5-6 gives us our spiritual compass: "Trust in the Lord with all your heart, and do not lean on your own understanding. In all your ways acknowledge him, and he will make straight your paths."

Here are the four points on our spiritual compass:

Point No. 1: *Trust in the Lord with all your heart.* We don't even consider that God might fail. His way is the only one.

Point No. 2: *Do not lean on your own understanding.* God sees the bigger picture. When he says move, just do it.

Point No. 3: *In all your ways acknowledge him.* God must be allowed along on every part of our journey. He is our all-consuming focus.

Point No. 4: *He will make straight your paths.* Distractions will fade away when we keep our attention on Jesus.

Life will throw obstructions in our way. Our spiritual compass helps us see past all obstructions. *Jesus is waiting*. Let's keep marching toward him.

We are on the right path when we follow the Jesus path.

April 18 – **5 Songs of the Lord**

WE CAN IMPROVE our memories with verses of song. It's in our vocal muscle memory. We can hear a fragment of a song from decades before, and we can sing it, **even though we'd forgotten we knew it**.

Singing praises to God triggers our love for him in the same way. Once we start, the rest falls into place, and **we release depths** of emotion we didn't expect. Psalm 145:3-4 gives us *5 Songs of the Lord:* "Great is the Lord, and greatly to be praised, and his greatness is unsearchable. One generation shall commend your works to another, and shall declare your mighty acts." We can come before him with praise, and **we will become joyful in the household of our mighty God**.

Our first song of the Lord tells the world of his **greatness**. The Lord's majesty **extends throughout the heavens**, for he resides in their embrace.

Our second song of the Lord comes from our heart, for he **deserves our praise**. His glory is **synonymous with his creation**, and in him, the world is glorified.

Our third song of the Lord flows from his **unsearchable mystery**. Man cannot **conceive the depths of the creator**. The Father's touch brings life, and in him, we are daily renewed.

Our fourth song of the Lord shares his **goodness** to all we meet. Our children, our coworkers, the people on the bus, and **the waitress at the restaurant**. We are secure in God's bounty.

The fifth and final song of praise records the **deeds** of God in the annals of history. We in**scribe his name in stone**, and we hold Jesus as the standard for others to emulate.

And if our tears fall as we lift our songs of praise? **That's our love for God coming through.** It's as it should be, as **natural as breathing**, that we should adore our creator in song.

Praise the Lord with a thousand voices, all who enter here.

April 19 – 2 Impacts from Trusting God

WHAT'S OUR purpose in serving God? How does our belief in a higher power impact our lives? How will we change when we come to salvation through the cross and blood of Jesus?

Our Christian walk can't be all *about fine cars, tony houses, and the bling* the world likes to scatter about. **Our calling in Christ must be something more.** 1 Timothy 4:9-10 reveals 2 impacts we must brace for when we place our trust in God. "The saying is trustworthy and deserving of full acceptance. For to this end we **toil** and **strive**, because we have our hope set on the living God, who is the Savior of all people, especially of those who believe."

The boldface is not in the original, but these are the two words we want to look at today.

Impact No. 1: God expects us to be on the job for him. *Toil* means to exert ourselves in labor, to work daily at a task, to become involved and to take responsibility to see our job through.

Impact No. 2: To *strive* involves conflict. We will face opposition in our Christian walk, and we must resolve to hit it head on. We can't sidestep the message of truth found in the Word.

If your faith is only Sunday deep, it's time to broaden your outlook. Jesus wants you to live for him *seven days a week*. Jesus will carry us through, but the journey is ours to begin.

April 20 – 3 Times Habakkuk Earned Our Respect

HABAKKUK IS relatively obscure to modern Christians. An Old Testament prophet, we're not even sure where his name originates, possibly translating as *"embrace"* or *"garden plant."* One thing is certain: **Habakkuk deserves his name.** He embraced his love for God and encouraged the people of Israel to *grow in their relationship with the Father*. Here are *3 Times Habakkuk Earned Our Respect:*

The 1st Time: *Habakkuk didn't mind standing up to God when he disagreed with God's responses.* Habakkuk 1:2 reveals the *fiery nature of the prophet.* "O Lord, how long shall I cry for help, and you will not hear? Or cry to you 'Violence!' and you will not save [us]?"

The 2nd Time: *Habakkuk called things as he saw them.* Habakkuk 1:8 illustrates the *fearless clarity in his vision of Israel's enemies.* "Their horses are swifter than leopards, more fierce than the evening wolves; their horsemen press proudly on. Their horsemen come from afar; they fly like an eagle swift to devour."

The 3rd Time: *Habakkuk was rooted in his trust in the Lord.* Habakkuk 1:5 proclaims his *awe for the power of the King of Kings.* "Look among the nations, and see; wonder and be astounded. For [the Lord is] doing a work in your days that you would not believe if told."

Open your Bible to Habakkuk from time to time. *Soak up the words of the prophet.* Get a feel for his connection with God. Habakkuk walked in communion with the Creator. If we follow his example, we will, too.

April 21 – A Blast of the Best

YOUR LIFE needs to be a subwoofer on overtime. The big kind, the Woodstock variety, eight feet tall, and vibrating with power that **shakes the grains of sand** underneath your feet.

That's subwoofer power.

Tweeters give out the high notes, and your regular speakers fill in the sounds in between, but it's *the subwoofer that gives substance to the sounds we hear*. Imagine the jet flying low overhead, and the windows rattle. That's **subwoofer impact** on our physical world.

A church organ swells in glorious resonance … when we can feel it in the pews, we're in **subwoofer heaven. That's how God wants us to live**, in subwoofer overtime, **vibrating our world with the reality of Christ every day**. Romans 1:16 says we should **shout it to the heavens**. "For I am not ashamed of the gospel, for it is the power of God for salvation to everyone who believes, to the Jew first and also to the Greek."

Revelation 1:3 tells us God's Word reveals the **truth of reality** to those who choose to pay attention. "Blessed is the one who reads aloud the words of this prophecy, and blessed are those who hear, and who keep what is written in it, for the time is near."

2 Peter 1:19 reveals the true path, the clear choice, **the truth that shines forth from the Word**. "And we have the prophetic word more fully confirmed, to which you will do well to pay attention as to a lamp shining in a dark place, until the day dawns and the morning star rises in your hearts."

Let's live **Christ on our sleeve**, let him shine on our faces, come through in our online posts, **shake the world around us. He is the best thing we can share with others.** We're closest to God when we're plugged into his high-volume power source, the Word of God.

April 22 – 2 Helps We Don't Want to Overlook

WATCH SMALL puppies. Their short legs limit their mobility. They can only go places their limbs will carry them. To get to the high places, like on a sofa or a bed, they need a hand up. They don't mind begging. They will take *assistance from anyone who will offer*.

Sometimes we need to be more like a puppy. We've become so independently minded that we refuse to allow anyone to come to our rescue. *We can do it*, we cry, often with defiance and a red face. **Or we go the opposite direction**, become entitled, and we expect the help because it's our right. We no longer see that we must play a part in taking that helping hand we desperately need.

You've failed me again, we cry, as tears roll down our face.

Jeremiah 17:14 says we already have *2 Helps We Don't Want to Overlook*. "Heal me, O Lord, and I shall be healed; save me, and I shall be saved, for you are my praise."

Are you sick, in pain, in need of physical relief? *"Heal me, O Lord, and I shall be healed."*

Are you spiritually adrift? Is your life out of control? *"Save me, and I shall be saved."*

Let's read the part we must play in receiving our help from God. *"For you are my praise."*

We tweak God's heart when we *lift our voice in praise unto him.*

God is our help, and in him, we find rescue in our need.

April 23 – 5 Touchdowns for Sunday School

WE UNDERSTAND the drive to be a winner. It's the **touchdown moment**, the thrill of accomplishment. It's the **payoff for the work** we've put in, and it overshadows the hours of effort we've expended.

Raising children is like football. We practice, we stumble, we fumble, and we recover if we can. We're hoping for a touchdown, that **moment of success** when we see our children maturing into what we hoped they would become.

Psalm 78:4-7 gives us **5 Touchdown Victories** that we get from keeping our children in Sunday school. "We will not hide them from their children, but tell to the coming generation the glorious deeds of the Lord, and his might, and the wonders that he has done. He established a testimony in Jacob and appointed a law in Israel, which he commanded our fathers to teach to their children, that the next generation might know them, the children yet unborn, and arise and tell them to their children, so that they should set their hope in God and not forget the works of God, but keep his commandments."

Touchdown Victory No. 1 – Our children will learn of the mighty works God has done for those who have come before us.

Touchdown Victory No. 2 – They will tell the stories to our grandchildren, passing on the knowledge of God's great works.

Touchdown Victory No. 3 – Each precious little one will set their hope in God, for they will have his story in their heart.

Touchdown Victory No. 4 – Our children will be forever reminded of God's power when situations in life challenge them.

Touchdown Victory No. 5 – Our children will keep the commandments of the Father for the rest of their days.

We can't let the opportunity pass them by. The history of the Bible is made real to them through the **passionate teachings of the great events** of Biblical history. Our touchdown in Christ comes when our children continue to walk in his footsteps.

April 24 – 3 Resolutions Stephen Made Before God

A RESOLUTION is a commitment. Merriam-Webster gives us insight into the word with the first (and most common) definition: *To take a complex idea and make it simpler.* So, when we make a resolution, we take the myriad motivations, facts, and experiences in our life, and we *decide on a course of action.* Our resolution comes about because of many things happening around us and how we respond to the accumulation of those experiences.

Here are *3 Resolutions Stephen Made Before God.*

Resolution No. 1: Stephen lived with God on his sleeve. *He kept his faith on display for anyone to see no matter the situation.* Acts 6:3-5 shows us the respect Stephen garnered. "Therefore, brothers, pick out from among you seven men of good repute, full of the Spirit and of wisdom, whom we will appoint to this duty. ... They chose Stephen, a man full of faith and of the Holy Spirit ..."

Resolution No. 2: Stephen offered God every part of who he was. Stephen had been given a vision of the power of God, and *he was willing to go "all in."* Acts 6:8 tells us of the power God released in Stephen's ministry. "And Stephen, full of grace and power, was doing great wonders and signs among the people."

Resolution No. 3: Stephen took the supremacy of God's presence in his life as fact, and *he trusted the Father to deliver him even in death.* Acts 7:59 reveals Stephen's final moments. "And as they were stoning Stephen, he called out, 'Lord Jesus, receive my spirit.'" Stephen's life was complex, filled with the experiences that led him to believe in and trust God no matter what came his way.

Stephen's ultimate resolutions in life were simple. We can choose to follow his example.

1. We must live boldly before God and Man.
2. We must give God every part of who we are without reserve.
3. We must trust in God in every circumstance.

Choose God. He will be your salvation in every situation.

April 25 – Your Lifeline to God

YOU ARE SPECIAL to God. He treasures you and *pays attention to what you endure in his name.* Sometimes we think, "Ah, why's everyone picking on me?" and we struggle to remember that the love of God flows through us. We wrestle with being kind in return. God says we've earned a special place in his heart when we are kind to those who lord it over us.

James 4:6 says: "But he gives more grace. Therefore it says, 'God opposes the proud but gives grace to the humble.' "

God wraps his grace around you each time someone picks on you. Can you feel it? It's the warmth of his love, *the protection of his arms each time you feel attacked.* The unrighteous will not forever remain on top. God says he views them with disdain and you with love. *You are God's treasure,* and he will lift you up. He is your lifeline when you call on him. You are connected directly to God. His love covers you in every situation.

April 26 – 5 Proofs that Levi Rocked the Ancient World

LEVI IS A popular name for both boys and girls. It means to join, to pull people together, **to draw from opposing concepts and forge a new beginning**. People named Levi carry in their name the essence of what the Christian experience is all about. Let's visit Levi in the Old Testament and look at **5 Proofs that Levi Rocked the Ancient World**.

Proof No. 1: Levi was the third son of Jacob and Leah, **the name number as the Holy Trinity**. Genesis 29:34 says: "Again she conceived and bore a son, and said, 'Now this time my husband will be attached to me, because I have borne him three sons.' Therefore his name was called Levi."

Proof No. 2: Levi **defended his sister's honor** to the death. Genesis 34:25 says: "On the third day, when they were sore, two of the sons of Jacob, Simeon and Levi, Dinah's brothers, took their swords and **came against the city while it felt secure** and killed all the males."

Proof No. 3: Levi didn't flinch **in the face of his father's anger**. Genesis 34:30-31 says: "Then Jacob said to Simeon and Levi, 'You have brought trouble on me by making me stink to the inhabitants of the land, the Canaanites and the Perizzites. My numbers are few, and if they gather themselves against me and attack me, I shall be destroyed, both I and my household.' **But they said, 'Should he treat our sister like a prostitute?' "**

Proof No. 4: Levi's legacy is bound up in the tribes of Israel, **impacting world history for thousands of years**. Genesis 35:23-26 says: "The sons of Leah: Reuben (Jacob's firstborn), Simeon, **Levi**, Judah, Issachar, and Zebulun. The sons of Rachel: Joseph and

Benjamin. The sons of Bilhah, Rachel's servant: Dan and Naphtali. The sons of Zilpah, Leah's servant: Gad and Asher. **These were the sons of Jacob** who were born to him in Paddan-aram."

Proof No. 5: Levi **bequeathed us Moses**, the savior of the Israelites from Egyptian captivity. Exodus 2:1-3 says: "Now a man from the house of Levi went and took as his wife a Levite woman. The woman conceived and bore a son, and when she saw that he was a fine child, she hid him three months. When she could hide him no longer, she took for him a basket made of bulrushes and daubed it with bitumen and pitch. She put the child in it and **placed it among the reeds by the river bank.**"

If you carry Levi's name, stand tall. You are the descendant of **one of history's earliest rock stars**. If you know someone named Levi, **you will see them differently from this day forward.** Levi rocked the ancient world, and **the same God that empowered Levi can help you do the same.** The difference you make comes not from yourself but from the Maker who infills you with the **authority to rock your world.**

Now is the time to step out on God's Word. You can become everything God wants you to be.

April 27 – **Leveling Up in Christ**

LEVELING UP is gaming terminology. Yes, computer games. Each character must achieve a final goal, and they work through "levels" reflecting the progress they've made. Each new level **gives them advantages** in terms of **supplies, speed, or knowledge**. The character performs better than they did before.

When we level up in Christ, we leave behind who we once were, and we become **better in him**. Let's look at James 2:15-16 for an example. "If a brother or sister is poorly clothed and lacking in daily food, and one of you says to them, 'Go in peace, be warmed and filled,' without giving them the things needed for the body, what good is that?"

Social media today is full of empty well-wishers. We click the "love" icon, or the "tears" icon, expressing our connection to a post. Do we ever **follow through with a physical expression** of that connection? It's like when someone greets us and asks how things are going for us. We start to tell them, their eyes glaze over, and they pat our shoulder and say, "Put it in God's hands." We just did – **by telling them**. Didn't they listen?

We are God's hands on this earth. God works **through us to achieve his desired ends**, and when we step around a need with little more than a verbal "God bless you," we are **losing out on God's best for us**.

We level up in Christ when we **follow through on our words of well-wishing**. Replace the leaking faucet. Take the kids for the evening. Do a grocery run. Offer to buy them gas. Use what you have, your skills and possessions, to **make people's lives better**. You will be a better person than you were before.

When we level up for Jesus, we improve through his grace and his love.

April 28 – 5 Insights from the Archangel Michael

WE EXCEL at putting people in their place. We slot them in and compare them by appearance, profession, or **the size of their bank account**. Powerful people get the best parking spaces, largest offices, and the most respect. We're acutely aware of who slots in **just above and below us** in humanity's hierarchy. Governor, bank president, or custodian. **We become what people think of us.**

How important does that make Michael the Archangel, higher than man and just under the King of Kings? Let's look at **5 Insights from the Archangel Michael:**

Insight No. 1: We have a defender. We will face trouble, yet God sends his messengers, the great princes of the air, to provide us aid. Daniel 12:1 says: "At that time shall arise Michael, the great prince who has charge of your people. And there shall be a time of trouble, such as never has been since there was a nation till that time. But at that time your people shall be delivered, everyone whose name shall be found written in the book."

Insight No. 2: We must **default to our Lord when temptation comes** against us. We have no power in ourselves, only in the Son of God. Jude 1:9 says: "But when the archangel Michael, contending with the devil, was disputing about the body of Moses, he did not presume to pronounce a blasphemous judgment, but said, 'The Lord rebuke you.' "

Insight No. 3: Our answer to prayer **comes through persistence**. The very angels from heaven fight for us in the battle between good and evil. Daniel 10:13-14 says: "The prince of the kingdom of Persia withstood me twenty-one days, but Michael, one of the chief princes, came to help me, for I was left there with the kings of Persia, and came to make you understand what is to happen to your people in the latter days. For the vision is for days yet to come."

Insight No. 4: The army of Christ is already victorious. Michael and his angels are the predetermined champions of the spiritual realm. Revelation 12:7-8 says: "Now war arose in heaven, Michael and his angels fighting against the dragon. And the dragon and his angels fought back, but he was defeated, and there was no longer any place for them in heaven."

Insight No. 5: We are not left alone in our battle against the world. We are **never abandoned**, no matter how bad our situation. Daniel 10:21 says: "But I will tell you what is inscribed in the book of truth: there is none who contends by my side against these except Michael, your prince."

We do not battle as men and women. We are surrounded by spiritual giants that slot in around us, and in their presence, we are undefeated in our pursuit of God's truth and holiness. Our grasp on the cross is made stronger by the angels that surround us. They are unequaled in their strength and power.

April 29 – **God's Tomorrow**

TODAY ONLY lasts twenty-four hours. Never less, never more. We can **time it with a stopwatch**. Today never runs too long, and we always have as much of it as we had yesterday.

It's tomorrow that's unlimited. It stretches in front of us for **weeks, months, years, and decades**. God looks out over the time he's given us, and he says **he has plans for us.**

Proverbs 3:1-2 connects our long life to **keeping his rules** and following his instructions. "My son, do not forget my teaching, but let your heart keep my commandments, for length of days and years of life and peace they will add to you."

1 John 2:17 promises us that the Lord will **be there for us** through it all. "And the world is passing away along with its desires, but whoever does the will of God abides forever."

Mark 9:23 assures us we can create **a better tomorrow in Jesus**. "And Jesus said to him, ' "If you can"! All things are possible for one who believes.' "

Jeremiah 29:11 says God will lead us to better things. "For I know the plans I have for you, declares the Lord, plans for welfare and not for evil, to give you a future and a hope."

John 14:2-3 is our guarantee that our rebirth into the heavenly kingdom will be grand and glorious. "In my Father's house are many rooms. If it were not so, would I have told you that I go to prepare a place for you? And if I go and prepare a place for you, I will come again and will take you to myself, that where I am you may be also."

We can't live in our yesterday, and our future is yet to come. Let's start with today and let God lead us into his tomorrow. Hand in hand with God is the only way to live.

April 30 – 2 Beliefs Vital to Every Christian

WE ARE TOLD that if we believe we can do a thing, it moves into the realm of possibility for us. Remember *The Little Train Who Could*. *"I think I can do it ..."* soon becomes *"I know I can do it."* It centers around our faith ... in God ... in ourselves ... *in what we've been promised by people, circumstances, and our own expectations.*

Hebrews 11:6 says that **"I know I can"** *applies to our relationship with the Father, also.* "And without faith it is impossible to please him, for whoever would draw near to God must believe that he exists and that he rewards those who seek him."

Having a spiritual awareness of a greater force in the universe is a start, but we've got to step it up. **We must graduate to the next level.** Just believing in God isn't enough. To please him, we must grasp *2 Beliefs Vital to Every Christian.*

Belief No. 1: We must believe that God exists, that he is who he says he is, and that he sent his Son to stand in our place and provide a redemption for our sins by his sacrifice on the cross. God is not a celestial force benignly ordering the universe. *He is much, much more.*

Belief No. 2: We must believe that God will reward us when we look for him; study the Bible to learn his nature; and strive to order our lives in accordance with the example we find in Christ. God desires our obedience, not our sacrifice. *He wants our praise, our trust, and our time.* **God wants to be at the center of who we are.**

Believing in God is just the start. We've got a lot of him to explore.

— *May* —

May 1 – God's Tender Heart

WE WANT to be understood. We ask, how can someone identify with me if they haven't **walked in my shoes?** Have they climbed my mountains? Stewed in the same pot? Looked through the lens of my life? When someone comes and **trades places with me**, that's when I'll believe they truly care about me.

"Uh-hem." … **clearing throat** … "**Already done. Check out the Bible.**" Hebrews 4:15-16 exposes **God's tender heart**. "For we do not have a high priest who is unable to sympathize with our weaknesses, but one who in every respect has been tempted as we are, yet without sin. Let us then with confidence draw near to the throne of grace, that we may receive mercy and find grace to help in time of need."

Jesus walked in our shoes. He left glory and **got his feet dusty** with good ole Planet Earth. He spent time with humanity, suffered **hunger and abuse**, and then came **The Cross**. What's so important about the cross? Besides our salvation, you mean? It's that question from earlier. **When someone comes and trades places with me … That's exactly what happened on the cross.** Jesus stepped in front of the train for us, took the bullet meant for humanity, and **learned exactly who we are**.

When we cry out in agony, and we lift our voice of despair to God, he can truly say he understands. **He's been there.** *He knows. He's looked through the lens of our life, and he's seen the human condition as we experience it.* When we reach out to God, his tender heart reaches back to us.

May 2 – 6 Inspiring Examples Caleb Set for Us

WE KNOW the story of Caleb from the Old Testament. Along with Joshua and ten other men, Caleb ventured into the Promised Land and *spied out the enemies the children of Israel needed to kick out* before reclaiming their heritage.

Caleb's life is rousing. Here are *6 Examples Caleb Set for Us* to inspire us to *do more and go further for the Lord.*

Example No. 1: *Caleb didn't hesitate to claim the promise of God.* Numbers 13:30 tells us: "But Caleb quieted the people before

Moses and said, 'Let us go up at once and occupy it, for we are well able to overcome it.' "

Example No. 2: *Caleb followed God unquestioningly and realized God's full promise.* Numbers 14:24 says: "But my servant Caleb, because he has a different spirit and has followed me fully, I will bring into the land into which he went ..."

Example No. 3: *Caleb sidestepped the punishment of God because of his obedience.* Numbers 32:12 reveals Caleb's reward: "None [entered the Promised Land] except Caleb the son of Jephunneh the Kenizzite and Joshua the son of Nun, for they have wholly followed the Lord."

Example No. 4: *Caleb actively discarded that which impeded his link with God.* Joshua 15:13-14 shows Caleb's conviction: "And Caleb drove out from [Hebron] the three sons of Anak, Sheshai and Ahiman and Talmai, the descendants of Anak."

Example No. 5: *Caleb encouraged those who struggled with faith in God's promise.* Numbers 14:7-9 is the encourager at work: "The land, which we passed through to spy it out, is an exceedingly good land. ... Do not rebel against the Lord ... [or] fear the people of the land, for they are bread for us. Their protection is removed from them, and the Lord is with us."

Example No. 6: *Caleb inspired his nephew (and son-in-law) to become the first judge in the book of Judges.* Judges 3:9 tells the tale: "... The Lord raised up a deliverer for the people of Israel, who saved them, Othniel the son of Kenaz, Caleb's younger brother."

Let's follow in Caleb's footsteps. Let's experience a life on fire for God.

May 3 – God Wants You to Become a Rock Star

A ROCK STAR? Are you kidding? Do you know the reputation rock stars have? On the website diymusician.com, we're told that "rock stars are mythical, dangerous, and everything most of us aren't."

That's exactly what God wants from us. Let me explain.

Rock stars are mythical. They do things most of us only aspire to. We marvel at their deeds. We think, "Wow! If only I could be like that." Mother Teresa taught the world how to care for the needy. Billy Graham spread the gospel to tens of millions. That's only a pipe dream for the rest of us. God's top followers achieve at mythic levels.

Rock stars are dangerous. They take chances, break boundaries, and disregard the criticisms of their detractors. They risk death to achieve success. David Wilkerson, author of *The Cross and the Switchblade*, lived on the edge among the gangs of New York City to reach the lost. We need to unlock our lives. God wants us to risk everything for him.

Rock stars are everything most of us aren't. Alistair Begg of Parkside Church in Cleveland **teaches the Bible over the radio**. Tony Evans of Dallas' Oak Cliff Bible Fellowship is the **chaplain for the Dallas Mavericks** basketball team. Barbara Brown Taylor, professor at Piedmont College and Columbia Theological Seminary, is ranked as **one of the top ten living preachers** by the Southern Baptist Convention. Joel C. Gregory of Baylor University's Truett Theological Seminary gave the **concluding message at the 2017 Baptist World Conference** in Durban, South Africa. Timothy Keller of New York chairs Redeemer City to City which **starts churches in urban centers worldwide**. Charles "Chuck" Swindoll preaches over the radio, has written 70 books, and was named **Clergyman of the Year in 1988**. Ralph Douglas West founded The Church Without Walls in Houston, ministering to **more than 24,000 families**.

Your Rock Star status is in your Christian DNA. Psalm 1:3 says to **step out for Christ**. "[You are] like a tree planted by streams of water that yields its fruit in its season, and its leaf does not wither. In all that [you do], [you will] prosper."

God has planted you. Now is your time to be successful for his work. Trust in the Lord. His promises will be fulfilled to completion.

Our plan is Jesus. Our astounding life comes through him.

May 4 – 5 Plans to Forget Your Fear

NO ONE likes being afraid. Not really. Sure, roller coasters are fun, and we get off, saying, "I was so frightened. I thought I would die." It's a game, not fear. We don't imagine for a moment we'll *really die. Real fear paralyzes us.* We can't think. Our body systems go haywire. To eat or drink is to tempt it to come back up.

We need to *kick fear out the door.* Scrub fear's residue off the floorboards. *Forget it was ever here.*

Here are *5 Plans to Forget Your Fear.*

Isaiah 54:14 says to *live your life by God's standards*, and fear won't come near you. "In righteousness you shall be established; you shall be far from oppression, for you shall not fear; and from terror,

97

for it shall not come near you."

Romans 8:15 assures us *our adoption into the kingdom* leaves no room for fear to linger in our lives. "For you did not receive the spirit of slavery to fall back into fear, but you have received the Spirit of adoption as sons, by whom we cry, 'Abba! Father!' "

Hebrews 13:6 is our shout that God *drives all fear from our lives*. "So we can confidently say, 'The Lord is my helper; I will not fear; what can man do to me?' "

Psalm 46:1 proclaims God's presence *in every difficult situation*. "God is our refuge and strength, a very present help in trouble."

Proverbs 29:25 guarantees our *trust is never misplaced* when we turn to God. "The fear of man lays a snare, but whoever trusts in the Lord is safe."

Let's review our 5 Plans: 1. Do what the Bible says. 2. Stick close to God. 3. Call on God in your time of trouble. 4. Never choose second best – make God top priority. 5. Take God at his word even when it feels chancy. **God wants us to trust him.** Our faith in him wipes away our fear.

May 5 – 3 Benefits of Moral Instruction

WATCH PARENTS with their children at the mall or an amusement park. Each one has a different take on the **best way to monitor their child**. Helicopter parents **hover over every activity**, shooting down any errant behaviors that make egress into their day. Tiger parents are the **tough-love type** who demand academic excellence above all else. Elephant parents are the opposite of tigers. They **encourage emotional well-being** above independence or other considerations. Dolphin parents come from the POD acronym. **Play** is important. **Others** take precedence. **Downtime** is vital. Lawnmower parents are what the name suggests. They **mow down any opposition** to their children, clearing a path for their success. Then we have the free-range parent. Freedom to roam and play, even at a young age, **promotes independence and self-reliance**.

The Bible tells us we can't afford to leave out good, moral instruction no matter our parenting style. Genesis 18:19 tells us: "For I have chosen him, that he may command his children and his household after him to keep the way of the Lord by doing righteousness and justice, so that the Lord may bring to Abraham what he has promised him."

Here are **3 Benefits of Moral Instruction:** *Our 1st Benefit:* Our children will **follow the teachings of Christ** when they mature into independent adults. *Our 2nd Benefit:* They will do **what's right for other people**, society, and their family when faced with difficult decisions. *Our 3rd Benefit:* Our children will place a high value on **justice and standing up for those** who have no voice of their own.

We can choose our parenting style, and who can tell us we are right or wrong? There's no definitive answer for that. There is a **good case for moral instruction**. Raise your children in the teachings of Christ, and **they will benefit from your choice for the rest of their days**.

Let's hold to Jesus, for his teachings are good and true.

May 6 – 7 Facts about Lazarus

THE EVENTS of the life of Lazarus have become iconic in secular literature. In the storytelling world, Lazarus is a man who lives on, to whom *death is a blip*, someone that has a *longer look toward the horizon than the rest of us*. In the Bible, he is the *good friend of Jesus*, a man the Master cared about.

The tale of Lazarus fascinates us with a man's death and rebirth at the hands of the Son of God. Here are *7 Facts about Lazarus* to encourage you in your walk with the Lord.

Fact No. 1: *Lazarus was an ordinary guy*. Nothing about him was superhuman. John 11:1 says: "Now a certain man was ill, Lazarus of Bethany, the village of Mary and her sister Martha."

Fact No. 2: *Lazarus was part of Jesus' plan*. The Master was in no rush. John 11:6 says: "So, when he heard that Lazarus was ill, he stayed two days longer in the place where he was."

Fact No. 3: Jesus gave Lazarus four days *to ensure he was really dead*. John 11:17 says: "Now when Jesus came, he found that Lazarus had already been in the tomb four days."

Fact No. 4: *Jesus acknowledged what was plainly obvious*. He didn't try to console Lazarus' friends. John 11:14 says: "Then Jesus told them plainly, 'Lazarus has died.' "

Fact No. 5: Jesus commanded *all obstacles to his healing power* to be removed. John 11:39 says: "Jesus said, 'Take away the stone.'"

Fact No. 6: *Jesus pronounced life where there was death*. John 11:43 says: "When [Jesus] had said these things, he cried out with a loud voice, 'Lazarus, come out.' "

Fact No. 7: Faith in God that leads to salvation *is more important than our temporary sorrow*. John 11:15 says: "For your sake I am glad that I was not there, so that you may believe. But let us go to him."

Our situation, no matter how devastating, is an avenue for God to work his will in our lives. Martha and Mary were heartbroken that Lazarus had died. *Jesus knew the joy he was about to bring.* When all we see is the despair of our sorrow, Jesus tells us new life is on the way.

May 7 – How to Get Healing

DOCTORS ARE gifted with the knowledge of God. The best surgeons have the **magnificent construction of God's nerves and tissues** to do the job they do. Scientists test and prove new medications for our healing. **They rely on God's instructions to the molecules and atoms to determine which chemicals are best for which ailment.** Yet, sometimes we are not healed. We visit the doctor, and she raises her hands in bewilderment. She has no answers for us, and we feel frustration wash over us. **Why can't we be healed?**

We can! God's Word tells us how in James 5:16. "Therefore, confess your sins to one another and pray for one another, that you may be healed. The prayer of a righteous person has great power as it is working."

This verse gives us two caveats for our healing. First, we must confess our sins one to another. **Just speaking them to God isn't enough.** Second, we must pray one for another. Trusting God on our own is only part of what God requires. **He wants us to share our prayer of faith with other believers.** This verse even supplies God's reasoning behind his instructions. "The prayer of a righteous person has great power as it is working." We become righteous in Christ **when we confess our sins and ask for forgiveness.** We become powerful in the Lord **when we fall to our knees in prayer.**

We can't let hidden sin keep us from the healing of God. The Father has a plan, and when we align ourselves with him, **he will work miracles through us.** God is our healing, and in him, we will find our good health.

May 8 – Our God-Given Guide

WE GET CONFLICTING instructions on how to live a Christian life. One teacher says do this, and another says to do that. Even our denominations are split on how to interpret the Word. "**What did**

100

God mean when he directed the Apostles to write the words in the gospel?" "Are we really supposed to do **that?**"

God knew there would be dissention about the meaning of the Word. Think about this: It's been **thousands of years** since the original words of the Bible were written. How have words, phrases, and expressions changed in that time?

King James, some teachers cry. It's the only version of the Bible we should use. Quit changing the Word of God. Yet, we attempt to read Shakespeare, and unless we're trained in the speech of the day, it's nearly impossible to understand. **Where do we get our training to understand the Word of God?** John 16:13 gives us God's solution. "When the Spirit of truth comes, he will guide you into all the truth, for he will not speak on his own authority, but whatever he hears he will speak, and he will declare to you the things that are to come."

Who is the Spirit of Truth? He is the Holy Ghost, called by many the Holy Spirit. He is our gift from the Father to **clarify what thousands of years of societal changes** have inflicted on God's Word. Let's read and study the Bible. Then allow the Holy Spirit to **guide us into understanding**. He is our revelation, our guide, our avenue into the **perfect understanding of the person of Jesus** and the **holy nature of our Lord**.

God is our guide, and in the Holy Spirit, his will becomes perfectly clear.

May 9 – **Our Divine Repairman**

IN SEPTEMBER of 2019, the owner of a low-mileage, garage-kept German sports car with a folding metal roof got an unwelcome surprise. He slipped inside his 16-year-old weekend car and felt something against his hair. Overnight, the headliner fabric had *turned loose and begun to sag.*

Search results on the Internet revealed the replacement headliner panel was *discontinued and unavailable.* One auto forum said to use push pins placed in an attractive pattern, and people would think it came that way from the factory. He was tempted, but only *for a moment. It wouldn't repair the damage to his standards.* He finally found a video telling how to lower the top halfway, undo nine screws, and remove the panel. A *local shop could reattach the vinyl* to the headliner panel at little cost.

Our lives are like that sometimes. We feel we've taken care of the little things, *protected our family*, <u>treated our friends with respect</u>, and *done what we could* to find success. Then the *headliner collapses around our ears*, and we think, "How did this happen?" It's tempting to consider the *easy options to put it all back together* again, even try to *make our repair attractive*, all the while aware that it's beyond our skill.

What we need to do is *remove the headliner and turn it over to God*. Psalm 27:1 tells us our **salvation in the hard times is found in our Lord**. "The Lord is my light and my salvation; whom shall I fear? The Lord is the stronghold of my life; of whom shall I be afraid?"

Are your finances collapsing around you? *Turn them over to God*. Is your family life coming apart at the seams? *Christ is your answer*. Did your employer's promises turn out to be empty assurances? The Lord of creation is the *stronghold of your life*.

Let's fix our lives the right way. Let's let God complete the repairs.

May 10 – **You Will Come Out Victorious**

HOW BAD is your situation? Are you swamped with responsibilities? Is your financial situation desperate? Is your family about to *crumble around you?* **God says you will be the victor in whatever situation you find yourself.**

We find a sample of God's saving power in Daniel 6:16-22:

"Then the king commanded, and Daniel was brought and cast into the den of lions. The king declared to Daniel, 'May your God, whom you serve continually, deliver you!'

"And a stone was brought and laid on the mouth of the den, and the king sealed it with his own signet and with the signet of his lords, that nothing might be changed concerning Daniel. Then the king went to his palace and spent the night fasting; no diversions were brought to him, and sleep fled from him.

"Then, at break of day, the king arose and went in haste to the den of lions. As he came near to the den where Daniel was, he cried out in a tone of anguish. The king declared to Daniel, 'O Daniel, servant of the living God, has your God, whom you serve continually, been able to deliver you from the lions?'

"Then Daniel said to the king, 'O king, live forever! My God sent his angel and shut the lions' mouths, and they have not harmed me, because I was found blameless before him; and also before you,

O king, I have done no harm.' "

Daniel faced being eaten by lions – real and gnarly lions. With one swipe of their paws, *they could have removed Daniel's head,* yet, the great beasts were calm as a cucumber, looking on the man of God as *a companion worthy of respect and honor.* What was the difference? What saved Daniel in his dire situation? His FAITH in the EVERLASTING GOD.

The king had been tricked into putting Daniel into the lion's den, and he wished the holy man well. **God knows the devil is a trickster, and our Lord wishes us success through the name of Jesus.** *The lions respected the power of God surrounding Daniel.* **The devil is forced to cower when we wear the full armor of God.** *No harm touched Daniel in the most horrific scenario possible.*

You will come out victorious whatever situation threatens your well-being. Trust in God. He will carry you when you can no longer walk alone.

May 11 – **4 Truths About God**

WE CALL God "The Great Mystery." Or perhaps we say he's the "Big Man Upstairs." How about these: **The Unseen, the Unknowable, or the Great Spirit in the Sky.**

How can we identify with a spirit? We're flesh and blood. What we want to know is **how God is like us**. What are our connection points? How are we the same? **What do we feel, experience, and enjoy that's the same as God?** Psalm 145:8 gives us the definitive view of God. "The Lord is gracious and merciful, slow to anger and abounding in steadfast love." Let's look at **4 Truths About God** one at a time.

Our First Truth: *The Lord is gracious.* Imagine Southern hospitality. We're invited in, told to take off our shoes, and we're given a tall glass of iced tea. **Yeah, that's God.**

Our Second Truth: *The Lord is merciful.* Picture standing before a judge. We did the crime. The book is about to land on us. Then the judge says, "I'm giving you a second chance." **That's exactly what God does.**

Our Third Truth: *The Lord is slow to anger.* You crash your grandfather's favorite model airplane. He sits down with you and takes out a tube of glue. Then he helps you reassemble the parts and praises you for a job well done. Imagine God doing that with your life. **He does that exactly.**

Our Fourth Truth: *The Lord abounds in steadfast love.* You get a new puppy and it messes the floor. You don't like the mess, but you love the puppy, so you clean it up. And the next time and the next time. You're seeing it now. **There's no end to God's love.**

God is not a fire-breathing dragon ready to scorch his children. His arms are open for us to come to him. Jesus treasures us even when we are hard to love.

May 12 – The Feather of Truth

WE ARE TOLD that the pen is mightier than the sword. A small thing we can balance on one finger can do more damage than a two-handed shaft of gleaming steel. Our tongue? It weighs only a few ounces, yet it can slice and dice. Our words can strike out and do more damage than a pen ever could. **How about something with no physical substance at all? How much damage can it do?** Let's look at Proverbs 25:18 to read about **truth**. "A man who bears false witness against his neighbor is like a war club, or a sword, or a sharp arrow."

False witness, or to lie. By definition, false witness is the opposite of the truth. If we lie about a situation, we might as well whip out a war club and batter our neighbor on the head. We should go ahead and skewer them with a sword. Fling a sharp arrow into their body to bring devastation upon them. **God says that's not what he gives us permission to do. We are to be better than that.**

Truth is a feather that gently brushes our cheeks, and in the touch, **we know the sweetness of God's love**. Let's be a feather and reveal God's truth in all that we say and do.

May 13 – 3 Incentives to Be Generous

WE FROWN at tightwads. Why do they grasp so tightly at their money **when they have enough to share?** A miser huddles around a single lightbulb when her bank accounts are **fat enough to light her entire home**. The cheapskate walks out of the restaurant without paying a tip because "they didn't get any value out of the service." **God says to stop it!** That's not his example. We are to be generous if we want to abound in the blessings of God. Here are **3 Incentives to Be Generous:**

Our 1st Incentive: Attempting to hold on to money will **cause it to slip away**. Proverbs 11:24-25 says: "One gives freely, yet grows all the richer; another withholds what he should give, and only

104

suffers want. Whoever brings blessing will be enriched, and one who waters will himself be watered."

Our 2nd Incentive: Our generosity is **rewarded in this life and in the life to come**. Psalm 37:25 tells us: "I have been young, and now am old, yet I have not seen the righteous forsaken or his children begging for bread."

Our 3rd Incentive: We become rich in the eyes of the Father **when we share with those who are in need**. 1 Timothy 6:17-18 is our promise from God: "As for the rich in this present age, charge them not to be haughty, nor to set their hopes on the uncertainty of riches, but on God, who richly provides us with everything to enjoy. They are to do good, to be rich in good works, to be generous and ready to share."

Tightwads do no one any good. Bah! **Don't be one of them**. Misers are more miserable than happy. **Sharing brings smiles**. The cheapskate is an offense to God. **Do not associate with such people. God loves generosity.** His nature is to give good things to his creation. He wants to bless you with more than enough through the generosity you show to others.

Jesus shared his life with humanity. It's time we offer ours to him.

May 14 – Checking Our Boots at the Door

OUR BOOTS are emblematic of our lives. When we travel enough of life, stuff begins to **stick to us**. The demands of our job, and expectations that don't quite fit Jesus' example of kindness and fair play. Our family situation that tempts us to bolt and run, leaving our responsibilities behind. The stress of the daily grind and our need for some sort of release, even when it involves harmful substances.

Then we show up at church wearing the same boots that have covered our feet all week. Do we even notice how filthy they are?

Jesus says, "I love you. Check your boots at the door. I want you to come into my presence clean and pure."

Is it really that easy to **toss off the bad behaviors, the disgusted attitude**, and the deeds we've done? Here's what Jeremiah 31:34 tells us: "… For I will forgive [your] iniquity, and I will remember [your] sin no more." Looking on down, Jeremiah 33:8 says: "I will cleanse [you] from all the guilt of [your] sin against me, and I will forgive all the guilt of [your] sin and rebellion against me."

We ask if it's really that easy … whether we can just check our boots at the door. **It seems so.** Look at what 1 John 2:12 has to say: "I am writing to you, little children, because your sins are forgiven for his name's sake."

No one's making this up. These nuggets of truth come directly from the Word of God. Move on to Isaiah 43:25 to grab the horns of God's love. "I, I am he who blots out your transgressions for my own sake, and I will not remember your sins."

Did you get that? God forgets your stained and tattered boots are **even outside the door**. 1 John 1:7 is the treasure you need to carry with you today. "But if we walk in the light, as he is in the light, we have fellowship with one another, and the blood of Jesus his Son cleanses us from all sin."

When we remove our boots and check them at the door, we begin to **walk in the light of Jesus' love**. We are cleansed from the muck we've walked through, and **we become pure in him**. Jesus is our clean-up man when we invite him into our lives.

May 15 – God Chooses You

A WOMAN and her husband were shopping at a big box store. As they wandered the aisles, she repeatedly found items that called to her. She lifted each one for her husband to look at, certain he would be just as interested, before returning many of them to the display when she saw the price. Occasionally, he glanced at the items, gave a disinterested reply, and returned to inspecting his fingernails, checking his phone, or idly riffling through the store's displays.

The two had **very different experiences** in the store. The wife was **searching for things** to interest her, and her shopping basket indicated the things she thought **gave her a good value.** The husband didn't want to be there. None of the items his wife held up, no matter how good its value, caught his attention. That is, until they reached the fishing section. The husband's eyes lit up, and he wanted to **inspect every item**. The price? **Unimportant**. It was **fishing gear.**

Advertisers know how to package products to make them appealing to their customers. A flashy label, a product review, maybe the words *new* or *improved.*

What makes God interested in us? What causes the Lord of Creation to pick us up and exclaim that we are the one he wants to take home, that we're worth the price? What's new and improved about us?

1 Corinthians 6:18-20 gives us a plan for raising our value. "Flee

from sexual immorality. Every other sin a person commits is outside the body, but the sexually immoral person sins against his own body. Or do you not know that your body is a temple of the Holy Spirit within you, whom you have from God? You are not your own, for you were bought with a price. So glorify God in your body."

Here's your value-raising packaging: 1. Up your morality game. Keep your relationships clean. 2. Respect yourself as God's temple. He lives in you. 3. Brand yourself with Christ-like actions. People will notice.

When people look at you, they should see Jesus. That's the appeal that will draw them to the cross. Raise your value to God. Live the way he wants you to live.

May 16 – 3 Motivations for the Lazy

FIRST OF ALL, get this right. This isn't about 3 motivations to *allow you to be lazy.* **Forget that.** People find enough reasons to lounge around with the remote in their hand and a cold glass at their fingertips.

This is about what happens when we choose to snooze while there's work to be done. Proverbs 24:30-34 reveals the dire situation that results. "I passed by the field of a sluggard, by the vineyard of a man lacking sense, and behold, it was all overgrown with thorns; the ground was covered with nettles, and its stone wall was broken down. Then I saw and considered it; I looked and received instruction. A little sleep, a little slumber, a little folding of the hands to rest, and poverty will come upon you like a robber, and want like an armed man."

That's a long passage, so let's break it down to reveal the sad things we find in the field of the sluggard, or as we would say today, *the lazy man.*

1. It's overgrown with thorns. A life overgrown with thorns is difficult to maneuver. Everything cuts us, and we want to *blame everyone but the person responsible.*

2. Nettles cover the ground. Nettles are the bad things that infiltrate our days. Wild parties, inappropriate websites, and foul language. *No one wants to be around us.*

3. Our stone walls are broken down. We've lost our morals, our resolve, our line in the sand that we refuse to cross. We are up for anything, *even when it's the bad thing.*

No one intends to fall into poverty. Not a person alive has said,

107

"I'm tired of a good life. I'll be desperately poor for a change." Poverty sneaks up on us with *"a little sleep, a little slumber, a little folding of the hands to rest."* Now's our time to wake up, to get motivated, and to *sidestep poverty's cruel noose.* Now's our chance to *kick out the armed man that would steal all the good from our lives.*

Wake up, wake up! God's time to work is now.

May 17 – **5 Pole Markers in Christ**

POLES ARE GREAT for marking things, especially locations hard to see. Take shopping, for instance. We're in a store, and the shelves obscure our view of what's beyond the nearest display. We can look for the store's pole markers with the names of items thrust toward the ceiling, and we know **just where to head**.

Athletes use pole markers, also. In snow events, they can be **thrust through the snow** to mark the location of obstacles or to form a course. In surfing, they **mark rocks or the location of rescue boats**.

Inter-island ferries love pole markers. They are navigation aids to **keep from going aground**. They are marked with colors or lights to tell the ferries to head to port or starboard to be safe.

What are our pole markers in our Christian experience? How can we find the **truth of Christ**, determine **where God needs us**, and get there safely? And as importantly, **what about us will lead others to Jesus?**

Isaiah 65:17 tells us God will **remove old obstructions** that might trip us up. "For behold, I create new heavens and a new earth, and the former things shall not be remembered or come into mind."

Ephesians 4:22-24 says we will look **more and more like Christ**. "To put off your old self, which belongs to your former manner of life and is corrupt through deceitful desires, and to be renewed in the spirit of your minds, and to put on the new self, created after the likeness of God in true righteousness and holiness."

Colossians 3:9-10 assures us God will **reveal himself to us** as we walk with him. "Do not lie to one another, seeing that you have put off the old self with its practices and have put on the new self, which is being renewed in knowledge after the image of its creator."

1 Peter 1:3 says our marker of our faith is our **hope of resurrection** in Jesus. "Blessed be the God and Father of our Lord Jesus Christ! According to his great mercy, he has caused us to be born

again to a living hope through the resurrection of Jesus Christ from the dead."

Revelation 21:4 promises us **peace in Christ** as a testament of our faith and trust in him. "He will wipe away every tear from their eyes, and death shall be no more, neither shall there be mourning, nor crying, nor pain anymore, for the former things have passed away."

We don't have to guess at our Christianity. It's not a mystery. When we choose to follow Christ, we become different, **our life veers a new direction**, and those people who knew us before will **see the change in us. We will become pole markers to lead others to Christ.**

Jesus is the prize, and we are to direct the lost to him.

May 18 – **3 Calls for Joy**

WE THINK about happiness, the laughter and smiles. It's our goal, what we **hope to find**. We'll be happy when we get that **new job**, a **larger home**, or visit our **dream destination**. It's out there **ahead of us,** and we can have it if we **work hard enough**.

Joy is our better choice.

What's the difference? Happiness is a **response to an immediate circumstance**. We meet an old friend ... our car gets especially good gas mileage ... or we find our favorite shoes on sale. Those things make us happy for a time. Joy is **long term**. If our friend disappoints us, our joy in our family remains. When our gas mileage slips or we must buy our shoes at full price, our sadness doesn't displace our anticipation of other good things in our life. The Word of God says joy is the better of the two. Let's look at **3 Calls for Joy** from the Bible.

Call No. 1: Habakkuk 3:18 tells us: "Yet I will rejoice in the Lord; I will take joy in the God of my salvation." Our salvation in the Lord is a treasure that **lasts for a lifetime** and beyond. It is a source of unending joy.

Call No. 2: Psalm 33:21 tells us: "For our heart is glad in him, because we trust in his holy name." Our trust in God can give us joy **even in the desperate moments** of our lives.

Call No. 3: 1 Peter 1:8 tells us: "Though you have not seen him, you love him. Though you do not now see him, you believe in him and rejoice with joy that is inexpressible and filled with glory." Because we believe in the Father, even though we have not seen him, we can **rejoice with upwelling joy**.

Happiness as a goal is great. We can anticipate the surge of emotions, but we cannot expect it to last. Our joy in God can be ours for a lifetime. **We find it through Jesus our Lord and Savior**.

When we focus on Christ, we uncover what's truly important in life.

May 19 – Respecting God's Choice

WHAT IS IT about marriage? How do we select our life mate? Is it no more than a chemical attraction? The hormones flood our system, and **that's the man or woman for us?** Or is God involved?

Many people believe we have a **soul mate**. Someone we are ideally matched with who will complete us, finish our sentences, and understand when we struggle with life. God says he gives us our spouse as our portion in life. The man or woman we marry is **our gift from God**. We are not to throw away God's gift.

Ecclesiastes 9:9 gives us God's definitive word on the matter: "Enjoy life with the wife whom you love, all the days of your vain life that he has given you under the sun, because that is your portion in life and in your toil at which you toil under the sun." This passage says your spouse is part of you. They are the person you turn to for enjoyment in your work, in your play, in all the activities of your "vanity" or your life's pursuits.

Checking out other people isn't God's way. We aren't allowed to "get bored and go a-looking." We must respect God's choice and renew our love in the spouse at our side. **If we're struggling, here are some options**.

- Bring flowers.
- Say "I love you."
- Go out just the two of you.
- Brag on your spouse to someone.
- Find the good in what they do then celebrate it.

Life can be miserable if you let it. You can choose something better. **Choose joy and take your spouse along with you**. God has given us our spouse, and we should strive to enjoy our time together.

May 20 – 3 Worries You Can Release Today

YOU LAY IN bed at night, and your worries are like raindrops on the windowpane. You hear each one louder than the one before. Just when you begin to doze, *plink*, another worry in the darkness, and you are wide awake once more.

God wants to give you a good night's sleep. **He wants to ease your mind.** He says, "My Son died to give you peace. Your worries are upon him. Give them up. They are no longer yours and cannot trouble you any longer."

Here are **3 Worries You Can Release Today**:

Worry No. 1: *People wish evil on you.* Proverbs 16:7 says: "When a man's ways please the Lord, he makes even his enemies to be at peace with him." When your heart dwells in God's garden, you will find favor in the eyes of those who wish you harm.

Worry No. 2: *Your hard work won't be rewarded.* Psalm 118:7 says: "The Lord is on my side as my helper; I shall look in triumph on those who hate me." God sees every good thing you do, and he is at your side, your helper along the way. God stands for you.

Worry No. 3: *Your life lived for Christ is of no effect.* Luke 1:74 says: "… That we, being delivered from the hand of our enemies, might serve him without fear." Darkness cannot exist in the presence of light. When you serve God with all your heart, you brighten every life around you.

A life lived for Christ is an umbrella that protects you from the worries of the world. Plink, plink, bah, those worries no longer apply to you. You are a child of the King. Sleep well. Your worries rest on the shoulders of Jesus. They are no longer yours.

Christ covers you and protects you from all harm.

May 21 – **Our Unlimited Time**

WE RUN OUR lives by the clock. We catch the alarm at six, and we know we must have the toast **started by half-past**. The subway departs at 7:20, and if we miss it, **we can't clock in on time**. Then there's the report due by noon, and we've barely had time to begin. If the printer's out of ink **again** we know how dicey this could be. **What if we had more time? Another day, another week, another year.** We awake one morning, and we realize we've chased our career and our **opportunity for children** has passed us by. Or our retirement looms, and our **bank account** is unprepared. **Another decade, we cry. We need more time to line things up.**

On our deathbed, we struggle with the things left undone. Projects, investments, family fractures unhealed. Yet there's **nothing we can do. How about our spiritual status?** Have we dealt with that? Have we let Jesus have control, or are we **still chasing our** own desires?

There's still time. **And here's the bonus we get. We'll never run out of time.** John 6:47 tells us: "Truly, truly, I say to you, whoever believes has eternal life." Eternal. Another day, another week, another year. There is no opportunity that has to pass us by. We get it all. **We receive unlimited time from the Lord.**

This life us just a precursor. It's a **buildup to the final event.** The opening act. The title card. The **prologue to the real story** about to unfold. Let's place our confidence in Christ. Let's jam with Jesus. It's time to huddle with the Holy Spirit **to ensure our relationship with God.**

We are in the right place when we are with our Lord.

May 22 – Forming a Love Pattern

LOVE IS LEARNED. Sure, we read about "instant attraction," where we fall head over heels … but that's not love.

What!?! How can you say that's not love?

Because it's not. **It's infatuation.** It can become love … notice that word **become.** Infatuation must change into something that will stand the test of time. **We must form a pattern of love if we want it to endure.** Proverbs 5:18-20 reveals our love pattern. "Let your fountain be blessed, and rejoice in the wife of your youth, a lovely deer, a graceful doe. Let her breasts fill you at all times with delight; be intoxicated always in her love. Why should you be intoxicated, my son, with a forbidden woman and embrace the bosom of an adulteress?"

Here's how it works: 1. Celebrate the person you love … over and over again. 2. Spend time with your love … lots of it. 3. Don't chase other people, no matter how strongly infatuation tries to steal your attention.

That's it. Simple as pie. That's your love pattern, **one that will become part of who you are, given time and perseverance.** God gives us a love plan. It's up to us to stick with it.

May 23 – The Lord Goes Before Us

WHAT'S THE ORDER of a battle? I mean, on the battlefield, **how do the men arrange themselves?** Who goes first, and who comes in behind? Study military history, and you'll find **the expendable guys are generally at the forefront of the fighting**, the **ones you can lose**, and the *battle can still go on*. The generals? The policy

112

makers? The ones who have the power to make the decisions where to go, how to fight, and whether the battle can be won? They are safely at the back of the fray, protected, and **not really in fear for their lives**.

Yet the most motivating leaders lead. They are at the forefront of the conflict, **risking their skin along with that of their soldiers**. Deuteronomy 20:4 tells us: "For the Lord your God is he who goes with you to fight for you against your enemies, to give you the victory."

God doesn't sacrifice his troops. He doesn't make tactical decisions about how many Christians he can lose and still win the battle. **This verse gives us three rousing encouragements in our walk with Christ. Our first encouragement** tells us that God goes with us. **He is always at our side. Our second encouragement** says God fights for us. **We do not wield the sword alone. Our third encouragement** shouts that God gives us the victory. The battle is decided. **We are the winner in the name of the Lord.**

We are in this together. We walk side-by-side with the Creator of the Universe. He **offers us his strong arm**, and **we are empowered in him. The outcome is certain, and we are on the winning side.**

Jesus is our Champion, and he breaks down every barrier in our way.

May 24 – **God Gives You a Fresh Start**

RE-DOS ARE FOR children's games. It's a learning process, a chance for **clarification of the rules**. A re-do also provides an opportunity for <u>renewed self-confidence</u>. We can know success, even if it's on the **second, fifth, or tenth try**.

Video game designers have this figured out, and the digital games we play allow us to **back up, reset, and replay** the most recent flub up we made. We get a fresh start so we can make **greater progress toward success**.

God figured this out a long time ago. He could have simply zapped wrongdoers with bolts of lightning, while calling out in peals of thunder, "I told you so." **God had a *better way*.** Nehemiah 9:17 introduces us to **God's re-do system of success management.** "They refused to obey and were not mindful of the wonders that you performed among them, but they stiffened their neck and appointed a leader to return to their slavery in Egypt. But you are a God ready to forgive, gracious and merciful, slow to anger and abounding in steadfast love, and did not forsake them."

Here are six things we learn about God in this verse. First, God is **ready to forgive**. There's no lightning hanging over our heads. **Second**, God is **gracious**. He is kind, polite, and courteous in dealing with our human nature. **Third**, God is **merciful**. In other words, he is lenient with our misunderstanding of the rules. **Fourth,** God is **slow to anger**. He prods us gently back onto his perfect path. He champions our success and wants us to succeed. **Fifth**, God abounds in **steadfast love**. Steadfast means unfaltering, persistent, and committed. He's there for us even when we can't imagine why. **Sixth**, God will **not forsake us**. Never. No matter how badly we behave, God keeps his hand outstretched, and all we need to do is take it.

Are you having a bad year, perhaps a bad life? **It's time for a re-do.** *God wants to give you a fresh start.* Now is your time. When you're ready to reset your life, God's willing to make it happen.

May 25 – 3 Fixes God Offers Us

ORDER SOMETHING by mail, and it's not unusual to see ASSEMBLY REQUIRED on the packaging. Our new "toy" is broken down into its individual parts for ease of shipment. When we reassemble it, **each part in its proper place**, we can enjoy what we've purchased. If we choose to bypass the assembly instructions, we might end up with a mess, one that doesn't work or serve the purpose for which it was intended.

Our brand-new salvation in Christ comes with an ASSEMBLY REQUIRED notice on the package. We become new in Christ when we **accept him as the authority** in our daily lives, but it's like that children's song: **"He's still working on me."** We're continually in assembly mode, and God is **adjusting and tweaking** to get us just right. Let's see how it goes in John 1:12-13: "But to all who did receive him, who believed in his name, he gave the right to become children of God, who were born, not of blood nor of the will of the flesh nor of the will of man, but of God." This passage tells us God is ready and willing to step in with a "fix" each time we stumble in endeavoring to lift ourselves to his standard.

Our 1st Fix from God: The Word says we are **not born into Christ because of blood**. Just because our parents are deacons in the church doesn't **automatically convey Christ's salvation upon us**. Our salvation comes when we **place our faith in God**.

Our 2nd Fix from God: The Word says we can't live a **good enough life to earn our salvation**. No matter how strong our desire is, we will fall short **without the help of the Lord**. When we believe on the name of Christ, **his salvation becomes ours**.

Our 3rd Fix from God: The Word says we can't **legislate people into living for Jesus**. The laws of the land don't make us followers of Christ in our hearts, **only in the actions forced upon us**. Our only source of salvation **flows from the Father above**.

We keep trying to earn salvation on our own, to improve our human condition, and God says, **"Here, let me fix that." He's the only one who can.** God wants to take control of our lives, and it's time for us to relinquish our authority to him.

May 26 – **Putting On Our Sin Shades**

HORSES GET THEM. We call them blinders, devices to block out what we don't want our horse to see. We use them in cars, visors, to block out the sun so we don't crash into things. How about on our computers? We call it a firewall, digital protection to keep out hackers and viruses.

How do we shield ourselves from temptation as Christians? Where's our protection there? Matthew 5:27-28 gives us an important guard for our souls. "You have heard that it was said, 'You shall not commit adultery.' But I say to you that everyone who looks at a woman with lustful intent has already committed adultery with her in his heart."

This verse talks about women and sexual sin, but our lesson is much wider. If we keep a dollar we haven't earned, we're tempted to want even more. If we sleep in for Sunday school, next time we might also forego the morning service. If we have one drink, we might down the entire bottle. One cigarette … one off-color joke … one trip to the gambling parlor.

If we even look … yes, that about sums it up. *God wants purity from us.* We must wear our sin shades and not look at all.

We're headed toward heaven. We can't afford to get distracted along the way.

May 27 – **2 Acts that Lifted the Jews Out of Danger**

WE LOVE THE story of Esther, a beautiful Jew who became queen of Persia. We commend her bravery in going before the king to plead for her people. Even as queen, she was in peril of death if the king took her plea as an affront to the power of the throne. We rarely focus on Mordecai's part in Esther's story. Without Mordecai's intervention, the queen would have seen her people wiped from the land at the hand of Haman, a vindictive vizier under the king. Here are *2 Acts that Lifted the Jews Out of Danger* and restored life to God's Chosen People.

The 1st Act: Mordecai saves the king's life. He uncovers a plot by the king's chamberlains to assassinate the king. Because of Mordecai, the evil scheme collapses before it can be carried out. Esther 2:21-22 says: "In those days, as Mordecai was sitting at the king's gate, Bigthan and Teresh, two of the king's eunuchs, who guarded the threshold, became angry and sought to lay hands on King Ahasuerus. And this came to the knowledge of Mordecai, and he told it to Queen Esther, and Esther told the king in the name of Mordecai."

The 2nd Act: Mordecai reveals the plot by Haman to commit genocide on all Jews by humiliating himself and wearing sackcloth with ashes to get Esther's attention. Esther 4:1, 4 says: "When Mordecai learned all that had been done, Mordecai tore his clothes and put on sackcloth and ashes, and went out into the midst of the city, and he cried out with a loud and bitter cry. When Esther's young women and her eunuchs came and told her, the queen was deeply distressed ..."

Esther steps up and intervenes with the king. Haman is hanged on the very gallows he had raised for Mordecai. Mordecai, Esther, and the Jews were saved by Mordecai's determination to **live by God's standard and his refusal to worship any other than the One True God**.

When God comes before everything else, we will find protection in the hand of our Lord.

May 28 – Casting Off the Bad News

SO, WE READ there's **global warming.** Then we turn the page to find another **terrorist attack** has taken lives. And **flesh-eating bacteria** have killed another innocent vacationer. We gasp to see images of **sharks where there have been none before**, and to best that, we're consuming micro-plastic in everything we eat. Are we going to die from just being alive?

Psalm 112:7 tells the believer **not to worry.** "He is not afraid of bad news; his heart is firm, trusting in the Lord."

Psalm 91:9-10 says we have two promises of good news from God. "Because you have made the Lord your dwelling place — the Most High, who is my refuge — no evil shall be allowed to befall you, no plague come near your tent."

Our promises **hinge on our trust in God**. Now that we've established that, let's identify our two promises.

Our 1st Promise of Good News: "No evil shall be allowed to befall you." It doesn't say some evil or not very much evil. It says **no evil.**

Our 2nd Promise of Good News: "No plague [shall] come near your tent." No sickness, no bad situation, **none of the bad news** that's going around the circuit will come into your house.

Let's turn to the news and read it like a comic strip. We don't have to be in that story, not when we place our trust in God. Our Heavenly Father has a new story written and ready for us to live. Let's place our trust in him. It's how we cast off the bad news and start the day with confidence in our heart. God is the author of our days, and in him, there is no evil thing.

May 29 – 2 Mysteries Revealed

WE LOVE the anticipation of a wrapped present. What could be inside? If someone took the time to box it up, decorate it with patterned paper, and tie it up with ribbon, **it must be really good**. Our heart races with our imagination, and as we pull the ribbon to untie the bow, our skin flushes, and our hand trembles with the possibilities.

God's present to us came two millennia ago. It remained a mystery throughout the life of Jesus. Our Lord revealed the love of God to all men and brought salvation through his sacrifice on the cross, but **God's present to his children was yet to be unwrapped**. The ribbon was pulled in the Upper Room with the infilling of the Holy Spirit as evidenced by tongues and fire. In that seminal event, the Holy Spirit was gifted to mankind. Here are **2 Mysteries Revealed** about our Helper from God.

1 John 2:27 reveals that the Spirit **teaches us about the nature of the Father** and leads us along paths of spiritual understanding. "But the anointing that you received from him abides in you, and you have no need that anyone should teach you. But as his anointing teaches you about everything, and is true, and is no lie—just as it has taught you, abide in him."

117

Romans 8:26-27 says the Spirit steps in when we need a connection with the Father, *one we cannot pinpoint or define*, and through the Spirit, **we receive intercession with God**. "Likewise the Spirit helps us in our weakness. For we do not know what to pray for as we ought, but the Spirit himself intercedes for us with groanings too deep for words. And he who searches hearts knows what is the mind of the Spirit, because the Spirit intercedes for the saints according to the will of God."

The Spirit is many things to the Christian. Foremost, we receive **understanding and a divine link to God's grace** when we let the Spirit work in our lives. We are empowered in knowledge, **make better choices in our spiritual walk**, and maintain our focus on God's plan for our lives. Being human will steer us off course. **The Holy Spirit will act as an override, able to bump steer us back onto course to our destiny with our Savior.**

Our focus is on Christ, and the Spirit is the gift that keeps our connection secure.

May 30 – Catching Our Reflection

CITY STREETS ARE good places to find out who we are. Or at least **how we look to others**. It's the sun and the glass, the dark interiors of the buildings. If a business has highly reflective window tint, that's even better. We're minding our own business, perhaps deep in thought, and we **happen to glance to our side**, and there we are, amid all the other people going about their business.

It's different than looking in the mirror in the morning. Then we've **prepared ourselves for what we will see**. The puffy eyes, the crumpled sleepwear. We shave, apply makeup, or whatever we do to prepare for the day, and we imagine ourselves as we want others to see us.

In that off-guard moment, glancing at our plate-glass reflection, we **find someone we don't expect**. Out, busy, in action. We blink, decide that's us, and we must **absorb the way everyone else** sees us.

Do we appear the same as in our morning mirror? Or does the reality jolt us? Proverbs 30:12-13 says: "There are those who are clean in their own eyes but are not washed of their filth. There are those—how lofty are their eyes, how high their eyelids lift!"

We have a standard, and it's not up for debate. **We can't remake right and wrong for our generation.** We are treading a dangerous line when we say, "That was wrong then, but now we're enlightened. We have new information." That's called **arrogance**. Putting ourselves above what's right and wrong. We're making a choice to bend the rules so we can pursue the pleasures of the world.

Read the Bible. Understand its standards. We must live them out in everything we do. When we look like Christ, that's the best reflection around.

May 31 – Looking Forward to God's Blessing

WE'VE HEARD it said that we can **speak things into existence**. That's rather like God. He spoke, and all creation flashed into being, from the earth under our feet to the distant stars in the heavens. **We can do that, only *it's not quite the same*.** Here's how it works with us. What we say begins to focus our thoughts and intentions. Once we speak a direction we want to go, we begin to travel that path.

For example, we dream of going to Hawaii. We never tell anyone, but **the dream remains**. We go to work, come home, mow the grass, and invite friends over for a cookout. Life is pleasant, we **never mention Hawaii**, and soon, our kids are grown, and **retirement is on the horizon**.

Now let's go a different direction. We have the same job, mow the same yard, and still invite our friends over, but we **talk about how much we'd enjoy** visiting Hawaii. We start saving, a friend tells us of a good deal on airline tickets, and soon **our vacation begins to seem real**.

The same happens with negative words. We talk of losing our job, and that affects **how we apply ourselves at work**. We moan of our bad health, and we begin to **give in to our aches and pains. God says we need to look up.** What we say speaks things into existence. Proverbs 10:24 says: "What the wicked dreads will come upon him, but the desire of the righteous will be granted."

Let's speak health. Let's talk about prosperity. *Let's discuss the goodness of God even when things aren't going well.* Our words will change our attitude, affect how we perceive the situation, and we will move **closer and closer to success in Christ**.

When we call upon the Lord, his power changes things in our lives.

— June —

June 1 – **Kick It Out the Door**

WHAT'S HOLDING you back from your best in Christ? KICK IT OUT THE DOOR. What do you look at and say, "I don't know if I can give this up." KICK IT OUT THE DOOR. Who's the person that pulls you back into your old ways, the place that draws you in, the job opportunity that forces you to **sacrifice your principles?** KICK IT OUT THE DOOR.

You've got better things on the way. God has stored up the riches of heaven, and he's ready to **pour them out on you**. God asks one thing, for you to show up completely and without reservations.

Cast off what's holding you back. Kick it out the door. Hang up the phone when it calls and **turn up the volume on Jesus**. Luke 18:29-30 says: "And he said to them, 'Truly, I say to you, there is no one who has left house or wife or brothers or parents or children, for the sake of the kingdom of God, who will not receive many times more in this time, and in the age to come eternal life.' "

Responsibility is vital to a Christian's actions and beliefs. Using your responsibilities as an excuse to be lazy in the Lord's work is another thing. Give it up. *Cast it off.* Take the road less traveled. Jump on the mission express. Offer your apologies to those who might not agree with your decisions and tell them you'll **see them on Skype**. God's got a plan for your life, and it's bigger than you can imagine. Go with God. **He's your better choice every time**.

Our future grows brighter the closer we are to God.

June 2 – **Getting Your Groove On with God**

THE PHRASE "getting your groove on" comes from the days of vinyl records. The sound reproduces in the grooves that circle the vinyl disk. That's where the music originates. We slip in the needle, the grooves vibrate the sapphire stylus, and music booms out of the speakers. When we are "in the groove," we are in *rhythm with the music*.

We are grooving, man, getting down with the song. We can sing or dance to the music and *never miss a beat*.

That's how we should be with God, in the groove, never missing a beat. Here are *5 Ways to Get Your Groove On with God.*

Groove No. 1: Acts 10:43 says you can *trust him to wipe away your sins.* "To him all the prophets bear witness that everyone who believes in him receives forgiveness of sins through his name."

Groove No. 2: Romans 6:6-7 says to look at your old ways as dead to you and *cut them loose.* "We know that our old self was crucified with him in order that the body of sin might be brought to nothing, so that we would no longer be enslaved to sin. For one who has died has been set free from sin."

Groove No. 3: 2 Corinthians 5:17 says you are to walk away from even the *appearance of wrongdoing.* "Therefore, if anyone is in Christ, he is a new creation. The old has passed away; behold, the new has come."

Groove No. 4: Romans 6:1-2 says to *pay attention when God convicts you* of something you used to do before you gave your life to Christ. "What shall we say then? Are we to continue in sin that grace may abound? By no means! How can we who died to sin still live in it?"

Groove No. 5: Romans 6:14 says to give up the legalism of the law and trust in the grace found in the *redemption of Christ.* "For sin will have no dominion over you, since you are not under law but under grace."

There's only one thing left to say. *Groovy,* man. We've got the groove on. We're in rhythm with Jesus, and we're gonna rock all the way to the throne.

Jesus provides us the melody, and he wants us to sing along.

June 3 – Looking at Us From the Outside

LISTEN TO YOURSELF on a video. Your voice sounds different than what you hear every day. Catch yourself in a glass storefront. **Do I really look like that? It's when we see ourselves from the outside that we can see ourselves as we are.**

How do people that read our social media posts imagine us? What do the drivers in rush hour traffic think of our manners? Our siblings? Are we still the little brother or sister they remember from two decades ago?

Isaiah 5:21 gives us **potent words to think over**. "Woe to those who are wise in their own eyes, and shrewd in their own sight!"

How can we find the wisdom to change who we are, to become someone who can be looked up to by others? Here are 3 ways:

1. Read the responses to your social media posts. Seriously. Don't discount them, and **don't lash back when you dislike them**. There's a reason you got the response you did.

2. Ask yourself, what if someone cut you off in traffic like you did this morning? Would you feel good about yourself? **Were you really in that much of a hurry?**

3. Are you still sniping at your siblings over hurts from 20 years ago? **Be a bigger person.** If they snipe, smile and let it go.

We must be as the Bible instructs us: kindhearted, generous, and thoughtful to others. In other words, **we must show love.**

When we rethink us, we become more like Christ.

June 4 – 3 Rocks in Our Spiritual Foundation

SOME PARTS of a foundation are more important than others. A keystone is the centerpiece of an arch. Remove it, and the rest is weakened. It will continue to stand for a while, but cracks will appear, and one day, it will come tumbling down. A cornerstone determines the accurate placement (and durability) of the entire foundation.

A couple in England bought a century-old house to renovate. The walls were cob-built, a functional material of mud and straw that can last centuries. Here's the key to making cob-build houses last: the cob must be **elevated on a stone base**, or water will soften the cob material, and the walls will weaken and crumble.

When the English couple began renovations and opened their walls, their cob rested directly on the ground. The cob had to be **completely replaced**, crippling their renovation budget.

A rock foundation is **vital to a building's staying power**, and that's true of our faith in Christ, as well. Here are **3 Rocks in Our Spiritual Foundation** to keep it strong.

Rock No. 1: Proverbs 28:5 says the understanding of life comes through **our relationship with God**. "Evil men do not understand justice, but those who seek the Lord understand it completely."

Rock No. 2: 1 John 5:20 tells us we connect with God when we **find salvation in Jesus, his Son.** "And we know that the Son of God has come and has given us understanding, so that we may know him who is true; and we are in him who is true, in his Son Jesus Christ. He is the true God and eternal life."

Rock No. 3: 2 Corinthians 4:6 reveals Jesus as the **source of spiritual revelation** and the knowledge and understanding of the

122

Father. "For God, who said, 'Let light shine out of darkness,' has shone in our hearts to give the light of the knowledge of the glory of God in the face of Jesus Christ."

We must underpin our faith with the foundation of the Word. Here are our 3 foundational rocks in a nutshell:

- Life is found in God.
- Salvation comes through Jesus.
- The majesty of God is revealed through the Son.

Let's upgrade our spiritual foundations. We build with Christ, the cornerstone of our faith in God.

June 5 – God's Rescue Team

MOUNTAIN CLIMBERS know that sometimes things go wrong. So do cross-country skiers. You get out there, and a **ski binding breaks**, you get a **sprained ankle** … something. Rally drivers. What can go haywire? It's a car. Under extreme performance. **Everything!** Now get in a motorhome. Take a cross-country trip. Travel the shore-to-shore dream vacation. *Beware*. You're bound to discover **a few hiccups along the way**.

We need a rescue team. A fallback plan. *Someone we can notify when our adventure is going bottoms up.* Who do we call? The old pop song says, "Ghostbusters." In reality, 9-1-1 will do. Your local **First Responders**. The fire department, the Coast Guard, perhaps your local police force. You can even sign up for an auto club to **send a wrecker** when your vehicle will no longer get you from Point A to Point B.

Where's our spiritual 9-1-1 rescue? Who comes to our aid when we flounder in our relationship to God? Psalm 91:14 tells us: "Because he holds fast to me in love, I will deliver him; I will protect him, because he knows my name."

This verse uses numerous pronouns. To clarify the meaning, let's replace them. "Because Clarice holds fast to Jesus in love, God will deliver her; God says, I will protect Clarice, because she knows my name."

That was for the women out there. Here's one for the guys: "Because Dawson holds fast to Jesus in love, God will deliver him; God says, I will protect Dawson, because he knows my name."

Now choose one of these and **plug in your own name**. Write it out on paper. Stick to your **fridge or your bathroom mirror**, perhaps slip it **in your wallet. This is your 9-1-1 reassurance. When** you call on the name of God, *he sends his rescue team to ensure your success.*

You are God's treasure, and he will guide you along life's way.

June 6 – Our Price for Success

SUCCESS IS ITS own reward. **So we are told.** If we work hard and achieve something of note, others don't need to pat us on the back. The knowledge of our achievement is all we need. **It's our private vindication for the hours we've put in.** If we fail, **that's part of the process.** We get back up, brush off the hecklers, and **jump back into the fray.**

God says our true reward comes when we're doing well, and we suffer for it anyway. People chide us. Our health takes a hit. Our finances tumble further down than we like, and we continue on our road to what's important.

Take college. You're divorced with three kids, and your way to better your future is night classes. You give up sleep, get your parents to watch the children, and you are tired constantly. What's your reward? **Classes successfully completed and the prospect of living better in years to come.**

It's the same with our work for Christ. It's a good thing, yet we often receive abuse from those who choose not to follow him. That doesn't negate the good we do, and **it pleases God to see us dedicated to his cause.**

1 Peter 2:20 says: "For what credit is it if, when you sin and are beaten for it, you endure? But if when you do good and suffer for it you endure, this is a gracious thing in the sight of God."

If our success is easy, that's nothing to crow about. God's pleasure comes when we **give up our safety and security** to do great things for him. God tallies every good deed we perform, and our reward will come in his good time.

June 7 – 7 Marriage Guidelines from the Bible

SO, YOU'RE ready to tie the knot. Or perhaps you've tied it, but you feel the knot **becoming frazzled.** Maybe you've even begun the untying process. You think there's **nothing to be done** for your marriage now.

The Bible says WAIT. No matter where you are in the process, you can enjoy a continuing, **better marriage**, one that can be a success for you, your spouse, and **everyone else involved**. Here are

7 Marriage Guidelines from the Bible to point your relationship to a successful future.

Marriage Guideline No. 1: Proverbs 5:15 says to **stay within the bounds** of your marriage. "Drink waters out of thine own cistern, and running waters out of thine own well."

Marriage Guideline No. 2: 1 Corinthians 7:3 says to **be kind** to one another. "Let the husband render unto the wife due benevolence: and likewise also the wife unto the husband."

Marriage Guideline No. 3: Ephesians 5:25 says a **Christ-like love** is vital between spouses. "Husbands, love your wives, even as Christ also loved the church, and gave himself for it."

Marriage Guideline No. 4: 1 Timothy 5:8 says we must **take care of our spouse** financially. "But if any provide not for his own, and specially for those of his own house, he hath denied the faith, and is worse than an infidel."

Marriage Guideline No. 5: Ephesians 5:28 says one spouse **cannot be more important** than the other. "So ought men to love their wives as their own bodies. He that loveth his wife loveth himself."

Marriage Guideline No. 6: Ephesians 5:31 says our **spouse takes precedence** over our parents and siblings. "For this cause shall a man leave his father and mother, and shall be joined unto his wife, and they two shall be one flesh."

Marriage Guideline No. 7: Ephesians 5:33 says we must be on **an equal footing** in every part of our marriage union. "Nevertheless let every one of you in particular so love his wife even as himself; and the wife see that she reverence her husband."

Go ahead and tie that marriage knot. Firm up the loose ends. Chuck the divorce proceedings and rediscover why you fell in love in the first place. You can do this. God's Word tells you how. The next step is up to you.

Step out on the Word. Your success is within your grasp.

June 8 – God's Seven Levels of Healing

OUR BODIES have a way of telling us something's wrong. Pain is our friend, although when it washes over us, *it's hard to tell*. Still, if we weren't aware of our physical problems, we'd go on and do more injury than our body could heal. Congenital analgesia (CIP) is a rare genetic disorder that allows some people to feel pressure against the skin but no pain. The condition CIPA also disables the body's ability

125

to cool itself by sweating, creating a real risk of heat-related impacts on the body. Healing is needed in more than one way. For some, it's to *take away pain*. For others, it's to *give it back*.

Isaiah 41:10 says *God will heal us by giving us strength*. "Fear not, for I am with you; be not dismayed, for I am your God; I will strengthen you, I will help you, I will uphold you with my righteous right hand."

Jeremiah 17:14 guarantees *our healing will come through salvation*. "Heal me, O Lord, and I shall be healed; save me, and I shall be saved, for you are my praise."

Jeremiah 33:6 offers *prosperity and security along with our healing*. "Behold, I will bring to it health and healing, and I will heal them and reveal to them abundance of prosperity and security."

1 Peter 2:24 *casts off our unrighteousness when we are healed*. "He himself bore our sins in his body on the tree, that we might die to sin and live to righteousness. By his wounds you have been healed."

Isaiah 53:5 *links our healing with the injuries Christ received* at the cross. "But he was wounded for our transgressions; he was crushed for our iniquities; upon him was the chastisement that brought us peace, and with his stripes we are healed."

Psalm 103:2-4 gives us our healing *along with God's love and mercy*. "Bless the Lord, O my soul, and forget not all his benefits, who forgives all your iniquity, who heals all your diseases, who redeems your life from the pit, who crowns you with steadfast love and mercy,"

James 5:15 imbues us with the *power to heal the sick through faith in the power of the Lord*. "And the prayer of faith will save the one who is sick, and the Lord will raise him up. And if he has committed sins, he will be forgiven."

No pain; no gain. That's an old body-builder's mantra. It's true for the Christian, also. **When we cry out in our suffering for Christ to heal us, all sorts of bonus blessings flow from God's hand along with his healing power.** Our hurting hearts draw us to Jesus, and he reaches to us to flood us with his steadfast love and compassion.

June 9 – 3 Reasons for Hope

DEATH AND TAXES are often quoted as the two unavoidable things in life. Brainyquote.com adds another: trash.

Mark Manson of markmanson.net says we are **born helpless**, we **discover ourselves**, we focus on **our abilities**, and we hope our legacy **outlives our death**.

The Word of God says **we have a hope for the future**. Life is more than death and taxes. **The trash of daily living doesn't have to send us sliding into depression.** We may be born helpless, but **we have a God with the power to save us** from the hopeless desperation of our limited number of days. Here are **3 Reasons for Hope** from the Word of God:

Reason No. 1: John 3:15 says the death of our bodies is **not the death of us**. "That whoever believes in him may have eternal life."

Reason No. 2: 2 Corinthians 4:16 says our rough circumstances on the outside **don't reflect the truth of our spiritual joy inside**. "So we do not lose heart. Though our outer self is wasting away, our inner self is being renewed day by day."

Reason No. 3: Psalm 37:37 says life might tumble us through the spin cycle, but **our ending with God is rooted in peace**. "Mark the blameless and behold the upright, for there is a future for the man of peace."

We aren't promised a life of perfection. Jesus didn't have that, and **we won't, either**. What we do have is a **hope for the future** in him and the promise of life without end. **Not even taxes or death can take that away.**

We have much to look forward to when we look forward to Christ.

June 10 – **Our Outstanding End**

WE ALL START the same, unformed and newly aware of the world around us. Our life's journey takes us along different avenues. Some of us travel tree-lined and shady streets, and others struggle along sunbaked and tortuous boulevards. You may be **flush with cash**, or you may be broke. You may have an **Ivy League degree**, or your chops may come through your experience.

Rolls-Royce or minivan. **Haute couture** or the dollar rack. **Fine dining** or fast food. **When we get to the end, none of it matters.** As we face our transition from this world to the next, our only concerns will be the final hug of a loved one, our next breath, and the rest we hope to find. Revelation 7:15-17 says we can **look forward to an outstanding upgrade** to what began many years before at our birth. "Therefore they are before the throne of God, and serve him day and night in his temple; and he who sits on the throne will shelter them with his presence. They shall hunger no more, neither thirst anymore; the sun shall not strike them, nor any scorching heat. For the Lamb in the midst of the throne will be their shepherd, and he will guide them to springs of living water, and God will wipe away every tear from their eyes."

Our upgrades include: 1. *We will hunger and thirst no more.* Essentially, our desires will be met, fully and without exception. 2. *The sun will not strike us, nor any scorching heat.* Hardships will be a thing of the past. We will have no more worries. 3. *We will drink at springs of living water.* We will receive strength and nourishment from an eternal source. 4. *Every tear will be wiped from our eyes.* Sorrows? Heartaches? Abusive experiences? All gone, completely forgotten, and as if they never were.

Presently we're on a path, a journey. We're traveling from one place to another, our beginning to our end. If we wind up with the Father, **we've found our success in *Our Outstanding End*.**

Jesus wants us along, and in him, our journey is sweet.

June 11 – 5 Wealth Nuggets from Proverbs

HEAR YE, HEAR YE, read all about it. There's more money out there than the world knows how to spend. That sounds silly, but it's true. The richest people in the world literally **can't give away their money fast enough.** By the time they've sorted out who deserves a few hundred million a year, their accounts have already **increased by more than they've given away**.

Then there's the rest of us, working hard for each dollar and wondering why God's not paying attention to how much **we would benefit** from a nice lottery payout. Here are **5 Wealth Nuggets from Proverbs** to help you see money from God's eyes.

Wealth Nugget No. 1: Proverbs 15:16 says money is not the cure-all that assures happiness. "Better is a little with the fear of the Lord than great treasure and trouble with it."

Wealth Nugget No. 2: Proverbs 22:2 tells us our personal worth isn't determined by our bank accounts. "The rich and the poor meet together; the Lord is the Maker of them all."

Wealth Nugget No. 3: Proverbs 11:28 cautions us about trusting in cash as our safety net. "Whoever trusts in his riches will fall, but the righteous will flourish like a green leaf."

Wealth Nugget No. 4: Proverbs 28:20 assures us God will bless us financially when we put him first. "A faithful man will abound with blessings, but whoever hastens to be rich will not go unpunished."

Wealth Nugget No. 5: Proverbs 11:4 guarantees that trusting in the Lord triumphs over riches every time. "Riches do not profit in the day of wrath, but righteousness delivers from death."

The riches are still out there. Perhaps you have your share. Here's the thing: We can't lose sight of our long-term goal. **It's better to bank on God, for he is our rescue in the time of the storm**. When our eye is on God, money will take second place to our relationship with him.

June 12 – 3 Redemptions When We Seek God

ARE YOU STILL waiting on the lottery? Have they not chosen your number? Did I hear that right? You've never even **purchased a ticket?** How will they know you want to win? How about that raise you've been expecting? Has your boss not offered it to you? Are you joking? You haven't even **asked for it?** Do you think he knows your desperate financial situation by default? What do you mean your landlord hasn't repaired your furnace? How can he be so callus? Oh, wait, you're telling me you **haven't reported it?** There's a good chance he doesn't know it's out.

What do we expect of God **without telling him?** Oh, we say, it's God we're talking about. We don't have to tell him. **He already knows.** Let's see what Jeremiah 29:13-14 says about that. "You will seek me and find me, when you seek me with all your heart. I will be found by you, declares the Lord, and I will restore your fortunes and gather you from all the nations and all the places where I have driven you, declares the Lord, and I will bring you back to the place from which I sent you into exile."

We are promised **3 Redemptions When We Seek God**.

1. **God will restore our fortunes.** We will be lifted out of our crushing debt, and we will be prosperous once more.

2. **God will take us out of the places that have stolen our joy and crushed our testimony.** We are released from the prison of our circumstances.

3. **God will return us to our rightful place as his children**. Our social standing, the respect we once enjoyed, it will all be returned.

Notice what this passage doesn't say. **God doesn't give us his 3 redemptions by default.** It's not an automatic win for those who

129

call him Lord. God says we must **SEEK HIM WITH ALL OUR HEART**. That's right. Seek God in the morning, at noon, and at night. Don't stop until you break down the doors of heaven and hear from God. Then, God's redemptions become yours. God wants to lift you up. When you seek him, he will show you how.

June 13 – A Little Dab of Jesus Makes the Love Go Round

HOW MUCH is a dab? Merriam-Webster says it's **a small amount**. Merriam-Webster also says we apply it with **a gentle touch**. Let's think about that for a moment. **We take a small amount of something and apply it gently.**

Have you ever attended a church service where you felt you were being pummeled with the words of the minister? How did you feel afterward? Better, or frightened that you were bereft of all hope? You felt like you had booked a voyage on the Titanic. You weren't underwater yet, but there was no way you were making it safely to the shore.

1 John 2:10 says we need to **dab the love of Jesus everywhere we go**. "Whoever loves his brother abides in the light, and in him there is no cause for stumbling." Read that verse clearly. We can't mistake the **message of truth** found in this sentence. If anything we do, no matter how well-intentioned, causes someone else to stumble, **we are not walking in the light of Jesus**. That includes brandishing the scriptures like a bull in a china shop. **That's not God's way.**

Do we have that in our heads, now? Are we understanding **the Jesus process?** It's like this: **Where in the Bible did Jesus take the baseball bat of God's truth and whack people in the head? It didn't happen. Full stop.** The woman at the well. The tax collector. The rulers of the synagogue. Jesus even spoke gently **to the Roman authorities** as they made the decision to crucify him.

How do we measure up to that? **A little dab of Jesus.** A small amount of his love. It's how Jesus treated the lost and hurting people at his side. **The gentle touch of his presence will draw people unto him.** Our Christian standard must flow from the perfect example of Jesus.

June 14 – 5 Characteristics Making Epaenetus a Pillar of the Church

DURING PAUL'S time, Rome was the center of the civilized world. Travel to and from the provinces usually **began and ended in**

130

Rome. As a premier missionary of the burgeoning Church, Paul had ample opportunity to meet and befriend new converts from across the region. **Epaenetus is only mentioned once in the scriptures**. Yet, this is the man who launched the Church's ministry into Asia. He was the Church's first convert to Christianity in Asia Minor, Rome's easternmost province.

Here's what we know about Epaenetus: 1. His name translates as **"praiseworthy."** 2. He is, by Paul's own words, **his close friend**. 3. He is a new convert, the first from the **initial missionary foray into Asia Minor**. 4. He is the opening gambit into a **cornucopia of God's harvest** in Asia. 5. He is well-known and **an example of Christ's faithfulness** among the early Christian believers.

Romans 16:5 tells us: "Greet also the church in their house. Greet my beloved Epaenetus, who was the first convert to Christ in Asia." Paul only writes **one sentence about his friend**, but his simple words, from a man **whose verbose style could run to pages**, tells us something. **Paul's friendship with Epaenetus was firmly established among the believers.** Paul could write a few words, and **his readers would understand the much larger picture. Praiseworthy. Close friend. Follower of Christ. The door to Asia, now opened and ready for a flood of believers. A person known and gladly accepted into the Christian fellowship.** In essence, **a pillar of the early Church**.

Let's live so the very mention of our name is all people need to hear. **Billy Graham**. Mother Teresa. **Thomas Beckett**. Joan of Arc. **William Tyndale**. Martin Luther. **The Apostle Paul.** His friend, **Epaenetus**. When we live like Christ, people will know we are different from the world.

June 15 – Cleaning Our Undercarriage

IF YOU LIVE up north, the best car washes come with a unique feature: a spray nozzle that **washes the underside** of our car. Why zap the underside of the car with soapy jets of water? We need to get rid of salt-encrusted gunk that will **rot our car from the inside out**.

Living on the coast is the same. If we drive on the beach, our first job when leaving the sand is to power scrub even the things **other people cannot see**. Just polishing the paint won't keep the hidden places we can't see from festering with rust and **weakening the integrity of our automobile**. Just because people can't see the insidious rust digging deeper and deeper into our frame, wiring, and

U-bolts doesn't mean we are safe from the rust's effects.

The Bible says **sin is like the salty encrustation** that lodges in the underside of our car. If left there, rust will form, and before long, we are **faltering with damage beyond repair**. Ezekiel 36:25-26 tells us: "I will sprinkle clean water on you, and you shall be clean from all your uncleannesses, and from all your idols I will cleanse you. And I will give you a new heart, and a new spirit I will put within you. And I will remove the heart of stone from your flesh and give you a heart of flesh."

God says he will **repair our frame damage**, replace **our rusty wires**, and ensure that **every U-bolt is returned to pristine**, factory-new condition. He makes the **heart of us look as good as the outside** of us. He renews our spirit with a **brand-new presence that lives in and through us. We become refreshed in his love, and we can love those around us once again.**

When we come to Christ, let's let him clean all the sin away, even the stuff no one else can see.

June 16 – The Importance of Salvation

SO, WHY BOTHER with salvation? What does the church have to offer us that we can't get elsewhere?

We can be good people. There are celebrated individuals worldwide who are recognized for their **good works and philanthropic deeds**. Is taking out time for attending church and donating to its upkeep even relevant in our modern culture? In previous centuries, church involvement offered a sense of community, but we have social media for that now. **Isn't that just as good?** Besides, we can attend church without the salvation part, can't we? That's in there just for feel-good measures, certainly.

Let's clarify where the Bible stands on the importance of salvation, and why it's the best part of Christian life. 2 Corinthians 5:21 says salvation imparts a very real change in our fundamental being. We become **better than before**. "For he hath made him to be sin for us, who knew no sin; that we might be made the righteousness of God in him."

Ephesians 2:1 says we are infused with the motivation to walk a better path. We want to **constantly improve**. "And you hath he quickened, who were dead in trespasses and sins."

1 Timothy 2:3-4 says we begin to see the world and our situation in a whole new way. We understand the **core truth** of our spiritual

existence. "For this is good and acceptable in the sight of God our Savior; Who will have all men to be saved, and to come unto the knowledge of the truth."

We can try to be good people without salvation, but we'll **always miss the mark**. We'll slip on the banana peel of conflicting emotions, and the damage will be done. Salvation is our better choice. We are infused with **spiritual power from a higher plane**, and God becomes our **mentor and guide**. Salvation is for everyone. Take hold of it today.

June 17 – **God's Perfect Law**

WE KNOW we must have law for society to have order, but that doesn't mean we always like it. The speed limit. What's the point in our high-powered sports car **if we can only do 40?** And homeowner's restrictions … or city parking laws. It's our home. **Why can't we do what we want?** Then there's the church. Rules for this and rules for that. We must wear our shirt fastened to this button, **our hair to a certain length**, and heaven forbid we show up at prayer meeting with too much eyeliner.

God wipes his hand across the church's lawbooks and says, **"Forget all that. I have a better way."** James 1:25 reveals God's plan for living according to his laws. "But the one who looks into the perfect law, the law of liberty, and perseveres, being no hearer who forgets but a doer who acts, he will be blessed in his doing."

God's law is a perfect law with none of our human imperfections. God's law gives us liberty **to be a better person**, a kinder person, and one who *lives a cleaner life*.

God's only speed limit is how fast we want to go to catch up to him.

June 18 – **God Will Make a Way**

DAVID, THE MASTER songsmith, the singer of praises, and the worship leader of Israel, gave us much of the Book of Psalms. A favorite verse from the man after God's own heart comes from Psalm 118:5. Let's look at four life-changing truths found in this verse.

Life-Changing Truth No. 1: "Out of my distress …" God is never far from us. **Our situation doesn't distance us from the Father. He is near at hand.**

Life-Changing Truth No. 2: "I called on the Lord." Our cry of need moves the Lord's heart. **We are his children. He wants us to**

draw unto him.

Life-Changing Truth No. 3: "The Lord answered me ..." Our needs are God's concern. **Our own children can call in the middle of the night, and we rush to them.** *How is God any different?*

Life-Changing Truth No. 4: "[He] set me free." What's holding us back? What's imprisoned us, bound our feet in the mire, and kept us from our success? **God wishes to cast it onto the dung heap.** *He will toss it as far from us as the east is from the west.*

The words of the prophet in Isaiah 43:19 give us God's new direction. "Behold, I am doing a new thing; now it springs forth, do you not perceive it? I will make a way in the wilderness and rivers in the desert." Our old life, our despair and distress, are part of our past. **God is moving us forward.** Even when we can't see it, **God is in control, and he is doing great things for us.** Our wilderness is our stressful job, our broken car, and our physical illness. Our desert is our lack of companionship, our empty bankbook, and our emotional devastation.

God says he will make a way! Our job is to trust in him, to follow him faithfully, and to praise him when each good thing comes our way. Our strength in God is our promise. Our praise is God's due.

June 19 – Standing in the Fire

IT'S EASY TO BE a Christian in the 21st century, or at least in modern society. We can attend services via computer, donate to missionaries with a click on our phone, and we never have to leave our cushy, air-conditioned surroundings. We click *Like* on social media, follow our favorite mega-evangelists, and even listen to the *latest Christian music on streaming services.* From the street, we're just another house with a nicely trimmed lawn, little different from every other residence on the block.

The early apostles stood in the fire. They took risks we will never face. Derision and death pummeled their doors in the dark of the night, and their only choice was to *trust in the faithfulness of the Lord.*

In Philippians 4:3, we learn of **Clement of Alexandria**, a highly educated Roman convert ministering to Paul and the saints at Philippi. "Yes, I ask you also, true companion, help these women, who have labored side by side with me in the gospel together with Clement and the rest of my fellow workers, whose names are in the book of life."

How many words are in the Bible? *Perhaps 800,000.* In the New Testament, there are fewer than half that. The Word says there's no room to include all of Jesus' miracles, and yet, Paul found space to include Clement's name in his letter to the church at Philippi.

Clement was a sturdy rock upon which the early church was built. He mentored Paul in his seminal days in the faith, took a hand in leading the Roman church, and *upheld the ideals of the perfect Christian.* His epistle to the church at Corinth, now preserved in the British Museum, was highly revered by early believers.

Clement stood in the fire, taking the heat of the ancient world's derision for the cause of Jesus. **Clement is an unsung pillar of the early church**, and without his dedication to Christ's cause, Christianity would have *struggled to spread across the known world at the time.*

Let's leap into the fire for Jesus. *When we burn with our faith, God can do miracles through us.* Our memory of those who came before us vaults us to do greater things for the kingdom of Jesus.

June 20 – **Taking Down Your Giants**

HEARTS FALTER when giants come calling. It happens to everyone. The singer on stage the first time. The soldier facing overwhelming odds. The entrepreneur when his business model is falling apart around him.

Let's look at the biggest giant of all, the monster of antiquity, the story of **taking down a giant of an opponent** in the ancient book of Samuel. The Philistines were a rough-and-tumble people. They crushed their opponents and left them quivering in the dust. They wanted the kingdom of Israel for a tasty snack. Goliath was their champion, and Israel quivered in their socks, unable to command anyone who would meet the challenge. **Then came David, a boy, a youth with more faith in God than fear of the enemy.**

1 Samuel 17:48-49 reveals the outcome of the day: "When the Philistine arose and came and drew near to meet David, David ran quickly toward the battle line to meet the Philistine. And David put his hand in his bag and took out a stone and slung it and struck the Philistine on his forehead. The stone sank into his forehead, and he fell on his face to the ground."

Here's our core takeaway from this passage. **When we base our authority in the rules of the Kingdom, we can run toward the**

battle. We chase down the evil one, we tackle our fears, and **we pummel what frightens us until it lies face to the ground**.

YOU ARE NOT A QUITTER. You are God's champion, filled with his supernatural power, and the victory you claim is the success God will give you. You will take down every giant when you have Jesus at your side.

June 21 – 4 Good Words from John

JOHN WAS a **close friend of Jesus**. He was one of the four musketeers, the four pinnacles of the modern church, the men who were Christ's **closest associates** and who wrote the Master's story and turned it into the four gospels: Matthew, Mark, Luke, and John. We revere them as the source of much of the New Testament's truths. These men **knew, walked with, and learned to trust** in our Lord. Jesus touched their hearts, spoke into their ears, ate with them, and **traveled the dusty roads of the ancient world** at their side.

When John speaks to us from the fourth gospel, we are hearing **the words of Christ** from his lips to John's ears to the Bible and **directly to us**.

Our 1st Good Word: John 14:23 tells us: "Jesus answered him, 'If anyone loves me, he will keep my word, and my Father will love him, and we will come to him and make our home with him.' "

Our 2nd Good Word: John 13:17 says: "If you know these things, blessed are you if you do them."

Our 3rd Good Word: John 15:10 instructs us: "If you keep my commandments, you will abide in my love, just as I have kept my Father's commandments and abide in his love."

Our 4th Good Word: John 5:24 promises: "Truly, truly, I say to you, whoever hears my word and believes him who sent me has eternal life. He does not come into judgment, but has passed from death to life."

These are the words of the Master. They may flow through John, but the man was there. He walked with Jesus, learned from him, and we can **take John's words at face value**. John shares truth with us. We are loved. **We are loved.** *We are loved.* We are loved. **That's straight from the mouth of Jesus.**

When we need a boost in our spiritual strength, the book of John is our **source of power and encouragement**. Let's break out the Bible and read it today.

We become stronger when we spend time in the Word.

136

June 22 – The Future of Us

TOMORROW'S a new day. The sun will rise in the morning, and we'll enjoy a **new opportunity for success**. It's like turning over a new leaf. We re-envision our goals and remodel our life. In computer terms, we **reboot our hard drive**. It's our future we're talking about. We take it in hand and make of it what we will. It's up to us to **become what we want** to be.

Then baby number 1 gets in the way of our goals, and **off course we go**. Our goals are skewered by baby number 2, and if there's a third, that's **all she wrote**. Our future just skittered out of our control.

But consider. Is that a bad thing? Are children following in our footsteps **a distraction or a reward?** Psalm 128:3 tells us our children are a bountiful addition to what we already possess. "… Your children will be like olive shoots around your table."

Psalm 127:3-5 says our children are an asset and a protection in every situation. "Behold, children are a heritage from the Lord, the fruit of the womb a reward. Like arrows in the hand of a warrior are the children of one's youth. Blessed is the man who fills his quiver with them! He shall not be put to shame when he speaks with his enemies in the gate."

Psalm 107:41 assures us our children are a gift from God. "He raises up the needy out of affliction and makes their families like flocks."

Proverbs 17:6 describes our children as a crown and a glory. "Grandchildren are the crown of the aged, and the glory of children is their fathers."

Maybe children are not part of your life, and you can pursue the dreams of your youth. If you do have children, you are **doubly blessed**. Our children become the future of us, and we find our treasure in them.

God ensures our future through those who follow in our footsteps.

June 23 – God Is Our Sun and Our Shield

WHAT'S THAT dark cloud hanging over your life? What's the storm that batters you day-to-day? What forms the muck that **sucks around your ankles** when you try to crawl out of bed? **God says that's not your life.** *It's not how he wants you to live.*

God says to **turn on the light,** get out of the darkness, get your

137

windshield wipers going and **get to the other side of your prob-lems**. You can, with the help of the almighty God. He will make a way for you to **move forward in your life**. Psalm 84:11-12 gives you God's good purpose for your life. "For the Lord God is a sun and shield; the Lord bestows favor and honor. No good thing does he withhold from those who walk uprightly. O Lord of hosts, blessed is the one who trusts in you!" There's so much good in this verse that we can grasp it better if we look at it in four parts.

Part 1: "For the Lord God is a sun and shield." God lights our path and wards off **all the bad things** that come against us.

Part 2: "The Lord bestows favor and honor." God **opens oppor-tunities before us** with his divine hand of grace, so that we may find security and safety through him.

Part 3: "No good thing does he withhold from those who walk uprightly." We are promised prosperity when we **align ourselves with Biblical principles**.

Part 4: "O Lord of hosts, blessed is the one who trusts in you!" Our faith in God's good intentions toward us will be rewarded with an outrush of **love, protection, and good things** from our Father in heaven.

So, our question again: What's that dark cloud? By now you should be saying, **"What dark cloud? God's shining so brightly in my life, he's all I can see."** It's time to stand up and shout. God is our salvation and our protecting shield against the evil one.

June 24 – 2 Helping Hands God Gives You

IT'S THE COFFEE with the zing that gets us going in the morning. It's the cake with the nuts that makes us crazy for a second slice. Sometimes it's the **kick in the seat** that forces us to get our project up and running, so that we can begin to **achieve the results God has promised us**.

God is eyeing the best for you. He surveys the landscape, and he **sees our future from a higher perspective**. God knows which direction to take us so that we can **find our best in him**. Our place is to follow his directions, even when they make no sense to us. God will be our guide, whether he uses the high-volume caffeine hit of that gourmet coffee, the tempting draw of a nut-infused confection, or a blatant kick in the pants to set us on the right path.

Deuteronomy 11:13-15 reveals the **2 Helping Hands God Gives You** to guide you to your best future ever. "And if you will indeed obey my commandments that I command you today, to love the Lord your God, and to serve him with all your heart and with all your soul, he will give the rain for your land in its season, the early rain and the later rain, that you may gather in your grain and your wine and your oil. And he will give grass in your fields for your livestock, and you shall eat and be full."

Helping Hand No. 1: He will give us the early and the later rain. This tells us God will be there **when we need him**. His help will show up at **just the right time**. It won't rain **all the time.** It will rain **at the right time.**

Helping Hand No. 2: He will give us grass in the fields. God will provide us the opportunities we need to be successful for him. **Educational opportunities.** Job connections. Even chance meetings **we must be prepared to act upon.**

God is **the zing** that gets us going along the path to success. He is **the sweet triumph** that tempts us forward. He is **the loving hand** that pushes us from our safe spot and into the opportunities that will **vault us into the life we want to achieve.** God offers his help. Reach out and take it.

June 25 – God's Heaven Guarantee

NOT ALL CHRISTIANS are guaranteed entrance through God's pearly gates. Wha-!?! How can you say that? I might not make heaven? I've confessed my faith. I believe in God and the Bible. I even attend church and wear a cross as a witness to strangers. Of course I'll make heaven my final home.

Let's see what Matthew 7:21 has to say. "Not everyone who says to me, 'Lord, Lord,' will enter the kingdom of heaven, but the one who does the will of my Father who is in heaven."

So, here's the question you need to ask yourself: **Am I doing the Lord's will?** The verse is very clear. We must do the will of the Father, or our heavenly entry pass is in mortal danger. 1 John 3:22 tells us how to determine if we're doing the Lord's will. "And whatever we ask we receive from him, because we keep his commandments and do what pleases him."

Ahh, our plan becomes clear-cut. We can trust the Ten Commandments. **We worship only Jehovah.** We reverence his name. **We set aside time to celebrate him.** We respect our parents. **We respect life and *the rights of others and more*.**

Jesus added one more commandment in Luke 6:31. "And as you

139

wish that others would do to you, do so to them."

How do we make sure heaven will be our final home? We treat others as we want to be treated. Say please and thank you. **Offer your seat on the bus.** Be patient with the elderly. **Offer to help those in financial difficulties**, even if the fault is their own. Speak to your neighbor over the fence. **Visit your grandmother in the hospital.** See? **You're getting it.** This is easy. *Be the kind person you want others to be to you.* God loves you, and he wants to welcome you home.

June 26 – Riding the Glory Express

MANY PEOPLE enjoy trains. The sounds. The noise. The experience of doing something that's outside their everyday activities. Who wants to wash clothes when we can RIDE THE TRAIN! Mow the lawn? Forget that. We're RIDING THE TRAIN! Grocery shopping? Vacuuming? Getting our teeth cleaned? No way. We have tickets to RIDE THE TRAIN!

Here's the thing. A train ride wasn't that exciting in previous centuries. Coal dust, black smoke, and roughly finished cars made for an excruciating journey. If you weren't in First Class, you were sore and worn out by your arrival. All that's changed. Modern trains have **air conditioning**, air-ride suspension, and **dining cars**. You can even reserve a **sleeping cabin and snooze the entire way**.

God says it's time to **set the everyday stuff aside** and get on his express train to glory. We get the upgraded car, the air-ride suspension, and **all the trimmings**. 1 Thessalonians 4:1 says: "Finally, then, brothers, we ask and urge you in the Lord Jesus, that as you received from us how you ought to walk and to please God, just as you are doing, that you do so more and more."

We've received the **message of salvation**. We know how to **get to the station**. We have our ticket, and it's time to **board God's Glory Express.** We please God by **accepting the message of the cross** and changing how we live. We please God when we **spend time in prayer** and in reading the Word. We please God when we **model our lives after the example of Jesus**.

When we board the Glory Express, we begin to do more and more for the kingdom. People are saved, the kingdom expands, and lives are made better. Now's the time. Forget the washing and vacuuming. **God has better things for us to do.** Our Jesus journey starts today on the Glory Express to heaven.

June 27 – 5 Benefits from Doing for Others

WE'RE FAMILIAR with the saying that you **get what you work for**. It's up to us to get ahead, because the **early bird gets the worm**. There's no easy ride to the top. You've gotta burn your candle at both ends, because **if you don't work, you don't eat**.

Whoa! God says to get off that roller coaster. He has another mantra we need to espouse. **It's better to give than receive.** Let's break down Psalm 41:1-2 to learn the **5 benefits we receive when we put others first**.

The passage starts off: "Blessed is the one who considers the poor!" **We could restate this introduction as "Blessed is the man who is generous to those who are in need."**

Benefit No. 1: "In the day of trouble the Lord delivers him." **When we face financial setbacks, God will restore our finances.**

Benefit No. 2: "The Lord protects him." **When danger is our companion, God is our safeguard and shield.**

Benefit No. 3: "The Lord … keeps him alive." **Our health and physical welfare become God's passion.**

Benefit No. 4: "He is called blessed in the land." **We receive public recognition for the good things God does for us.**

Benefit No. 5: "You do not give him up to the will of his enemies." **Those who oppose us are crushed by God's holy power.**

Jesus had it right. We must *do unto others what we want them to do unto us*. When we treat our fellow man with kindness and consideration, even to **giving them our time and money** when they are in need, God's heart is moved, and his blessing will cover us.

When we do right by others, we do right by God.

June 28 – 3 Notches on Our Financial Yardstick

RECORDKEEPING follows the trends of technology. Move a stone from one basket to another. Tie knots in strings. Perhaps work a cord through seashells to measure how many fish you've caught. Pocket-knives stepped up our technological advantage, and we had a **new way to keep track** of events around us. We notched a section of wood, perhaps a stick of slivered timber. Each notch meant something important. Make enough, and we became a **person of importance**. People began to **look up to us**.

How do we notch our achievements in the modern day? That's

easy. We buy a glitzier car. Move into a more exclusive neighborhood. Wear high fashion so the world can see the notches of our success.

The Word of God gives us different notches. Having money is okay. Great, even. It's what we **do with it** that changes when we create our notches **according to God's standards**. Ecclesiastes 5:12-14 gives **3 notches we want to find on our financial yardstick**. "Sweet is the sleep of a laborer, whether he eats little or much, but the full stomach of the rich will not let him sleep. There is a grievous evil that I have seen under the sun: riches were kept by their owner to his hurt, and those riches were lost in a bad venture. And he is father of a son, but he has nothing in his hand."

Let's look at our notches **one at a time**.

Notch No. 1: Putting our best effort into our financial endeavors is vital, whether we work with our hands, our head, or our heart. **We must give it our all. "Sweet is the sleep of a laborer."**

Notch No. 2: Piling up our bank accounts when there is need at our door is a disastrous choice. Our generous blessings from God are for the **benefit of our fellow man. "Riches were kept by their owner to his hurt."**

Notch No. 3: We can't be lured by get-rich-quick schemes. If all we desire is more money, our caution will evaporate, and **we will stumble** in our endeavors. **"Riches were lost in a bad venture."**

How do we make our notches count? What do we change to perform to God's standard? 1. **Work hard to show honesty in financial matters. 2. Share with those in need. 3. Seek Biblical guidance in new business ventures**. God is our measuring stick. Let's do right by him.

June 29 – 4 Motivations to Come to Jesus

AT A RECENT team-building exercise, the participants were paired together. One person was blindfolded, and the other was given a set of instructions for them. The goal was trust, to be able to **put yourself into the care of another**, and to **follow them (literally) blindly**. That doesn't come naturally to most of us. We scoff at how gullible someone is, how **naïve or innocent**, when they take someone at their word without proof. We need a reason to place our life in the hands of someone else. We need them to have **experience, verifiable skills, a history of consummate proportions**. We want nothing left out.

What are Jesus' credentials? What is there about the man that might convince us to **place our future in his care?** Here are *4 Motivations to Come to Jesus* and follow him. Isaiah 53:5-6 says: "But he was pierced for our transgressions; he was crushed for our iniquities; upon him was the chastisement that brought us peace, and with his wounds we are healed. All we like sheep have gone astray; we have turned—everyone—to his own way; and the Lord has laid on him the iniquity of us all."

Our 1st Motivation says he was **pierced for our transgressions**. Jesus took one for the team, and he accepted the pain for us.

Our 2nd Motivation reveals he was **crushed for our iniquities**. He bore the weight of our wrongdoing, and he did it willingly.

Our 3rd Motivation is his chastisement that **brought us peace**. Jesus was mocked and cursed so that we don't have to live in fear.

Our 4th Motivation is the **wounds he bore** in his flesh. The whipping, the scourging, the crown of thorns — Jesus bled for our physical renewal through him.

This is Jesus' list of credentials, his set of **verifiable skills**. And if those aren't enough, this passage in Isaiah has one more award-winning experience Jesus took on to prove his love for us. **Jesus bore every sin ever committed by humanity so that we could be forgiven by his Father in heaven.**

Team-building exercise complete! Jump aboard. We can trust Jesus no matter where he might lead us.

June 30 – Jesus, Mountain Chucker

WHAT'S IMPOSSIBLE is what you haven't tried. In 1842, the French philosopher Auguste Comte said we could **never know the composition of stars**. We can now identify each chemical element in the sun. Meteorites were once **dismissed as folklore** by the French Academy of Sciences, saying, "Rocks don't fall from the sky." Clearly, they were wrong. In 1895, Lord Kelvin stated, **"Heavier-than-air flying machines are impossible."** He was proven wrong by the Wright brothers eight years later. Space flight, nuclear energy, black holes, force fields … we now know these are possible and/or exist. They were deemed fantasy not long ago.

Now, about that Bible verse about **chucking mountains into the sea.** How did that one work out? Let's read about it in Mark 11:22-23. "And Jesus answered them, 'Have faith in God. Truly, I say to you, whoever says to this mountain, "Be taken up and thrown into the sea," and does not doubt in his heart, but believes that what he says will come to pass, it will be done for him.' "

Was Jesus talking about **real mountains here**, or was it something else? Like, perhaps, problems that are so overwhelming that we **can't see through them to the other side?**

How did we discover the chemical elements that make up the sun? By throwing our hands up and quitting? About those meteorites ... they had the proof in their hands. Yet, they had to be hit over the head before they saw it. The Wright brothers continued to believe ... and risked their reputation and fortune on doing the impossible.

Jesus, mountain chucker. He wants us to **have faith in him**. To trust him. To continue claiming his salvation **even when life tries to steal our faith from us**. We become mountain chuckers when we **refuse to turn loose of our faith in Jesus**. He is our example, and when we follow him, we will have the strength to do all things.

Our faith in Jesus is the certainty that we can become what he requires of us.

— July —

July 1 – The Importance of the Word

WE HAVE access to a multitude of teachings about God. We can tune in to spiritual guides on our television and enjoy their teachings *24 hours a day*. *We can soak it in.* If we grow weary of our television, the Internet is jam-packed with revelations God has shown to *wise men and women of faith*. There is no verse in the Word that is left in the darkness. Everything within the book is revealed.

Yet, here's the problem. How can we find time for the Word when we're knee-deep in what *others are teaching about the Word?* That said, is reading the Bible important in our modern day and age? Our great spiritual teachers reference the Word, so we're getting it there. *That's enough ... isn't it?*

Let's see what Colossians 1:6 says. "[The gospel] which has come to you, as indeed in the whole world it is bearing fruit and increasing—as it also does among you, since the day you heard it and understood the grace of God in truth."

The truth of God spreads across the world *through the gospel*. It finds its way into people's hearts *through the Word of God*. We cannot discount the Bible. Our study time in the Book is _vital to our relationship with the Heavenly Father_. The true nature of God is found in _all the words in the Bible_, not just in the warm and fuzzy nuggets presented on the Internet. It's up to us to learn what the Word teaches, to understand the *mysteries of what's not taught*, and uncover *the truth and reality of the grace of God*. That's where our salvation lies. We gain it through our _understanding of God's Word_. We grasp understanding by _study and time in prayer_, so that we can **become more like our Lord**.

Christ is our example, and we learn of him between the covers of the Bible.

July 2 – Seeing the World Through New Eyes

WHO WE ARE affects how the world appears to us. Take a family on the way to Disney World. The children see **stars and sparkles**. The parents? The lines for the rides, the cost of the tickets, and parking when they arrive.

How about the future? A healthy person sees plans put into play, and they have no trouble with **an endgame years away**. Someone seriously ill sees today and tomorrow, maybe not much past that. They don't have a lifetime to fill. **Today might be their last.**

Parents see their children, and **it affects every decision** they make. Bosses are **wrapped up in profits**. Teachers see **educational value**. Ministers see **relationships**. **What does God want us to see?**

Matthew 9:28-30 says: "When he entered the house, the blind men came to him, and Jesus said to them, 'Do you believe that I am able to do this?' They said to him, 'Yes, Lord.' Then he touched their eyes, saying, 'According to your faith be it done to you.' And their eyes were opened ..."

Jesus wants us to open our eyes and see him. His work. His plan for our lives. How do we learn to see the world through our newly opened eyes? How can we find Jesus in the world?

First, we spend time reading and studying the Word of God. Second, we set aside a portion of each day to focus on God in prayer. It's when we're wrapped up in Jesus that we begin to understand his vision for humanity. We draw **close to him**, he **touches our eyes**, and *we see as he sees*.

The world is our harvest, and it's time for us to gather. Jesus needs us to reach the world for him. Today is our day.

July 3 – **Our Spiritual Safe House**

UNDERCOVER AGENTS – spies, as we like to call them – have a special status while they are in the field. They place themselves **in the middle of danger**, even if no one can see it. They lead normal lives (or so it seems) as **teachers, construction workers, or government officials**. Yet, they are just an Internet firewall away from **exposure and confiscation** of their **life, liberty, and pursuit of happiness**.

In 2011, the terrorist organization Hezbollah identified and captured **two American spies**. The damage began to spread as the CIA scrambled to **protect the identities of even more** undercover agents. In 2009, seven CIA employees were **killed** and six others **wounded** in Afghanistan. In 2007, the US, Britain, and Israel began **losing contact** with their spies in Iran.

The spies needed a safe house, a place to **hunker down for safety** until the storm clouds of exposure and capture passed them by. **As Christians, there are times we need to *hunker down against the world's assaults*.**

146

Ezekiel 34:28 says we will dwell in the Lord, and WE WILL BE SAFE. "They shall no more be a prey to the nations, nor shall the beasts of the land devour them. They shall dwell securely, and none shall make them afraid."

Proverbs 1:33 says God puts his protection around us, and NO EVIL CAN TOUCH US. "Whoever listens to me will dwell secure and will be at ease, without dread of disaster."

Psalm 4:8 says we can rest in safety, and OUR SLEEP WILL BE UNDISTURBED. "In peace I will both lie down and sleep; for you alone, O Lord, make me dwell in safety."

Jesus is our spiritual safe house. He is our haven of protection. In him, we need not fear **anything life throws our way.**

Jesus is our rock of redemption, for his arms protect us from harm.

July 4 – **Finding Joy in Our Old Age**

BEING YOUNG is outstanding. It's hard to define when you're there, but what youth really means is that our **joints don't hurt**, we don't **worry about our energy levels**, and **nothing we eat makes us fat.** Or in other words, we **don't have to think about our bodies.** We can just **enjoy them, get on with life, and have fun.** We can't imagine the effort it takes for old people to simply get through the day.

What!?! Where'd that come from? We were talking about how great it is to be young.

Here's the thing. We think we'll be young forever when we're in the middle of it. Old age? Ha! Never. Not me. Then we turn twenty and we **injure our ankle**. It's never quite the same. At thirty, we must **diet every spring** to get back into our summer clothes. Bummer! At forty, **getting out of bed is a chore**. If only we could get a full night's sleep. Fifty is an eye-opener. **Everything hurts**. Retirement starts to look appealing.

Let's not get into the sixties and on. Life **becomes a torture**, from looking into the mirror to wondering how we were able to consume **anything** in our youth and not get sick.

What good thing can we find about growing old? Proverbs 17:6 says there is plenty of good in our senior years. "Grandchildren are the crown of the aged, and the glory of children is their fathers." Our joy comes in their **arms around our necks** and their **excitement in our hearts**. There's a reason why grandparents indulge their grand-

147

children. **They return the joy of being alive when life tries to take our joy from us.**

Our children are God's gift, and our grandchildren are a double blessing from the Lord.

July 5 – **And God Said . . .**

THE CHRISTIAN MUSIC group Kutless put out a well-received song in 2012. One section of the lyrics references the times our healing doesn't come from God. It's all about *having faith in our Lord no matter what happens in our lives.*

Yet we cannot afford to doubt that God will do as he has proclaimed. That's a path to self-fulfillment and a license to sin. *God's laws are true, and his promises will come to pass.* Nebuchadnezzar was witness to the miracle of Shadrach, Meshach, and Abednego, the three Hebrews saved from the fiery furnace. He spoke so highly of them that he proclaimed that any man who spoke against the God of the Hebrews would be killed and cut into pieces. Gruesome, huh? It showed that Nebuchadnezzar believed in the power of God. However, he *refused to accept the authority of God.*

In Daniel 4:31 we read God's judgment against the king: "While the word was in the king's mouth, there fell a voice from heaven, saying, O, king Nebuchadnezzar, to you it is spoken; the kingdom is departed from you."

That's a scary place to find ourselves. We witness the power of the Lord, and we choose to look away. We believe, then we turn our back. Nebuchadnezzar did this, and his kingdom was stripped away **that very day.** Daniel 4:33 lays out God's timeframe: "The same hour was the thing fulfilled upon Nebuchadnezzar: and he was driven from men, and did eat grass as oxen, and his body was wet with the dew of heaven, till his hairs were grown like eagles' feathers, and his nails like birds' claws."

Woe to the king! All was lost! Or was it? The very next verse tells us that *when Nebuchadnezzar lifted his eyes unto God, his kingdom was restored.* Read of his transformation in Daniel 4:34: "And at the end of the days I Nebuchadnezzar lifted up my eyes unto heaven, and my understanding returned unto me, and I blessed him who lives for ever, whose dominion is an everlasting dominion, and his kingdom is from generation to generation."

Kutless hit the nail on the head with their song. Even when we don't feel the healing of the Lord, he hasn't left us. *He waits for us to lift our eyes unto him.* It's all about having faith in our Lord no matter what happens in our lives. When we search for God, he'll always allow himself to be found.

July 6 – **Jesus Lights Up Our Darkness**

WHAT'S WITH the scary stories? **Who's sharing tales of woe and woebegone?** We're scaring ourselves, and **that's not God's plan for our lives**. Quit telling about your broken marriage. There's no need to expound on the year everything went wrong. We're stepping backwards when we do. We're reliving the worst that happened to us, and we bring ourselves down. We stir up the old fears we once knew before Jesus changed us into something new.

Let's cheer the good things happening to us. The bill that **got paid**. The cancer **in remission**. The friendship **renewed after a dozen years. Let's learn to look forward, not backward. Let's step into the morning, not fall back into night.** 2 Timothy 1:7 tells us we have a God of **hope and brightness**. He wants to **lift us into the light**. "For God gave us a spirit not of fear but of power and love and self-control."

Our fear is gone. God has replaced it with something better. Bah! **We kick out our memories of childhood hunger**. Ouch! **There go our failed relationships**. Shazam! **Every bad thing from our past is turned to dust**. The future is ours, and it is bright with three gifts from God.

1. Power: God gives us the strength to **overcome every bad thing. 2. Love:** Our connection with our fellow travelers is **strong and enduring. 3. Self-control:** "We are focused on Christ and guided by him **every step of the way**.

We are to be proactive for Jesus, positive in our everyday thinking, and all about Christ every moment of the day. It is our smile that tells the world Jesus lights up our darkness.

July 7 – **3 Bonuses When We Exercise Our Faith**

EXERCISE MAKES us stronger. Just ask an Olympic athlete, a long-distance runner, or someone who works at labor-intensive jobs. The more we do, **the more we can do**. Our muscles grow in girth and strength **because we use them**.

Scientists say our brains are the same. The more we exercise them, the stronger they get. Stronger here means greater memory retention, quicker thought processes, and increased judgment capacity. There's even evidence that using our brains regularly keeps them from getting flabby (i.e., developing Alzheimer's).

How does that work with our spiritual muscles? When we exercise our faith, **what good results do we experience?** Ephesians 3:17-19 reveals **3 Bonuses When We Exercise Our Faith**. "So that Christ may dwell in your hearts through faith—that you, being rooted and grounded in love, may have strength to comprehend with all the saints what is the breadth and length and height and depth, and to know the love of Christ that surpasses knowledge, that you may be filled with all the fullness of God."

Bonus No. 1: Christ dwells in our hearts. We can invite Jesus to walk by our side only if we exercise our faith in the invisible made visible. We choose to believe in what we cannot see.

Bonus No. 2: We begin to understand the depths of Christ's love for us. Studying the scriptures is only the beginning of learning about God's love. Our faith, when exercised, opens our hearts to a greater, never before seen love.

Bonus No. 3: We are filled with the fullness of God. The Father becomes more than an abstract concept. He becomes real to us. We learn to depend on him, and we take on the likeness of his Son.

We're all athletes for Jesus when we exercise our faith in him. We get stronger. **Our love grows deeper**. And best of all, we dominate the devil when he tries to come against us.

God is our faith-building machine, and we become spiritual giants in him.

July 8 – 4 Phases of Joy in Christ

THE MOON SHINES on the world with the reflected light of the sun. It moves through phases, from the new moon, quarter moon, half moon, to a full moon. Our seasons are the same. There's fall, winter, spring, and summer. All build on one another, and **each has a distinct purpose**.

How about the cardinal directions? North, east, south, and west. They help us define **where we are** and **where we're going**.

We also uncover **4 Phases of Joy in Christ** when we spend time with him. Isaiah 55:12 says: "For you shall go out in joy and be led forth in peace; the mountains and the hills before you shall break forth into singing, and all the trees of the field shall clap their hands."

Our 1st Phase of Joy: We shall go out. Out of our homes. Out of our churches. Out into the world to share the love of God. That's where our joy is found.

Our 2nd Phase of Joy: We are led by God. Only in following the leading of the Lord can we be at peace with our existence and find true joy in him. If we insist on our own way, we will run rock-solid into despair.

Our 3rd Phase of Joy: We choose to break out of our somber worldview. God is not a god of sadness. He is the Champion of life that created the waterfalls, the mountains, and the beauty of the sunsets. It's time for us to pay attention to his gifts to us.

Our 4th Phase of Joy: We exult in the world God has given us. God wants us to sing and dance, to **"clap our hands"** in joy before him. Even the wind in the trees creates a joyful noise to the Father. We must do the same.

God is the lifter of our souls. When we **follow his plan**, our joy in him will be complete. Our opportunities for joy are endless when we place our trust in God.

July 9 – The View from the High Waterfall

HIKE THE FOOTHILLS of the Appalachian Mountains in the eastern United States, and you'll come across numerous waterfalls. Search in Georgia, alone, where the mountain range begins, and you'll discover 36 significant (and beautiful) waterfalls. That doesn't include the small fry, the little cascades **scattered along every tumbling stream and river**.

Amicalola Falls, from the Cherokee "tumbling waters," is the largest in the state, at 729 feet. It plunges down **seven cascades**, ending in a reflection pool at the bottom. Start at the bottom, and the path **is easy**. The mountain air is cool, and you **hardly break a sweat**. Around you are thickly wooded slopes, and you might come across a sign showing you are at the trailhead of the Appalachian Trail that runs **all the way to Maine**.

It's when you start up the mountainside to the top of the waterfall that **you begin to see what you were missing** at the bottom. As beautiful as the reflecting pool is, on the way up, the trees begin to open to **glimpses of the distant hills** undulating across the landscape in their forested beauty – **as far as the eye can see**. Then, at the top, you look down the waterfall, and the reflecting pool at the base **disappears into the rising mist**. Before you stretches the unimpeded landscape, **disappearing into the horizon miles away**. It takes work to get to the top of Amicalola Falls, but the reward is worth every step.

Zephaniah 3:17 is a testament to the **unending beauty of our glorious God**. "The Lord your God is in your midst, a mighty one who will save; he will rejoice over you with gladness; he will quiet you by his love; he will exult over you with loud singing." When we break out of our comfort zone to hike up God's mountain, we'll find our **ultimate reward at the end**. It will be beyond compare. God is worth every step we take toward him.

July 10 – 4 Moments We Will Find Joy

DAVID IN THE Bible is the song meister, **the writer of poems**, the man who teaches us that **we can release joy in worshipping God**. David is the principle author of the Book of Psalms. Today, let's look at Psalm 97:11-12. "Light is sown for the righteous, and joy for the upright in heart. Rejoice in the Lord, O you righteous, and give thanks to his holy name!" This passage gives us **4 Moments We Can Find Joy**.

Our 1st Moment: When we **live by God's rules**, we will know joy. We will experience the light of God's love.

Our 2nd Moment: Our **desire to become more like our Lord** will daily flood us with the peace and joy of Christ.

Our 3rd Moment: Singing praises to God will **lift us into his joy** and fill us with his eternal and warming presence.

Our 4th Moment: Acknowledging God's authority and benevolence in our lives **brings us closer to him and his infilling joy**.

Joy doesn't have to be a mystery. It's a definitive byproduct of our interactions with the holy God of all creation. **When we move closer to him, we cannot help but be covered with his indescribable joy.**

God's joy rubs off on us when we reach out to him.

July 11 – Crediting God for His Goodness

PEOPLE GENERALLY work for a living. We walk outside our front door each morning, make our way to our place of employment, and we spend the day **trading our time and skills for the money** to make it through another month. If we have a job we enjoy, it's easy. We relish our time on the job, and the money is a bonus that seems to **flow like a mountain spring**. If our job wears us down, well, most of us know what that's like. It hardly seems the money is **worth the time** it steals from us.

152

How does God see our money? Better, how does God see **our relationship to our money?** Does God see it as **a possession**, something that's come to us because **we deserve it** and no one else has a right to it? Or does our Lord see it as **a gift**, a blessing that's better when it's **shared with others** ... like a birthday cake or lottery winnings? **Let's see what the Bible has to say.**

Psalm 12:5 tells us God takes a great deal of interest in **how we treat those who struggle** to make ends meet. " 'Because the poor are plundered, because the needy groan, I will now arise,' says the Lord; 'I will place him in the safety for which he longs.' "

Proverbs 17:5 says God takes **mistreatment of the poor** as a personal affront. "Whoever mocks the poor insults his Maker; he who is glad at calamity will not go unpunished."

1 Chronicles 29:12 reminds us that even when we labor for our pay, **God is the source** of the funds we receive. "Both riches and honor come from you, and you rule over all. In your hand are power and might, and in your hand it is to make great and to give strength to all."

Mine, yours, or ours. How do you see your money? **It all comes down to God.** He is the source of your life, through both your good days and your struggles. Our paycheck was God's before it became ours. Let's remember the Father's goodness as we review our accounts.

July 12 – A Perfectionist's Prayer

WHAT ARE YOU picky about? What small details get your goat? What **must be so perfect** that it consumes you? **What does your radar zero in on that blinds you to everything else?**

The automotive blog vinwiki.com tells the story of a man who bought a high-end exotic sports car. He brought it back the next day to return it. "Why," his sales representative wanted to know. "You loved it yesterday." The buyer had surrounded it with high-intensity lights in his garage and found flaws, real or imagined, that ruined the car for him.

Are you like that with the blessings of God? They are only good enough if they gleam with **flawless perfection?** That spouse you prayed for ... underwear on the bathroom floor ... **time for a trade.** Your financial foundations ... you find a crack in your investments, and **you rail at God.**

God says to release it to him. You no longer need to seek solace in the details of his gifts to you. Philippians 4:6-7 says: "Do not be anxious about anything, but in everything by prayer and supplication with thanksgiving let your requests be made known to God. And the peace of God, which surpasses all understanding, will guard your hearts and your minds in Christ Jesus." Here are three things to take away from this passage:

1. We must **cast worry out the window**. It's **not our responsibility** any longer. 2. We must **turn our needs over to God**. He is the **guardian of all that we are**. 3. We must **keep focused on Jesus**. He will keep us **protected from every evil thing**.

It's time to reveal **The Perfectionist's Prayer**, one on which we can choose to model our own daily prayers: *Dear Father, I turn loose of my need to be in control. You know my concerns and petitions. I will keep my eyes on Jesus through prayer and study of your Word. Worry is no longer my master, for you are supreme in my life.*

There you go. **You've forged a new connection to God**. Two thumbs up. **God approves.**

When Jesus shows up on our screen, he overshadows every other blip on the radar.

July 13 – Safety Net Not Required

HOW'S YOUR retirement plan coming along? Do your children have a **college fund tucked away** and ready to go? What about your car's **extended warranty**, and the one on your water heater, your air conditioner, and your riding mower? Are all your **safety nets in place** so that nothing bad can happen in your life?

We carry medical insurance, with a rider that pays for long-term care … **just in case**. We back up our digital life on multiple hard drives and even pay monthly for an online back-up service so that nothing's lost. Along the coast, people install whole-house generators. If the electricity fails during a storm, **life can go on at the push of a button**.

It's all about our safety net, Plan B, our **escape clause** when things don't go according to our expectations.

What's happened to our faith, our trust in God? What back-up plan do we require of him? What guarantees must God sign off on before we turn our lives over to his care?

Hebrews 11:6 tells us it's **time to get back to basics with God**. "And without faith it is impossible to please him, for whoever would

154

draw near to God must believe that he exists and that he rewards those who seek him."

What is faith? It is accepting without proof, without a guarantee, **without a safety net** just in case we got it wrong and need to fall back on Plan B. 2 Corinthians 5:7 **puts us on the right track**. "For we walk by faith, not by sight." So, write that check to **fund the new roof on the church**. Agree to that mission's trip **to a third-world country**. **Go out on a limb for Jesus**. Witness to a coworker. Make Christ a bigger part of your life than he's ever been before.

If we spend too much time worrying about our safety net, we'll never accomplish what God has planned for us. Let's leap for Jesus. He will enable our success in him.

July 14 – 2 Reasons to Follow God's Instructions

A GARDEN CENTER is a wonderful place to visit. Every plant is one we can try. Our yard will explode with color if we **choose this or that** or maybe the **one over there**. All we need is our bank card, and they can **all be ours**.

Here's the conundrum. Not every plant will survive in our yard. We must study the planting directions to know the soil, light, and water requirements for each plant. Ignore those, and your plantings will look great for a time, but your beautiful yard will begin to fade. Did the ground need to be constantly moist, or was it supposed to be well-drained and occasionally allowed to dry? Is fertilizer required year-round or just in the fall?

Some plants like the longleaf pine can be damaged by applying fertilizer or water at any time of the year. Plant it and leave it alone. Fertilizer will force the tree to leaf out rather than drive its roots into the ground. The roots won't grow deep enough to balance the upper structure, and the tree will come down when the storms begin to blow.

What does God require from us for our spiritual growth? Deuteronomy 6:18 tells us: "And you shall do what is right and good in the sight of the Lord, that it may go well with you, and that you may go in and take possession of the good land that the Lord swore to give to your fathers."

Here are our **2 Reasons to Follow God's Instructions**.

First, things will go well with us. When we follow God's instructions, our job opportunities will line up, our family relationships will improve, and we will find God has cleared the path he

155

wishes for us to follow.

Second, we will take possession of the land God has for us. Following God's instructions brings the fulfillment of the promises of God. That promotion, that prime piece of property for our new church auditorium, that opportunity to minister on the mission field … God goes before us and leads us into success.

If we want a beautiful garden, we need to **select the right plants** and **tend them carefully**. If we want a beautiful life, we need to **select God** and **follow his instructions**. Our future is beautiful when we are planted in God.

July 15 – **Your Honest Streak**

ARE YOU RESPECTED for your honesty? Do people count on you to **return to the store when you've been given too much change?** Are you always chosen to be treasurer … **because the cash is safe in your hands?** If so, you might have an honest streak running through everything you do, and God says he loves you all the more for it. Leviticus 19:35 expresses **God's desire for honesty to pervade every part of your life.** "You shall do no wrong in judgment, in measures of length or weight or quantity."

If you break a cookie in two, do you offer the larger half? Do you pull out the hidden candy when your daughter asks what you're eating? Do you buy extra fries on the way home from work to share with your spouse? **You are living up to God's standard. You portray honesty in every measure of your life.** You are living out the will of God as an example before everyone you meet.

The rest of us are trying to get there. **Be patient. With God's help, we will make it one day.** God is our encourager, and he praises us when we take steps to become more like him.

July 16 – **God Remembers Your Name**

HOW'S THE crowd around you? Do they hustle and bustle? Keep the status quo? Do they drive the latest cars, eat at trendy restaurants, and shop to deck themselves out in the most current fashion possible? Jewel tones are from last season. Get with it. **The crowd is moving on.** Keep up.

The bigger issue is **getting lost in the crowd.** Try this. Park your car at the mall and **go inside for an hour.** Don't record where you parked. Just **walk away** from your car. It's yours, right? You know what it looks like.

Come back to it from a different side of the mall. See how easy it is to find ... or does it **fit in with the crowd**, just another SUV or sedan that looks eerily like all the others?

God says he notices you. He keeps track of who you are, where you live, and the **troubles that are weighing you down. God remembers your name.** Read in Isaiah 43:1: "But now thus says the Lord, he who created you, O Jacob, he who formed you, O Israel: 'Fear not, for I have redeemed you; I have called you by name, you are mine.'"

Think about it like your children. You can recognize them by **their haircut**, the way **they walk**, even the **back of their hand**. If you hear your **son's voice** or your **daughter's laughter** in a crowded room, you can **pick them out in an instant. That's how God is with us.** He can pick us out of a crowd. **Just. Like. That.** We are special to God. He is our Father, and he calls us his children. He never loses track of us.

July 17 – God's Rescue Clause

WOULDN'T IT BE nice to have a built-in 9-1-1 button on our phone? **One that's dedicated just to us?** Like a credit card that guarantees **everything we buy**, no matter how it gets damaged ... or even lost ... **even if we're careless.** Or a car warranty that covers **everything.** Just press the button, and we have a replacement car ready and waiting while ours is in the shop.

We do have those things, those built-in rescue clauses. The button on our phone, the credit card guarantee, even the warranty that gives us a replacement car to drive. **They are perks to attract business.** One company compared their rescue clause to a woman wearing a shoe. She breaks a heel, and before she can get the shoe off, a hand reaches into view and hands her a replacement shoe.

That's exactly what God does for us. Psalm 37:40 gives us **our rescue clause.** "The Lord helps them and delivers them; he delivers them from the wicked and saves them, because they take refuge in him."

Here's what you must get from this verse. We must buy the right phone, carry the premium credit card, and drive the luxury brand to get our 9-1-1 guarantees. **They don't come with the cheap stuff.** For us to invoke God's rescue clause, we must choose to **take refuge in him.** That's it. There's no other way. We must accept **salvation through Christ**, live by **God's standards**, and place our **trust in**

him. Then God's rescue clause becomes ours, and he will **deliver us from every wicked thing**. Cheaters. Liars. People who gossip about us behind our back. **God. Will. Rescue. Us.** That's in our contract, and we can **count on it**.

We are never on our own when we walk side by side with Jesus.

July 18 – **Our Path to Peace**

PEACE, ACCORDING to Merriam-Webster, is a state of tranquility or quiet. In other words, things are in a **calm state**, with no rowdiness anywhere near. We can close our eyes and **think without being disturbed**. Merriam-Webster goes on to give us some **specific examples of peace. 1. Freedom from civil disruption. 2. Order and security in our community. 3. Contentment in our thoughts and emotions. 4. Harmony in our personal relations. 5. Mutual respect between governments.**

So, how do we achieve this **state of tranquility** or quiet? What's our path to **casting out the rowdiness** that drives us nuts? Colossians 3:12-13 gives us a good start. "Put on then, as God's chosen ones, holy and beloved, compassionate hearts, kindness, humility, meekness, and patience, bearing with one another and, if one has a complaint against another, forgiving each other; as the Lord has forgiven you, so you also must forgive."

First, we must change ourselves. We must **take on the attributes that we expect from others:** compassion, patience, etc. **Next, we must forgive the hurts others have done to us.** Turn them loose. You know, the way Jesus **forgives us when we wrong him**. We can't find peace inside if we **fail to pursue it on the outside**. **Civil disruption**. We must follow the laws of the land. **Our community**. We have customs and behavioral boundaries for a reason. **In our heads**. We can choose to become a kinder, nicer person. **Personal relations**. Say please and thank you. Then mean it. **Between governments**. Vote for government leaders that will do the right thing.

Peace can be ours. God gives us a plan. Let's start down the path to peace today. Our peace comes from Christ and spreads to every life we touch.

July 19 – **Driven to Be Better**

WE ARE MADE of flesh and bone. No one questions that. Our bodies work by **chemical signals**, and by pumping **blood, nutrients,** and oxygen to the extreme parts of our frame. **Our fingers and our toes. Our ears. And every part in between.** Every reaction we have is understood by science. Anger is a series of actions and **released hormones**. The chemical signals that elevate our heart rate, change our body temperature, and flood us with adrenalin are measurable.

The feeling of anger is something else entirely. The same is true for **physical attraction**. It's all measurable responses to certain stimuli. Our eyes register a certain shape, our body releases specific chemicals, and the responses in our bodies cascade to their expected end. "It's out of our control," we bemoan. "The devil made me do it," is something else we say. 1 Corinthians 6:13 says we must **exercise control over our bodies**. "… The body is not meant for sexual immorality, but for the Lord, and the Lord for the body."

God formed us from the dust of the ground. He made Adam **in his own image**, and Eve was created **from Adam's rib**. God understands when we behave and react like we do. We are created in his image. That doesn't, however, mean we can chase willy-nilly after every chemical impulse that stirs inside our body. **Just because a chemical floods us doesn't give us the right to satisfy its cry for gratification.** We are formed for a higher purpose. We must **refocus**. Set boundaries. Understand that there are behaviors **not permitted no matter how much** we are tempted. We must be driven to be better than our emotions demand us to be.

Our standard is the Word. **Our actions reveal who we are.** Let's be like Jesus, holy and pure every day.

July 20 – 5 Orders of Belief in Jesus

YOU WOULD never apply peanut butter to bread before taking it out of the wrapper. **What!?!** That doesn't make any sense. **No one would even try that**. A 1st grade teacher laid out the supplies for making peanut butter sandwiches and asked his students to write out directions. Then the teacher **followed the students' instructions exactly**. One set of directions had him applying the peanut butter **directly to his hand**. Another had him eating the bread **before opening the peanut butter jar**. Still another saw him spreading the peanut butter **with his fingers**.

Doing things in the proper order makes a difference. We must **open the peanut butter jar** before we can spread it. We must **remove the bread** from the wrapper. We must **pick up our knife** as well as **separate the two slices** of bread.

What's the **order of salvation?** Of belief in Jesus? Of **placing our faith in him**? John 3:36 says we must **believe that Jesus is the Son of God**. "Whoever believes in the Son has eternal life; whoever does not obey the Son shall not see life, but the wrath of God remains on him."

1 Peter 2:6 says we must **accept the Christ as the cornerstone** of our faith. "Behold, I am laying in Zion a stone, a cornerstone chosen and precious, and whoever believes in him will not be put to shame."

Acts 16:31 says we **cannot waver from our belief** in our Lord. "And they said, 'Believe in the Lord Jesus, and you will be saved, you and your household.' "

John 12:46 says we must **cast off anything that occludes the light** of Jesus in our lives. "I have come into the world as light, so that whoever believes in me may not remain in darkness."

John 6:35 says our source of spiritual sustenance must flow **from Jesus and Jesus alone**. "Jesus said to them, 'I am the bread of life; whoever comes to me shall not hunger, and whoever believes in me shall never thirst.' "

Without these five things, we will falter in our Christian walk. Let's summarize them, **write them down**, and **carry them with us**. Jesus is … the **Son of God** … the **cornerstone of our faith** … the **source of our salvation** … the **light of our existence** … the **bread of life**. There is no other through whom we can be saved. Our redemption flows from Jesus alone. When we get our life in order, we'll find Jesus at the top of our list.

July 21 – 5 Situations to Praise God

DAVID IN THE Bible struggled with his role as God's chosen ruler over Israel. The man was a warrior and king, and he united the 12 fractured tribes of Israel. He also wove the religious faith of Israel into the daily lives of the people and its government. He even composed much of Israel's greatest prayer text, the Book of Psalms. Today we remember him as the greatest of Israel's kings, a **"man after God's own heart."** *Even Jesus was honored to be called the Son of David.*

What, then, should we think about the David who committed murder and rape, was a weak father who raised a resentful son, and who invited court intrigue that haunted him until his death? Let's see how David handled 5 desperate situations in Psalm 42:9-11.

160

Situation No. 1: "I say to God, my rock: Why have you forgotten me?" David knew what it was like to feel abandoned. He responded, **"[I find] hope in God; for I shall again praise him, my salvation and my God."**

Situation No. 2: "Why do I go mourning because of the oppression of the enemy?" The Great Poet understood what it was like to have everyone come against him. He responded, **"[I find] hope in God; for I shall again praise him, my salvation and my God."**

Situation No. 3: "As with a deadly wound in my bones, my adversaries taunt me." The Man after God's Own Heart suffered the lances of his detractors, and their pain caused him distress. He responded, **"[I find] hope in God; for I shall again praise him, my salvation and my God."**

Situation No. 4: "While they say to me all the day long, Where is your God?" God's Warrior knew the shuttering blankness of heaven when there was no answer to his prayers. He responded, **"[I find] hope in God; for I shall again praise him, my salvation and my God."**

Situation No. 5: "Why are you cast down, O my soul, and why are you in turmoil within me?" The Uniter of Israel was overwhelmed by the turmoil of life, and he could find no rhyme or reason to continue. He responded, **"[I find] hope in God; for I shall again praise him, my salvation and my God."**

David retains his position of excellence in the annals of the Bible not because of who he was or what he did. He remains a great man of historical note **because of the God he acknowledged as his source of power and coming redemption**. David's most redeeming quality is seen in his heartfelt proclamation in the final verse in this passage. "[I find] hope in God; for I shall again praise him, my salvation and my God."

Let's be like David. Let's find our hope in God in every situation, no matter how dark the night. God is our lifter, and he raises us to new heights in him.

July 22 – How to Grow in God

STEP INTO your garden during a dry spell. If you don't have a garden, give your flowerbeds a good look-see. Pay attention to the plants. Which ones are doing best, still surviving in the heat? Those in full sun, in the intensity of the dry spell, or those near a water source, perhaps the air conditioner drain lines or a water faucet?

161

When our flowers begin to droop, we understand the best way to bring them back to life. Pull out the hose, put it at the base of the plants, and let it run slowly for an hour or so. Within a short time, the plants will revive, lifting their branches once more toward the sky. They won't mind the dry spell when they have plenty of water at their roots.

That's how we grow in God. The world can scorch us, and it can try to wither us with the heat of many trials. It's **our roots that are our survival**, and when we keep them planted in the Word of God and spend time in prayer, we will bloom in the Lord. Psalm 1:3 paints this example in the most beautiful way. "And he shall be like a tree planted by the rivers of water, that bringeth forth his fruit in his season; his leaf also shall not wither; and whatsoever he doeth shall prosper."

It doesn't matter what's happening in the sky, whether sunshine or rain. **It's the roots that matter.** It's our roots that keep us healthy spiritually.

Here are four things you can do to grow in God. **1. Get involved in a Bible study. 2. Be part of a prayer group. 3. Attend Wednesday night services. 4. Get a devotional and follow it every day.**

You've got this. **You can be a success**. You will grow in God and bloom in the glory of his presence. Jesus is our source, and we must remain rooted in him.

July 23 – **You Will Be Rewarded**

HAS YOUR BOSS demanded you volunteer for extra duties at work? Are you frustrated that **no one else will volunteer to do the lawn?** You are always running the washer, fueling the car, and working in grocery store runs, while everyone else seems to be **at the mall or playing a video gam**e. Then an online client emails you for an urgent revision to a report **just before you head out for lunch** with your spouse. When can you choose to disregard the extra duties and take time out for yourself?

God says your time is coming. Have patience, and your reward will surround you. You will be **enveloped in the peace of God**, and you will **never know another troubled day**.

Jeremiah 31:12 says your time of rest in God is on the way. "They shall come and sing aloud on the height of Zion, and they shall be radiant over the goodness of the Lord, over the grain, the wine, and the oil, and over the young of the flock and the herd; their life shall be like a watered garden, and they shall languish no more."

You will sing with joy at the coming of the Lord. Your face will be radiant with the glory of your coming King. Life will be coming up roses. Your tired limbs and lack of sleep? Banished to the darkness, never to be seen again.

Your job is to hang in there. **Find small moments of rest. Share the workload.** Admit that some things *don't have to be done to perfection.* Someone else will eventually get around to it if you can't. Trust me, they will.

God is your rest and reward. Never forget to take out time for him.

July 24 – Taking On Our Superpowers

RECENTLY, MARVEL COMICS has had an amazing run in theaters. The cast of superheroes in the Marvel lineup is **strong, courageous, and a model we can strive to emulate.**

Ant-Man, for example. He can **change size to challenge** any opponent. **Black Panther** wears a Vibranium suit **impervious to any attack. Captain America** is immune to most diseases and **heals astoundingly fast. Daredevil** has a "radar" sense that allows him to see what's around him **even though he is blind. Hawkeye** excels by his masterful use of the **tools he's been given. Human Torch** can **control any flame** within his field of vision. **Iron Man** uses technology to be **quicker and more powerful** than his opponents. **Quicksilver** runs faster than sound and can **outrun gravity. Silver Surfer** can **tap into cosmic energy** and go for years without resting. **Spider-Man** has a super-sense that **alerts him to incoming dangers.**

The gamut of Marvel's superpowers includes **the following and more:** innate abilities; special equipment; power drawn from creation, itself. **What does the book of Psalms say about our Christian superpowers?**

Psalm 31:23 says we **have invulnerability.** "Love the Lord, all you his saints! The Lord **preserves the faithful** but abundantly repays the one who acts in pride."

Psalm 28:7 says we **wear an impenetrable shield.** "The Lord is **my strength and my shield**; in him my heart trusts, and I am helped; my heart exults, and with my song I give thanks to him."

Psalm 138:7 says the cosmic energy of the Creator of the

universe is **at our disposal**. "Though I walk in the midst of trouble, you preserve my life; you stretch out your hand against the wrath of my enemies, and **your right hand delivers me**."

The devil isn't in control of us. There is no weapon aimed our direction that can break through God's protection. **We are immune to the attacks of the evil one, because God is our champion**. Let's use our fist of God's iron and smash the devil into dust.

July 25 – **Jesus, Broken-Hearted Redemption**

ENDURE THE LOSS of a loved one, and tears flood your eyes. You can barely endure the preparations for your final good-bye: deciding the flowers, the songs, the color of the bunting on the casket. Then comes the day, and you wonder if your eyes will **ever be dry again**. Grief consumes you, and the prospect of going forward darkens every moment you live.

Or you're at the doctor, and you dread the news you might hear. Cancer is the big one, the battle you don't know you can win. Even if you do, **how horrible will the skirmishes be?** Chemo, meds, and your hair … will it all fall out? Perhaps … perhaps … letting it go is better … offering escape from the hurt and desperation.

In September of 2019, a 16-year-old teen in Tennessee was devastated by social media bullying. Channing, a junior at Coffee County Central High, was swallowed by desperation and couldn't find the strength to face another day. His broken heart took his life from him.

Psalm 22:24 tells us we have a **redemption for our broken heart**. "For he has not despised or abhorred the affliction of the afflicted, and he has not hidden his face from him, but has heard, when he cried to him." Jesus hears us when we come to him. Our voices ring in his ears, and he **offers his hand to us**.

Your loved one won't come back to you. **That's not what Jesus offers.** Your cancer treatment? That's God's **gift for your survival**, as bad as it might get. Betrayal? Jesus says to **put it on his shoulders**. He can carry you when you are weak, and he will never stumble or fall.

Jesus is our redemption when life lets us down.

July 26 – **Your Day Is About to Get Better**

NOT EVERY DAY will be perfect. Clouds will occlude the sky, your tires will go flat, and you'll eat something that disagrees with you. **That's life.** We all face challenges. It's how we **deal with them** that makes the difference. Understand this. When you can look past the things that try to trip you up, you will find that **your day is about to get better** than you ever imagined.

Romans 8:31-32 assures you **God will give you all good things.** "What then shall we say to these things? If God is for us, who can be against us? He who did not spare his own Son but gave him up for us all, how will he not also with him graciously give us all things?"

What do you need today? A kind word? A helping hand? A new direction for your life? **Ask God. He loves you very much.** Joshua 10:8 says there are **no barriers too tall for you to scramble over.** "And the Lord said to Joshua, 'Do not fear them, for I have given them into your hands. Not a man of them shall stand before you.' " Re-read what that verse says. **Not a man of them shall stand before you.** God has already cleared the way for you to move forward.

Proverbs 21:31 assures us that trusting in **God is our preparation for every fight.** "The horse is made ready for the day of battle, but the victory belongs to the Lord." Your job isn't to win the battle. God expects you to focus on him and **place your life in his hands. He will give you the victory**.

You can't make your days perfect. That's not our human existence. **You can trust in God.** That's his desire and motivation for **taking your day and making it better** each time you turn to him.

We reveal the best things in life when we look up to find the Father.

July 27 – 6 Things God Desires of the Wealthy

A RICH MAN or woman can be a Christian. Well, duh, **of course,** we think. Money has nothing to do with your salvation. Here's the thing. **Your salvation has everything to do with your money.** 1 Timothy 6:17-19 tells us **6 Things God Desires of the Wealthy.** "As for the rich in this present age, charge them not to be haughty, nor to set their hopes on the uncertainty of riches, but on God, who richly provides us with everything to enjoy. They are to do good, to be rich in good works, to be generous and ready to share, thus storing up treasure for themselves as a good foundation for the future, so that they may take hold of that which is truly life."

Our Christianity changes us on the inside, our **desires, goals, and dreams.** We walk to a **higher calling,** one that lifts our fellow man to a **greater level of importance.** That changes how we reflect

165

on the money in our bank accounts.

The 1st Thing God Desires of the Wealthy: We can't think more of ourselves than others with less money.

The 2nd Thing God Desires of the Wealthy: We can't place our confidence in our money over our confidence in God.

The 3rd Thing God Desires of the Wealthy: We must use our money to do as much good for others as we can.

The 4th Thing God Desires of the Wealthy: We are to donate to good causes, to spread our good fortune around.

The 5th Thing God Desires of the Wealthy: We must see our wealth in what we have done for others, not in the resources at our disposal.

The 6th Thing God Desires of the Wealthy: We are to treasure the things in life that really matter: respect for our fellow man, care and concern for the less fortunate, and a desire to be Christ-like in everything we do.

God blesses us according to our abilities. When money comes our way, it should flow **through us**, not just **to us**. Our wealth is our opportunity to bless others. Let's start today.

July 28 – 3 Lessons We Can Learn from Esau

ESAU IS PAINTED as the negative side of the Jacob coin. The scriptures tell us the two were **different from before their birth**. Genesis 25:22 says the brothers struggled even in their mother's womb. "The children struggled together within her ..." Esau was firstborn, red and hairy, and his brother was nothing like him in appearance, bearing smooth skin. Yet they were twins, born of the same mother, and conceived by the same father.

Genesis 25:27 tells us Esau was cunning, and Jacob was a plain man who preferred his tent. "When the boys grew up, Esau was a skillful hunter, a man of the field, while Jacob was a quiet man, dwelling in tents."

Genesis 25:28 proclaims Isaac's love for his eldest, Esau; but Rebekah was drawn towards Jacob. "Isaac loved Esau because he ate of his game, but Rebekah loved Jacob."

No good could come of this family situation. Here are **3 Lessons We Can Learn from Esau:**

Lesson No. 1: Genesis 25:32 reveals Esau's short-sightedness. "Esau said, 'I am about to die; of what use is a birthright to me?' " When we disdain tomorrow and forget that today has consequences, we edge perilously close to disaster. We must remember the future and prepare for it.

Lesson No. 2: Genesis 27:37 shows that some things cannot be undone. "Isaac answered and said to Esau, 'Behold, I have made [Jacob] lord over you …' " Our past will come back to haunt us. What "happens in Vegas" doesn't always stay in Vegas.

Lesson No. 3: Genesis 33:4 assures us forgiveness is always an option. "But Esau ran to meet [Jacob] and embraced him and fell on his neck and kissed him, and they wept." No knife thrust is too deep for our wound to heal. Our physician is Jesus, and his faithfulness is more than skin deep.

Esau went on to become the father of a great nation. The journey was often a bumpy one, clashing with Jacob's path toward his future history. We can be like Esau or Jacob. The difference comes in allowing God to be our guide. Following God's direction takes us on the right path to success in the Son.

July 29 – The Shadow of Our Sin

SHADOWS FOLLOW us everywhere. We get used to them and don't pay them any attention. You might even say **we don't notice them anymore**. The only time we give them any consideration is when they get in our way.

Perhaps we're reading, and our arm blocks the light. **We adjust the lamp and move on**. Or we walk in front of the window, and we block the warmth for someone else. **"Move," we hear.**

Normally, however, our shadow is an unobtrusive companion without form or substance, an **untouchable second skin**. Here's the thing. That shadow, that second skin we can't touch or feel, affects everything around us. Keep something in our shadow long enough, and it will begin to wither and die.

That's what sin is like. We can't feel or touch it, but it's always there, a shadow, getting between us and other people, and raising the specter of death when it remains too long. Proverbs 13:21 says: "Disaster pursues sinners, but the righteous are rewarded with good."

If we disregard the teachings of the Lord, we invite disaster to shadow our days. We open ourselves to situations that will rain trouble on our head. It's the righteous that stand in the light. God says he will **reward right living with good things**. We do well to trust in God. His teachings are good and true. His faithfulness is **our backbone of strength**. In him we will live a long life filled with blessings from above.

Take God's hand. He will banish all darkness and lead you into the light.

July 30 – The Fight Has Already Been Won

YOU CAN UNCLENCH your fists now. You can remove your shoulder pads, put away your helmet, and step away from the fight. You can kick off your training shoes, rest on the sidelines, and let your weary muscles take a break. **The battle's not all up to you.** You don't have to do everything, win every conflict. You are **one of a team**, and Jesus says he's **already won every battle** we will fight.

John 16:33 says Jesus has overcome the world. "I have said these things to you, that in me you may have peace. In the world you will have tribulation. But take heart; I have overcome the world."

Ephesians 6:13 tells us we are covered in the full armor of God. "Therefore take up the whole armor of God, that you may be able to withstand in the evil day, and having done all, to stand firm."

Deuteronomy 20:4 is our promise that God's victory is already ours. "For the Lord your God is he who goes with you to fight for you against your enemies, to give you the victory."

What's got you battered? Is your pantry bare? Are you being shunned by your family? Are your investments crashing like a falling tree? **Look up, look up! God fights for you.** He has overcome the world, and he has **offered his armor unto you** for your protection and security. Jesus is on your team. **Take up his cause.** Join his line. His offense is the best battle-ready cause you can take on. When you battle with Jesus at your side, the outcome is always in your favor.

July 31 – Why God Chooses Us

PEOPLE MATCH up with other people for various reasons. They desire friendship. They are looking for a mentor. Perhaps it's a job opportunity, or even physical attraction.

The **reason for our matchup** affects how we choose our companion. A friend should **share common interests**, perhaps sporting skills or shopping chops. A mentor must be **outside our peer group** so they can guide us without worrying if they might hurt our feelings. Those we match up with for job purposes ... our **skillsets need to complement** each other. How about physical attraction? Or to say it another way, **romantic interest** ... the desire to **pursue a lifelong commitment** of love, family, and shared interests. We need to choose carefully, making certain we can mesh our lives successfully.

What's God's standard for choosing us, for bonding us to him through redemption? Are we required to clean up our lives, become better than we were … in essence, to **prove ourselves by righteous living** before we can become part of the church? Titus 3:4-6 tells us: "But when the goodness and loving kindness of God our Savior appeared, he saved us, not because of works done by us in righteousness, but according to his own mercy, by the washing of regeneration and renewal of the Holy Spirit, whom he poured out on us richly through Jesus Christ our Savior."

Let's focus on these seven words: **"… according to his mercy he saved us …"** That's God's whole reason for choosing to reach out to us and offer us his redemption. We need to **quit trying to prove ourselves** to God in hopes he will **"come through"** for us. God loves us because he loves us, even when we aren't living by his standards.

So, here's the plan: Accept the hand of Christ just as you are. You don't need to "clean up" first. There's plenty of time for that after you accept God's offer of salvation. Before we can live like Jesus, we must become connected to him through our spiritual rebirth in Christ.

— August —

August 1 – **Standing Out in the Crowd**

DRIVING A CAR that's a popular color can give us a headache. We come out of the mall and look for a tan SUV, only to find there are **dozens of them**.

Search for white SUVs on CARFAX, and as of late 2019, you could find **538,934 examples**. It's no wonder people install glittery wheels, giant spoilers, and decorative stickers on their paintwork. They want to stand out in the crowd. They want to be able to **find their cars amid all the others** in the lot.

Here's what God says about standing out in the crowd. Notice the seven boldface words in the center of the passage. We're reading in Romans 12:1-2. "I appeal to you therefore, brothers, by the mercies of God, to present your bodies as a living sacrifice, holy and acceptable to God, which is your spiritual worship. **Do not be conformed to this world**, but be transformed by the renewal of your mind, that by testing you may discern what is the will of God, what is good and acceptable and perfect."

We can't afford to be **another car in the lot**, another church member in the pews, another upwardly mobile status-seeker just like everyone else. How will people pick us out as Christians? How will we look any different than the rest? 1 Peter 1:14-15 doubles up on our **plan for improvement**. "As obedient children, do not be conformed to the passions of your former ignorance, but as he who called you is holy, you also be holy in all your conduct."

As obedient children. We are obedient when we **study the Word of God** and let it **change how we live**. Then we will be holy in everything we do, and we'll **stand out in the crowd and draw others** unto our Lord.

Jesus is the difference that changes each of us.

August 2 – **Spread the Goodness of the Lord**

WHEN SOMEONE throws a party and sets out a good spread, we know exactly what we're saying. There's **food aplenty**. More than enough. **No one will go away hungry** unless they refuse to eat. The host has shared without reserve, and the guests are invited to **join in the feast**.

1 Peter 4:9-10 reflects on the importance of **spreading around the goodness the Lord blesses us with**. "Show hospitality to one another without grumbling. As each has received a gift, use it to serve one another, as good stewards of God's varied grace."

That leads us to ask what God has gifted us with. This isn't all about money. **Are you great at sewing?** Offer your skills to **mend items for the church or the elderly. Do you have a riding mower?** Volunteer to **clip the church lawn** or stop by a sick church member's home to **tidy their yard. What about a beach house?** If you have one, have you invited your Sunday school class for an **afternoon on the sand? Others of us might be skilled at phone conversations.** We can call and chat with those who missed the Sunday service and **bring them up to date** on the pastor's message.

Here are some other ways we can **Spread the Goodness of the Lord**. 1. Offer an hour or two of babysitting. 2. Do a grocery run for a shut-in. 3. Accompany the pastor on a hospital visit. 4. Donate some good items of clothing to a church family. 5. Offer church members a ride on Sunday morning.

You can do this. If you have money, spread it around. If not, there are **plenty of other ways to share the love of God** with people around you. Our duty is to God. It's revealed in our love for those at our side.

August 3 – God Wants to Be Good to You

THE UNIVERSE is a grand and glorious creation. It's **bigger than we can imagine**. We're only now uncovering the massive depths of stars in our field of vision. The well-known Hubble telescope has revealed an estimated **100 billion galaxies**, and that's **only the start**. New telescope technology is likely to reveal twice that many. That's **200 billion galaxies**. We can't even guess the number of stars involved. The total is too large to comprehend. Yet – **and this is a big one** – the Creator of the cosmos found his way to Earth to bless his creation with the **gift of his Son**.

How do we know God still loves us after 2,000 years have passed? The Bible reveals **three verses that tell us he still wants to be good to us**.

Psalm 103:13 says God looks at us with **kindness and love** in his gaze. "As a father shows compassion to his children, so the Lord shows compassion to those who fear him."

Exodus 33:19 says the Father **forgives our stumbling attempts**

171

to follow him and lifts us up. "And [the Lord] said, 'I will make all my goodness pass before you and will proclaim before you my name "The Lord." And I will be gracious to whom I will be gracious, and will show mercy on whom I will show mercy.' "

Isaiah 48:9 says our Redeemer will **never cast us aside** for better followers or more dedicated adherents to his name. "For my name's sake I defer my anger; for the sake of my praise I restrain it for you, that I may not cut you off."

Write these on a sticky note and **put it on your mirror**, slip it in your wallet, and **keep a copy in your car**. Look at it often. It's your reminder that you are loved by the Creator of the Cosmos.

Here's God's love verses summarized for your sticky note.
1. **God has a soft spot for you.**
2. **God rolls out his carpet of goodness for you.**
3. **God claims you permanently, without end, full stop.**

Put your trust in the Father. He will return your faith with whole-hearted love.

August 4 – **Our Most Precious Bundle**

BABIES ARE cute. Their little dimpled smiles and those fat little fingers. Their adorability can be scientifically evaluated.

What!?! No way! *Yes way.* It can be measured. **Put to a standard and recorded on paper.**

What makes a child adorable? Let's think about baby animals for a comparison. What makes a kitten cute, or a puppy, calf, fawn, or any other newborn animal? It's the **size of their head**, the relative dimension of their **face to the rest of them**, the **placement of their eyes** and so on. We can measure their cuteness by the **shape of who they are**. Then there's the lack of coordination, the stumpy movements, and the wobbling walk. It tweaks our heart and **invites our love to spill out** of us.

God forbid that we don't like children. Seriously. Read about God's instructions in Mark 10:14-16. "But when Jesus saw it, he was indignant and said to them, 'Let the children come to me; do not hinder them, for to such belongs the kingdom of God. Truly, I say to you, whoever does not receive the kingdom of God like a child shall not enter it.' And he took them in his arms and blessed them, laying his hands on them."

Our children are the most precious things we possess. We are to teach them of the Lord, show them the love of God, and then turn

172

them loose into the world to **become mighty warriors** for the sake of the cross. We mustn't let ourselves forget that just like newborn animals, childhood is brief. Let's love our little ones while we can and instill in them our **commitment to our Lord**.

We take one step, and those who follow us are right behind.

August 5 – 3 Gifts That Come with Age

CHILDHOOD IS A time of looking forward. We can ride our bike to the corner this year, then **to the store the next**. We look forward to our first car. Then comes dating, and the **possibilities are endless**. Then we level up to college. **Freedom!** There's no one looking over our shoulder. **We can do what we want.** In our twenties, we reach our physical apex. Our bodies are taller, stronger, better looking than they will be ever again.

After we hit thirty, we must **fight to retain what came so easily** a decade before. The further we move along life's timeline, the harder the challenge becomes. **What good is there in our future?** The Bible gives us **3 Gifts that Come with Age**. We can achieve them no other way.

Proverbs 16:31 says our **high standards and moral lifestyle are a prized achievement**. "Gray hair is a crown of glory; it is gained in a righteous life."

Job 11:17 assures us we will receive **recognition for our good works**. "And your life will be brighter than the noonday; its darkness will be like the morning."

Proverbs 3:1-2 tells us we will live in the **golden glow of our achievements** in the Lord. "My son, do not forget my teaching, but let your heart keep my commandments, for length of days and years of life and peace they will add to you."

Life doesn't wind down at twenty or even thirty. *Forty isn't our peak decade nor is fifty.* God has our prize waiting. **Our golden years will be the best of all.** God's reward will **flow from heaven when we live by his Word**. Jesus is our future, and our happiness comes through him.

August 6 – The Sunrise Belongs to You

YOU ARE NOT a person of the dark. **Your days are lived in the light of the comforting love of Jesus.** Night and day are the cycle of life, but the sunrise **always comes with the morning**. The sunrise belongs to you.

Jeremiah 29:11 says God is **leading you with the light of his glory**. "For I know the plans I have for you, declares the Lord, plans for welfare and not for evil, to give you a future and a hope."

1 Peter 1:3-4 tells you the **resurrection of Christ is your bright and shining hope**. "Blessed be the God and Father of our Lord Jesus Christ! According to his great mercy, he has caused us to be born again to a living hope through the resurrection of Jesus Christ from the dead, to an inheritance that is imperishable, undefiled, and unfading, kept in heaven for you."

Philippians 3:20 assures you **heaven shines brightly before you**. "But our citizenship is in heaven, and from it we await a Savior, the Lord Jesus Christ."

Zephaniah 3:17 renews the promise of **God's bright and shining love** for you. "The Lord your God is in your midst, a mighty one who will save; he will rejoice over you with gladness; he will quiet you by his love; he will exult over you with loud singing."

Romans 15:13 is your hope and peace in the **shining promise of the power of the Holy Spirit**. "May the God of hope fill you with all joy and peace in believing, so that by the power of the Holy Spirit you may abound in hope."

Isaiah 40:31 guarantees that you will be like an eagle, **soaring triumphantly in the brilliance of the coming day**. "But they who wait for the Lord shall renew their strength; they shall mount up with wings like eagles; they shall run and not be weary; they shall walk and not faint."

No dark thing can take your joy from you. Bad things will happen. Expect them. Just know that **God is on the other side**. The dawn is about to break, and the sunrise belongs to you. Your faith in God reveals his light through the darkest gloom.

August 7 – **And Sickness Shall Flee**

AN EDUCATOR in a small town just west of Fort Worth, Texas, had worked hard to improve her family's fortunes. In 2013, after years of extra university work, she accepted an administrative position in her school district. She celebrated her success (and her extra pay) with a new car of exceptional style. **Then disaster struck.** In 2015, she was *diagnosed with cancer*. How could this be? She had a husband and a young daughter. Her fortunes were on the rise. *She even professed a church background.* Where had God gone, that this should happen to her?

174

Luke 5:24 tells us: "But that you may know that the Son of Man has power upon earth to forgive sins, …I say unto you, Arise, and take up your couch, and go into your house."

God's presence in our life isn't determined by our sickness or our health. His love for us *isn't reflected by our bank book*, whether we have money or we don't. God doesn't bless the faithful with a loving family, while the weak of heart are forced to live alone. That's not the modus operandi of our Heavenly Father. *He does, however, understand who we are as flawed humanity.* He knows we need to feel his reassuring hand. He connects with our needs, **and he sees how easily we doubt his presence in our lives**.

That small-town educator recovered. It wasn't easy. The treatments were tedious and wearing. Some days she could barely walk the floor. Yet, she had a husband who was her rock. Her daughter, now a young teen, pampered her with pedicures (and a lot of love!). Her job awaited her. *God still loved her.*

Why does God heal the sick*? **Because we need it.** Because our faith will falter if he doesn't. *Because it proves that he is the God who has power over sin and death.* God heals the sick because he is God, and he needs no other reason. **When he speaks, sickness shall flee.** When he speaks, sin is banished. *When he speaks, our world is made right, and we know him as the Awesome One, the Bright and Morning Star, the Holy One, Adonai.*

God's love to us is proved by his touch on every portion of everything we do.

August 8 – The Gift of Bread

WE ALL LIKE to eat. It's more than that. **We need to eat**. If we don't eat, we will die. Seriously. Starvation happens all the time.

Here's the thing. **Bread isn't free. We cannot afford to feel entitled to what we haven't earned, and that's from the Word of God.** 2 Thessalonians 3:10-12 says our bread is conditional on the work we've completed. "For even when we were with you, we would give you this command: If anyone is not willing to work, let him not eat. For we hear that some among you walk in idleness, not busy at work, but busybodies. Now such persons we command and encourage in the Lord Jesus Christ to do their work quietly and to earn their own living."

Yup, that's what it says. **No work = no eat.** To clarify this stern declaration, **intentional laziness is not of God**. He doesn't approve,

175

nor will he condone an able-bodied person not doing their share. If you can and don't, then **no one else is obligated to feed you. That's right out of the Word of God, so buck up and get busy**. God has work for you to do. Our gift of bread is our due when we jump in to get the job done.

August 9 – 3 Times Prayer Is Our Salvation

PRAYER. It's a tenet of our Christian walk. It's expected, part of the wallpaper. **Of course we spend time in prayer**.

Then we have our salvation. That's the reason Jesus came to live among us. It's the purpose of his death on the cross. **Who doesn't know that?**

Yet, there's more to salvation. According to Merriam-Webster, it's foremost deliverance from sin, but it's also **freedom from ignorance, illusion, destruction, or failure**. If we don't see that a bridge is out, and a good Samaritan waves us toward the detour, **that's a type of salvation**. If we're dating someone bad for us, and we are too in love to see their flaws, a friend's **eye-opening pointers** serve as our relational salvation. **We are rescued from the brink of despair**. So, what three times is prayer our salvation?

Psalm 55:17 says: "Evening and morning and at noon I utter my complaint and moan, and he hears my voice." These aren't general prayer opportunities, rote prayers over a meal or at bedtime. These must be **real, heartfelt prayers** that come from deep within.

Psalm 145:18-19 describes God's response to our prayers. "The Lord is near to all who call on him, to all who call on him in truth. He fulfills the desire of those who fear him; he also hears their cry and saves them."

Each time we pray, we receive **three benefits from God**. 1. God draws near to us. 2. God fulfills our desire. 3. God saves us from our desperate circumstance.

Prayer is our salvation 3 times a day. If we tally over a lifetime the times prayer is our salvation, our salvation opportunities through prayer become **too many to count**.

When we turn to God for our help, he grants our every request.

August 10 – **Who Needs Cruella?**

WE KNOW THE story of the dalmatians. 101, in fact. The movie is iconic, the story of a wealthy socialite that desires to **take what doesn't belong to her**.

176

Or sing Beethoven's song. That's a movie, too. An adored dog saves a family from the clutches of an evil couple to whom **money is more important than kindness**. We root for the poor person, not the wealthy snoot. Who hasn't seen **It's a Wonderful Life** and cheered on George as he <u>fights for the little guy</u>?

Proverbs 16:19 tells us why we have this divide in the cheering section. "It is better to be of a lowly spirit with the poor than to divide the spoil with the proud."

We've watched the good ole boys of Hazard County run from Boss Hogg, and we never want to see Boss win. **Never**. Even if the sheriff has all the money. And the fancy car. And the big house. It's not cool to hold your nose in the air and **put on airs**. Why else do we find Tiny Tim so heartwarming and Scrooge (rich and prosperous) so infuriating? **You got what you deserve**, we yell at the screen, when Christmas Future reveals the beggars grubbing over his life's leftovers.

Let's live with grace. **Let's exemplify kindness**. Let's be the person others want to spend time with, the aunt, the uncle, the grandfather that **holds out open arms and gives away whatever they have**.

We are closer to God when we draw others to us.

August 11 – Getting the Extreme Clean

THERE'S A GOOD reason to wash your car. It will last longer and perform better. You read that right. Get the dirt out of the springs, clean the grime from the hinges and under the wiper blades, and your car will **weather the years and be in better shape** than the average car. Then there's your headlights and taillights. **Safety first!** If you can't see well at night, that's dangerous. If your taillights are obscured with road grime, you risk not being seen in the dark.

What about the inside? Does that matter? <u>Absolutely</u>! Hit the brakes and watch empty containers fly around your interior. You've just become a distracted driver. What about the empty bottle under your brake pedal? Or the dirt gumming up your power seat or your steering wheel?

Thank God we have **automatic car washing facilities**. We drive in, pay for a wash, and we **drive away shiny and clean**. We must be diligent to avoid the light wash. If we only clean the outside, and we ignore the rest, we will look good going down the road, but <u>we've left much of our cleaning undone</u>.

Isaiah 5:21 says: "Woe to those who are wise in their own eyes, and shrewd in their own sight!"

Our life is the same. If we wash our hair, put on clean clothes, and even paint on some makeup, **we've only just started**. We've done the light wash. We want the extreme clean, the one where the trash is removed, the carpet is steamed, and the inside of the windows are wiped clean. **Only then can we operate at our maximum efficiency for the Lord.**

God's standard is our measuring stick. Let's use it to stand tall in him.

August 12 – 3 Praise Truths

AMERICA HAS A turnaround culture. We pull ourselves up by our bootstraps. Put on a new leaf. Turn to the sun. Get up on the other side of the bed. Each of these means the same. We change our situation by **hard work and determination**. We improve ourselves by **sheer will**. **We make a difference in our situation because we desire it.**

A good first step is to offer praise unto the holy God who gives us life. Harold Herring in **7 Keys to Activating the Cyrus Anointing** says, "God inhabits the praises of His people, and the spirit of dread and fear cannot stay in that environment."

Praise will **turn your life around.** 1. God will be there when you lift him up in praise. Let me say that again. **God will be there ... with you ... because you praised him.** 2. You will no longer dread tomorrow when you praise God. Why? **Because God's presence will give you hope for the future.** 3. Fear is banished from your life ... all fear ... financial ... emotional . . . physical. **God will fill you with courage to face every situation.**

2 Timothy 1:7 says it this way: "For God gave us a spirit not of fear but of power and love and self-control." That's bootstrap control! We can rise out of the mess we're in. We can have a brighter sunrise, a warmer hug, and a better job situation because we've become different **through praise to our holy God.**

Let's get our bootstraps out. The time to praise God is now.

August 13 – All Things Become New

LET'S REDECORATE the house. Top to bottom, from the **light fixtures** to the **baseboard trim**. We don't want to leave anything the same. We want new windows, new countertops, and new carpet on

178

the floor.

How would it be to slick up the walls and leave the bathrooms alone? **Rip them out.** All new tubs, tile, and sinks. Even our HVAC system. Toss it in the dumpster. We don't want the old one anywhere around. **We want our house to feel brand new.**

That's what God does for us when we come to him. We ask Jesus to come into our hearts, and we change our way of living. The weekend parties? **Tossed out the door.** Inappropriate clothes? **On the trash heap.** Juicy gossip shared? **Banished to the wind.** We change the way we dress, where we go, even the words we speak. We no longer use the vulgar expressions we thought so funny when we were mired in the world.

2 Corinthians 5:17 says it exactly like it is. "Therefore, if anyone is in Christ, he is a new creation. The old has passed away; behold, the new has come."

That's what God wants from us when we accept salvation in him. From top to bottom, we don't leave anything the same. We don't slick up the outside and leave the inside alone. We clean up **our thoughts, plans, and dreams**, also. **We become a new person because God makes us brand new.** That's what God does for us when we come to him.

When God scrubs away sin, we are sparkly clean in him.

August 14 – Maxing Out Our Jesus Quotient

WE NEED TO start off by looking at today's title. **Maxing out ... our Jesus ... quotient.** Each part of this five-word title has a specific and vital meaning in today's teaching.

Maxing out. What meaning can we pull from this? First, we need to look at the origin of maxing. It comes from maximum, which Merriam-Webster says is the **upper limit allowed**, or the **greatest quantity**. In other words, we want **as much as possible.** We want to stretch the limits, push the boundaries, and swell the coffers to overflowing.

Our Jesus. This sounds simple, but don't skip over these words too quickly. What is Jesus to us? We must make a **life-changing commitment** to better ourselves through studying the example Jesus lived and **copying his loving attitude** toward people. In other words, we must dump our old ways of thinking and behaving and let Jesus **take over every part** of who we are.

Quotient. This is a math term, a result of dividing two numbers.

179

Merriam-Webster says it's also a portion, a share, or **how much of something we have**. In other words, we must be reduced, and Jesus must be increased in everything we do. **Jesus is our gold standard** for how to live.

John 15:11 says it beautifully. "These things I have spoken to you, that my joy may be in you, and that your joy may be full."

When we study the Bible, learn God's nature, and begin to model ourselves after Jesus, God will **find his joy in us**, and we will **find our joy in him**. We will max out our Jesus quotient and become the best we can be.

Jesus is our example, and we are to become like him.

August 15 – **Your New Life Starts Today**

WHAT'S WITH your old dead self? That's not you anymore. You are brand new in Christ. Toss out that condemnation. Slough off the world's criticism. God has made you perfect in him. You are so full of the power of God and his living waters that **everyone who walks near you will soon be soaked with Jesus**.

John 7:38 says: "He who believes in Me, as the Scripture has said, out of his heart will flow rivers of living water."

You will speak peace, and it will calm anxious minds. **You will call out healing**, and miracles will happen. **You will proclaim the love of God**, and sinners will fall to their knees.

It's not you. It's God when you let him loose in your life. **Jesus is the living water**, and when you release him in your life, you **will become a mighty force for good in his name**. So, never mind what you used to be. Forget where you started. Jesus has places for you to go, and your new life starts today.

August 16 – **Jesus Cheers Us On**

CHILDREN NEED "face time" with their parents. They also need "skin time," little hugs to show them they are **loved and appreciated**.

A news story appeared the morning of September 10, 2019. The successful and busy parents of twin 8-year-old boys were devastated when one of their sons died in his sleep. The Oregon couple's biggest regret was the time they spent at their jobs and not with their children. They pleaded with other parents to **make time to enjoy their children** while they have them.

How much regret must Jesus suffer when people reach the end of their days and slip away without deciding for salvation? **Jesus wants to spend time with us.** He pleads before the Father for us that we will **feel his love** and know that **he treasures us**. 1 John 2:1-2 reveals the depths of Jesus' passion for his followers. "My little children, I am writing these things to you so that you may not sin. But if anyone does sin, we have an advocate with the Father, Jesus Christ the righteous. He is the propitiation for our sins, and not for ours only but also for the sins of the whole world."

Jesus is our advocate. He supports us in our time of need. He **promotes us before God.** He believes in us and actively backs our attempts to live rightly before God. **Jesus is also the propitiation for our sins.** His sacrifice on the cross **appeases God's need for justice.** Jesus' love for us pacifies God's affront to our sins. It is through the **loving nature of Jesus** that we are allowed access to the throne room of the Father.

Face time. Skin time. It is **our connection to Jesus** that enables us to **weather the tough times** and losses that life brings our way.

Let's spend time with Jesus. He is our strength and our joy.

August 17 – **Turning Over Our Christ Card**

A DECK OF CARDS is an interesting setup. Lots of numbers. Pictures of royalty. Jokers, too. Then there are four suits. Diamonds. Clubs. Spades. Hearts. Finally, we have our ace, **different from all the rest**.

How you pair the cards during a game determines their value. Whether you are playing Bridge, Five Hundred, or Thirteen, you must **know the convention for that game.** Even Go Fish has rules and conventions that determine what cards win and those that don't. Draw the wrong card, and you can crash your chances of having a winning hand.

What's our winning hand in our Christian walk? How do we lay down a victory hand when we play against the world? **What's the best card to draw that trumps all the rest?** John 13:34-35 reveals our best card to play. "A new commandment I give to you, that you love one another: just as I have loved you, you also are to love one another. By this all people will know that you are my disciples, if you have love for one another."

When we draw love from the deck, and we turn it over to reveal it in our lives, we have trumped every other card. It's our **Christ Card**, the singular ace that is different from all the rest. With it, we take all the good we can do in every area of our lives, and we **bump it up a notch**. We become better when we are **infused with the love of our Lord**. We become like Jesus, and the world is better. Not just for us, but for those who interact with us.

Jesus is our source, and though him, the love of God empowers us to overcome the world.

August 18 – **Your Troubles Will Turn Around**

JUST BECAUSE you've stumbled into the dirt doesn't mean God intends for you to stay there. **God will lift you up. He has better things on the way.** Wipe off the dusty remains of yesterday's argument. Rinse your hands of your financial failure. Sweep your spiritual hiccups into the trash bin and prepare for a fresh beginning. Psalm 68:13 in the much-loved King James Version says: "Though you lie down among the sheepfolds, you will be like the wings of a dove covered with silver, and her feathers with yellow gold."

Your past cannot stick to you. You will spread your wings and glisten with the glory of God. **Silver is your adornment. You will sparkle with the majesty of God's future as it comes over you.** As you launch into flight, the yellow gold of God's good fortune will **reflect the love of God in every action you take**.

Your future is bright when you are released from your troubles by the powerful hand of God. Step out, step out. God has places for you to go.

August 19 – **4 Riddles to Set Your Children on God's Path**

CHILDREN LOVE to be pranked. A surprise gift, a joke told at *just the right time*, or an unexpected visit to the ice cream shop. Tell your kids the perfume sample from the department store is stink juice. Play it up before you open it, then put some on, all the while *acting like it's the worst smell in the world*. Then hug them so they can get a whiff of how pleasant it really is. *They will remember your prank for years to come.*

Here are **4 Riddles to Set Your Children on God's Path**.

Riddle No. 1: *What measures one-half, yet is bigger than two?* The answer is a child. When he honors his parents, the Lord gives him double blessings. Deuteronomy 5:16 says: "Honor your father and your mother, as the Lord your God commanded you, that your days may be long, and that it may go well with you in the land that the Lord your God is giving you."

182

Riddle No. 2: *What can you keep but never put in your pocket?* Your parents' example for how to live. Proverbs 6:20 says: "My son, keep your father's commandment, and forsake not your mother's teaching."

Riddle No. 3: *What grows best when you cultivate something else?* God's pleasure when you grow in obedience to your parents. Colossians 3:20 says: "Children, obey your parents in everything, for this pleases the Lord."

Riddle No. 4: *The more you fill it, the more you have left. What is it?* Your life, when you fill it with obedience and honor for your parents. Ephesians 6:1-3 tells us: "Children, obey your parents in the Lord, for this is right. Honor your father and mother (this is the first commandment with a promise), that it may go well with you and that you may live long in the land."

So get out there and prank your kids. Give them some riddles to solve. They will have fun figuring them out, and they will *learn to walk on God's path at the same time.*

What we think on is what we learn. Let's think on Jesus.

August 20 – **A Dose of God's Goodness**

VACCINATIONS are generally considered a good thing. We get a small dose of medicine, and it **protects us from a larger illness**.

Getting poked by a needle's not fun, however, even when we know the good it will bring. That's where **sugar cubes come in**. It's like that song from **Mary Poppins**, when we sing, "A spoonful of sugar helps the medicine go down …"

In schools across the nation, during the 1960s, school children received vaccinations via sugar cubes. A drop of the medicine was placed on the sweet white square, and they were eagerly eaten with no complaints.

God wants to give us a dose of his goodness. He wants us to **skip the bad things** that come our way. He offers us a **way out of the problems** he knows will trip us up. Proverbs 12:2 says we receive God's favor when we **follow the precepts of the Word**. "A good man obtains favor from the Lord, but a man of evil devices he condemns."

Matthew 6:33 assures us we will receive God's blessings if we **put our Lord first** in our list of priorities. "But seek first the kingdom of God and his righteousness, and all these things will be added to you."

183

Proverbs 11:28 is our instruction to **put our trust in God**, not in the wealth of this world. "Whoever trusts in his riches will fall, but the righteous will flourish like a green leaf."

Here's God's plan. He wrote the Bible as a **source of medicine**, just a **jot on a cube** of sugar, **easy to swallow, one truth at a time**. When we take in his truths and <u>let them change us</u>, we can sidestep the pitfalls we find along the way. The Bible is our source of goodness. We get a good dose when we **study its truth**. We become healthy in God when they **become part of us**.

Our spiritual health flows from God. It's waiting for us to reach out and take it.

August 21 – **Jamming Down in Prayer**

TO JAM DOWN is a slang phrase that crept into popular culture in the music scene. We play music informally with other people, and in the process, we create something beautiful. Let's break this down into **five vital layers** of meaning.

1. We play our instrument. 2. We keep it casual, meaning without a formal plan. 3. We are not alone. Other people are involved. 4. We progress through multiple stages of achievement. 5. We wind up with a better result than we started with.

Good prayer follows this **same sequence**. Let's look at James 5:16. "Therefore, confess your sins to one another and pray for one another, that you may be healed. The prayer of a righteous person has great power as it is working."

Can you see the similarity? Here's how we jam down in prayer. 1. We **speak aloud** our needs. 2. We do so **in private**, not from the pulpit. 3. We pray for the **sins of others**, and they return the favor. 4. We endeavor to **lift ourselves** to a higher calling. 5. We **receive the answer** as God responds to our prayers.

Luke 11:9 says our prayers are answered if we have the courage to **ask and believe**. "And I tell you, ask, and it will be given to you; seek, and you will find; knock, and it will be opened to you."

John 15:7 says it's all about our **involvement with Jesus**. "If you abide in me, and my words abide in you, ask whatever you wish, and it will be done for you."

Here's what we need to get from this. **Prayer isn't a solitary activity.** We need to jam down, involve our peers, keep it on a one-to-one basis, show we really care for each other. Formal prayers are rote and **come across as such. God is a personal God**, and he

184

answers our prayers **on a personal level**. Let's spend time with Jesus, and we will become beautiful.

August 22 – 7 Amazing Facts about Elijah

ELIJAH IS THE storied prophet of the Old Testament. He was sent to Israel to lead God's people out of corruption and suffering. Elijah was the man for the job. Here are 7 Amazing Facts about Elijah that qualified him to be God's Man.

Fact No. 1: God trusted Elijah with control over the weather. 1 Kings 17:1 tells us: "Now Elijah … said to Ahab, 'As the Lord, the God of Israel, ... before whom I stand, there shall be neither dew nor rain these years, except by my word.' "

Fact No. 2: Elijah commanded a pot to not run out of food until the rains came. 1 Kings 17:16 tells us: "The jar of flour was not spent, neither did the jug of oil become empty, according to the word of the Lord that he spoke by Elijah."

Fact No. 3: Elijah brought a child back to life by breathing on him. 1 Kings 17:22 tells us: "And the Lord listened to the voice of Elijah. And the life of the child came into him again, and he revived."

Fact No. 4: Elijah faced off 450 false prophets with fire from heaven. 1 Kings 18:21-22, 38 tells us: "And Elijah came near to all the people and said, '… If the Lord is God, follow him; but if Baal, then follow him.' … Then Elijah said to the people, 'I, even I only, am left a prophet of the Lord, but Baal's prophets are 450 men.' … Then the fire of the Lord fell and consumed the burnt offering …'"

Fact No. 5: Elijah never died; he rode a whirlwind into heaven. 2 Kings 2:11 tells us: "And as they still went on and talked, behold, chariots of fire and horses of fire separated the two of them. And Elijah went up by a whirlwind into heaven."

Fact No. 6: The angel of the Lord compared John the Baptist to Elijah. Luke 1:17 tells us: "And [John] will go before him in the spirit and power of Elijah, to turn the hearts of the fathers to the children, and the disobedient to the wisdom of the just, to make ready for the Lord a people prepared."

Fact No. 7: James modeled Elijah as one of the greatest prayer warriors of all time. James 5:17 tells us: "Elijah was a man with a nature like ours, and he prayed fervently that it might not rain, and for three years and six months it did not rain on the earth."

We can do worse than to emulate Elijah in our Christian walk.

There's only one way we can do better. Model our lives after Christ, our Savior.

We become today's warriors for Christ when we live like God's champions of old.

August 23 – 4 Streams of Help from God

GOD'S LOVE is a rushing flood. It crashes down from heaven, and we are **consumed with its power and majesty**. There is nowhere God's love cannot reach, no hidden place it cannot uncover, and **no dark corner it cannot brighten**. Every river, every rushing flood starts with a trickle, a stream that grows and builds **until we are overwhelmed. That's God's love.** Let's look at **4 Streams of Help from God**.

Stream No. 1: Lamentations 3:31-33 reveals the **Lord's compassion**. "For the Lord will not cast off forever, but, though he cause grief, he will have compassion according to the abundance of his steadfast love; for he does not afflict from his heart or grieve the children of men." Our troubles are matched only by the love and compassion of God. Our lifted voice stirs God's heart to **answer our prayers in a flood of compassion**.

Stream No. 2: Psalm 18:2 underscores the **level of trust we can place in God**. "The Lord is my rock and my fortress and my deliverer, my God, my rock, in whom I take refuge, my shield, and the horn of my salvation, my stronghold." Rock. Fortress. Deliverer. Shield. Salvation. Stronghold. Each of these words **embodies the rushing flood of God's love**.

Stream No. 3: Micah 7:8-9 says God **sees our distress and will lift us up**. "Rejoice not over me, O my enemy; when I fall, I shall rise; when I sit in darkness, the Lord will be a light to me. ... He will bring me out to the light; I shall look upon his vindication." Our dry season will know the rain of God's empowering love. Our roots will be watered by the **flood of God's enduring help**.

Stream No. 4: John 16:33 reminds us that Jesus went before us, and **he knows our situation**. "I have said these things to you, that in me you may have peace. In the world you will have tribulation. But take heart; I have overcome the world." We are awash in the power of God. His love swirls around our feet, and when we step out in faith, **we will be carried forward by the rushing tide of his glory and grace**.

God does not abandon his children. He instills in us a powerful link to heaven **through the cross and our relationship with Jesus**. Let's open our arms. His flood is headed our way. We can rest assured that God has us covered no matter what our troubles might be.

August 24 – 3 Calls for Honesty

SPORTS ARE A good venue for learning about living a good life. You may be thinking of the lessons of **fair play** and **good sportsmanship**, and there's no question sports can teach those. They are good life skills, **among the very best**.

What about the referees and umpires? The coaches and team captains? **What about the plays they call,** *the instructions for helping their team be a success?* **How often do you think a team will win if they ignore their instructions and decide to go it on their own?**

Here are *3 Calls for Honesty* that God gives us from Proverbs.

Proverbs 11:1 tells us we must be **fair in our dealings in business**. "False balance is an abomination to the Lord, but a just weight is his delight."

Proverbs 3:27 says to pay what we owe **as soon as the money is available**. "Do not withhold good from those to whom it is due, when it is in your power to do it."

Proverbs 16:8 states the shame of **living by hook or crook** to get by. "Better is a little with righteousness than great revenues with injustice."

We are on a team. **Everyone of us**. *We must play together.* What we do affects everyone else. Spouse. Children. Coworkers. Church family. Let's play well. Let's play fairly. Let's **play by God's rules**, *and he calls on us to play honestly.*

We can walk with pride when we walk in the truth of the Word.

August 25 – Working for Our Blessings

WE SHALL receive showers of blessings. **Who-ee!** It's like the lottery. Stuff comes our way – **lots of it** – and all we need to do is wait for it to arrive.

WRONG! That's not what the Bible says. Not even close. Let's look at how God's blessings really come to us. Genesis 2:3 **starts off with the Big Guy.** (Note: He had to rest from all his work.) "So God blessed the seventh day and made it holy, because on it God rested from all his work that he had done in creation."

187

Deuteronomy 28:12 reminds us **God blesses our hard work**, not our sofa-bound dreams. "The Lord will open to you his good treasury, the heavens, to give the rain to your land in its season and to bless all the work of your hands. And you shall lend to many nations, but you shall not borrow."

2 Chronicles 15:7 tells us **preparation is vital** if we want to receive good blessings from God. "But you, take courage! Do not let your hands be weak, for your work shall be rewarded."

John 4:34 shows us that **Jesus worked for his goals** to become reality. "Jesus said to them, 'My food is to do the will of him who sent me and to accomplish his work.' "

1 Corinthians 15:58 says **we mustn't slow down** in doing the work God requires of us. "Therefore, my beloved brothers, be steadfast, immovable, always abounding in the work of the Lord, knowing that in the Lord your labor is not in vain."

The blessings of God aren't the stuff of fairy tales. We don't wake up one day to a bounty of presents filling our house. The financial houses of the world won't automatically funnel their ill-gotten gains into our checking account.

Here's a list of how we can get the blessings of God: 1. We work. 2. God blesses us.

It's as simple as that. Now's our time to prepare to receive the blessings of God. **Here's how.** 1. Get training. Go to school. Consult successful people already in the business. 2. Practice at what we want to do. Volunteer. Try a work-study program. 3. Be in it for the long haul. Success builds on hard work.

Today's your day in God. Your future begins now.

August 26 – **Our Footsteps Toward the Father**

THE IDEA OF TRAVEL to a distant land ... how exciting! Elephants! Rocky beaches, or sand, if we prefer! Voices in new and unfamiliar languages! It seems an exotic escape, and we can imagine how glorious it will be.

Then the trip draws closer, and we begin to drag. Packing. Airline reservations. Choosing our accommodations ... have we selected a good part of town or bad? We can become overwhelmed **before we even get on the road**. We must choose to forge ahead, push aside the thought of ten, twelve, or fourteen hours in the air, and **make that first step** outside our door.

Philippians 3:14-16 describes our Christian walk much the same.

"I press on toward the goal for the prize of the upward call of God in Christ Jesus. Let those of us who are mature think this way, and if in anything you think otherwise, God will reveal that also to you. Only let us hold true to what we have attained."

We are caught up in the excitement of Jesus when we first find salvation. We want to spend time with him, **talk to other believers**, and **imagine ourselves in the splendor of heaven**. Then come the travel details. Putting aside our old life. Choosing to forge a new direction in Christ. Time in prayer and the Word. **It's easy to become overwhelmed**. Yet, our verse tells us what we must do. "I press on toward the goal for the prize …"

We choose to **step outside our comfort zone**, mention the goodness of God to those we meet, and **keep our eye on our heavenly destination**. Ten, twelve, or fourteen years … even **a lifetime of travel with Jesus** is a minor inconvenience with how exciting our destination will be.

Salvation is our first step on our journey toward our exotic destination.

August 27 – Spread the Goodness of the Lord

WHEN SOMEONE throws a party and sets out a good spread, we know exactly what we're saying. There's **food aplenty**. More than enough. **No one will go away hungry** unless they refuse to eat. The host has shared without reserve, and the guests are invited to **join in the feast**.

1 Peter 4:9-10 reflects on the importance of **spreading around the goodness the Lord blesses us with**. "Show hospitality to one another without grumbling. As each has received a gift, use it to serve one another, as good stewards of God's varied grace."

That leads us to ask what God has gifted us with. This isn't all about money. **Are you great at sewing?** Offer your skills to *mend items for the church or the elderly*. **Do you have a riding mower?** Volunteer to *clip the church lawn* or stop by a sick church member's home to *tidy their yard*. **What about a beach house?** If you have one, have you invited your Sunday school class for an *afternoon on the sand*? **Others of us might be skilled at phone conversations.** We can call and chat with those who missed the Sunday service and *bring them up to date* on the pastor's message.

Here are some other ways we can **Spread the Goodness of the Lord**. 1. Offer an hour or two of babysitting. 2. Do a grocery run for

189

a shut-in. 3. Accompany the pastor on a hospital visit. 4. Donate some good items of clothing to a church family. 5. Offer church members a ride on Sunday morning.

You can do this. If you have money, spread it around. If not, there are **plenty of other ways to share the love of God** with people around you. Our duty is to God. It's revealed in our love for those at our side.

August 28 – God's Gift of Children

KIDDOS CAN BE a mess. There's **no end to the mischief** they can dream up. **Golf balls in the toilet. Toilet paper trailed through the house. Mud everywhere.** Even our dinner table is no safety zone. One sneeze, and **our meal is contaminated**. Literally. Who wants to eat that?

So, what good are children? Acts 16:31 says **they are saved along with their parents**. "Believe in the Lord Jesus, and you will be saved, you and your household." Acts 2:39 tells us the promises that flow from God to us **also flow to our children**. "For the promise is for you and for your children and for all who are far off, everyone whom the Lord our God calls to himself." Isaiah 54:13 says our children **will be at peace** when we teach them of the Lord. "All your children shall be taught by the Lord, and great shall be the peace of your children." Isaiah 44:3 tells us our children **become our legacy** through the blessings of the Lord. "For I will pour water on the thirsty land, and streams on the dry ground; I will pour my Spirit upon your offspring, and my blessing on your descendants.

Are children a mess? **Absolutely. They are also an opportunity. Let's recap the four gifts that flow through us unto our children**.

1. They receive God's salvation through our faith in Christ.
2. God's promises to us are also to our children.
3. The truth of God will bring our children peace.
4. Our legacy in Christ is found in our children.

Our children need our love. They are God's gift unto us. Let's treasure them daily. Jesus welcomed the children. Let's hold out our hands, also.

August 29 – 4 Victories When We Feel Defeated

DO YOU FEEL like the accused? Things in your life go awry, and you feel all eyes looking to you? "It's her fault. If only she wasn't involved." "He does that every time. Why can't he stay away?" Hear something enough, and we internalize it, even when we know it's not true. It becomes truth to us, even if it wouldn't hold up in a court of law. "You're stupid." "I wish you'd never been born." "Not even Jesus wants you now."

Stop. **Stop, stop, stop!** God says **that's not how you should feel**. Let's look at 4 victories that can lift us up when we feel defeated.

Victory No. 1: Romans 9:33 says our past can no longer bring us down when we place our faith in Christ. "As it is written, 'Behold, I am laying in Zion a stone of stumbling, and a rock of offense; and whoever believes in him will not be put to shame.' "

Victory No. 2: 2 Timothy 2:15 tells us our confidence comes from the study of God's Word. "Do your best to present yourself to God as one approved, a worker who has no need to be ashamed, rightly handling the word of truth."

Victory No. 3: Psalm 119:80 plants our feet (and our lives) firmly on the rock of the promises that flow from the cross of Jesus. "May my heart be blameless in your statutes, that I may not be put to shame!"

Victory No. 4: 1 Peter 4:16 instructs us to lift our hands in praise to the Creator when we feel trouble hounding our footsteps. "Yet if anyone suffers as a Christian, let him not be ashamed, but let him glorify God in that name."

People can be cruel. When fingers point your way, look towards the Master. *His is the only hand that counts, and it draws you unto him.* Jesus is our source of success when life beats us down.

August 30 – 3 Rescues Guaranteed by God

SAILORS KNOW the value of a good life preserver. A lifeboat is reassuring when the **water is rising around us**. Steven Callahan tells of being adrift at sea in a 6-person raft for more than 76 days in his 1986 memoir *Lost at Sea*. He was able to retrieve supplies from his sinking sailboat: an emergency kit, charts, a spear gun, and an emergency rescue beacon. He was lost despite his gear. There was **no rescue on the horizon**.

That's how life makes us feel at times. The water is rising, and all the safeguards we've put in place seem useless. **Our savings accounts, our extended warranties, and our marriage.** They are insubstantial helps, and still the sea surrounds us. **The Word of God**

says we have 3 rescues on the way.

Rescue No. 1: Luke 1:71 says our **haters will be cast adrift** by our mighty God. "That we should be saved from our enemies and from the hand of all who hate us."

Rescue No. 2: Acts 18:10 is our **promise of protection** when the waters rise. "For I am with you, and no one will attack you to harm you, for I have many in this city who are my people."

Rescue No. 3: Hebrews 13:6 tells us **God is greater** than anything men can bring against us. "So we can confidently say, 'The Lord is my helper; I will not fear; what can man do to me?' "

Callahan might have been tempted to give up hope after 76 days. His resources were exhausted, and no help had come. **Then he saw lights on the horizon.** The next day, a fishing vessel pulled up by his side and took him aboard.

Now is not the time to despair. The storm is already brushed aside. Jesus is our **light on the horizon**, and **his arms will lift us** into the protection of the Father. Trust in God. He guarantees our safety in Christ.

August 31 – 3 Layers of God's Love

NOT ALL LOVE is the same. One is not better than the other, they are just different. We love our kids and want to protect them. Our love for our pets creates a warm feeling in our lives. When we love our job, it no longer feels like work. Spousal love, the real kind, makes even their foibles adorable.

What type of love does God feel toward us? There are **3 Layers of God's Love** that he bestows on us. **One is not better than the other. Understanding all three are vital to understanding our relationship with God.**

Love Layer No. 1: God loves us because we **believe on Jesus**. John 16:27 says: "For the Father himself loves you, because you have loved me and have believed that I came from God."

Love Layer No. 2: God loves us because he **loves his Son**. John 17:26 says: "I made known to them your name, and I will continue to make it known, that the love with which you have loved me may be in them, and I in them."

Love Layer No. 3: God loves us to prove the **divine nature of the Christ**. John 17:23 says: "I in them and you in me, that they may become perfectly one, so that the world may know that you sent me and loved them even as you loved me."

We can write these as **three love nuggets** to carry with us always. God loves us because we **believe** on his **Son**, his **divine emissary** to all people. We become wrapped in the love of God. Our choice to follow Jesus **strengthens the cords that bind us** to our Father in heaven. Coming to Christ cocoons us in multiple layers of God's eternal, unbounding love.

— September —

September 1 – God Will Lift You Up

IN HIS 2015 BOOK, *Fool's Talk*, Os Guinness says, "From the shortest texts and tweets to the humblest website, to the angriest blog, to the most visited social networks, the daily communications of the wired world attest that everyone is now in the business of relentless self-promotion." Email, Skype, cell phones … as Guinness says in his book, **"I post, therefore I am."**

Sometimes our public posts aren't received well, or people put up "revenge posts," revealing scathing details about our lives, **whether real or invented.** Our reputation is dragged through the electronic mud, and we emerge scorched and worse for the wear. What do we do when our Christian character is besmirched? What must be our response when our faith in Jesus is **mocked and ridiculed?**

Ask Tim Tebow, professional football player. He won the Heisman Trophy in 2007 and has appeared on BCS National Championship-winning teams. He's admittedly one of the most **outstanding players of modern American football.** He is regularly mocked on social media for his Christian beliefs.

1 Peter 4:14 tells us: "If you are insulted for the name of Christ, you are blessed, because the Spirit of glory and of God rests upon you."

Peter is telling us that if we **wear our Christian faith proudly enough**, it will rub people the wrong way. We will get noticed, and not always in a good way. That's the way it's supposed to be. It's the reality of the Christian experience. Os Guinness might have said, "I post my Christian beliefs, therefore I walk with Christ." Tim Tebow wears his faith **proudly on his sleeve**, and America's media notices.

It's time for **God-promotion**, not self-promotion. **Let's put the Father first in everything we do.** Write God all over your life, and he will lift you into the realm of his glory.

September 2 – Trading Our Cross for Gold

BILLS WERE once called silver certificates. We could take the bill to the bank and receive silver in exchange. One 1934 bill with a face value of $10,000 is stamped on the front with the words Gold

Certificate. At the time, you could take it down and trade it in. The bills were considered **equivalent to the precious metals**. One had the same value as the other.

Let's apply that to our Christian walk. We know following Christ isn't a trouble-free endeavor. We face **stumbling blocks every day**. Yet God gives us a **Heaven Certificate**. What we go through here on earth is **cash in our hands** to be traded at heaven's gate for entry inside.

2 Corinthians 4:16-17 tells us: "So we do not lose heart. Though our outer self is wasting away, our inner self is being renewed day by day. For this light momentary affliction is preparing for us an eternal weight of glory beyond all comparison."

Someone could walk around with a Gold Certificate in their pocket, and if they never took it out and traded it in, they **would never gain any benefit** from possessing that $10,000 bill.

Let's get our Christianity out. Let's put it in action. **Let's get the maximum benefit from our walk with God.** Heaven's coming. That's our due. The work of Jesus is waiting on us right now, and we can **bank our reward until we meet our Savior face-to-face**.

God's promise is our confidence, and we will be rewarded in him.

September 3 – Our Source of All Power

EXPERTS ONCE claimed that goldfish have a three-second memory. They track their world in three second intervals. One – two – three – bam! The world begins again. We know now that's not true. Five months is the current benchmark. In one study, a sound was played each time the animals were fed. After five months without the sound, when it was replayed, the fish immediately swam towards the feeding station.

What the fish displayed was more than just memory. Returning to the feeding station when it heard the sound revealed a level of trust the creature had developed. **The bell rings, and I'll get food.** That's how we need to respond to the presence of God. Our memory of our disappointments in life needs to be about three seconds long. Our trust in the goodness of Jesus needs to draw us to him no matter how long it's been since he's answered our prayers.

Proverbs 28:25-26 reveals the person who chooses to trust in God. "A greedy man stirs up strife, but the one who trusts in the Lord will be enriched. Whoever trusts in his own mind is a fool, but

195

he who walks in wisdom will be delivered."

Trusting in God **enriches our lives**. We learn to depend on him in the small things and the large ones. People cross us wrongly, and we continue to **see the good** in them. Our finances hit a rough spot, and we can see **God's protecting hand** despite our troubles. The answers to our prayers are a long time in coming, and doubt **never enters our mind**.

The passage tells us **we are wise to trust in God**. It also says only a fool would trust in himself as his total source of strength, knowledge, and power. We are **fulfilled, made better, and enriched** when we base our hopes and dreams on the will of the Father.

Trust comes from knowledge, and the Lord is our source of both.

September 4 – The Argument for Family

GET MARRIED or go it alone. **That's a valid question in today's divorce-afflicted society.** Want to pay alimony? Child support? Give up half your retirement account? It doesn't matter if your spouse has worked inside or outside the home, half belongs to them. Isn't it better to live alone? Keep what you earn safe? See to your best interests rather than risk what you've put your heart and soul into?

Ecclesiastes 4:9-12 argues for **being part of a family**. Let's look at this passage one verse at a time.

Verse 9 says: "Two are better than one, because they have a good reward for their toil." One can give aid to the other and pick up the slack when times get tough. They will be repaid double and more for their effort.

Verse 10 says: "For if they fall, one will lift up his fellow. But woe to him who is alone when he falls and has not another to lift him up!" The banana peels in life are frequent and unexpected. Life is easier when we have a helping hand at our side.

Verse 11 says: "Again, if two lie together, they keep warm, but how can one keep warm alone?" Loneliness is a strong precursor to depression, a top-tier killer of young people. Suicide is the 2nd leading cause of death among teens and 10th in the overall population.

Verse 12 says: "And though a man might prevail against one who is alone, two will withstand him—a threefold cord is not quickly broken." A spouse makes for a better life, and children can complete the bond. A good family will benefit us along life's journey.

A treasured companion becomes a helper through the tangles of daily living. Together we avoid pitfalls that bring others down. **Live alone or as part of a family? Each person must decide**. The argument for family is strong. When we hold hands, life's path is easier than walking alone.

September 5 – **Our Way to God's Heart**

THE TRINITY of the Lord is widely accepted in the Christian world. **God** is the Father, the central focus of the Trinity. **The Son** is the Father's most treasured joy, and he is a reflection of the Father. **The Holy Spirit** is the empowering focus of God's enduring nature, able and willing to give strength to all who ask. The three, together, form the nexus that **radiates power and glory** to the far reaches of creation.

What we ask of one, the remaining two know. To make a request of Jesus is **to speak to the Father**, and to reach out to the Son is to **embrace the nature of the Spirit**. That's why we read the words of Jesus in John 16:23-24. "In that day you will ask nothing of me. Truly, truly, I say to you, whatever you ask of the Father in my name, he will give it to you. Until now you have asked nothing in my name. Ask, and you will receive, that your joy may be full."

When Jesus walked with the disciples, they counted on the Master to answer their questions, provide for their needs, and be their connection to the heavenly realm. Jesus says **we can go directly to the Father**. The Spirit is on our speed dial. We pray, saying, "Jesus, put me through," and **our prayer is already at the throne of the Living God**. That's pretty awesome. We have no wait time, no navigating the insulating sycophants we encounter in the world, just **a direct line to the Father** *through Jesus the Son*. Whatever you ask of the Father in Jesus' name … God will give it to you. How's that for a good day? It can be yours, **a power session direct to the heart of God**. Prayer works. Let's take time on our knees today.

September 6 – **3 Proverbs for Prosperity**

SO, YOU'RE NOT rich, yet. You've come to Christ, become his follower, and you **still have the same car** you drove before you accepted him as your savior. What's up, God? **Where are the riches we're supposed to have? God smiles at our question.** *It's too silly for a response*. He's already told us where our wealth comes from. We only need to look in the Bible to find God's message to us about prosperity and how it can become ours.

Prosperity Proverb No. 1: Proverbs 15:6 tells us **living by the rules** makes us rich. "In the house of the righteous there is much treasure, but trouble befalls the income of the wicked." We can become rich by deceit. It works. Just look at the people who are in power today. However, God says **those riches will eat us alive. Peace doesn't belong to the wicked.**

Prosperity Proverb No. 2: Proverbs 22:4 tells us we must **respect the laws of the Lord** to be rich. "The reward for humility and fear of the Lord is riches and honor and life." If we want to be respected, live a long, good life, and have everything we need, we must cast our pride in the garbage and live by God's standards. When we lift up the Lord, **we are lifted up with him**.

Prosperity Proverb No. 3: Proverbs 8:18-19 tells us riches **can't compete with the goodness** of God. "Riches and honor are with me, enduring wealth and righteousness. My fruit is better than gold, even fine gold, and my yield than choice silver." If all we care for is wealth, it's too easy to let God slip by the wayside. Our bank balance is only a small part of who we are. God will satisfy us as pocket change never will. Having the biggest house, the shiniest car, and the best hairstyle will leave us empty **without God at our side**.

The world tells us to gain wealth at any cost. The Bible says we must *put God first*. **We can't afford to put the wrong priority at the top of our to-do list**. We are wealthy in the world when we become wealthy in God.

September 7 – Getting the Best that God Has for You

LIFE IS ABOUT improving our situation. That's generational as well as personal. What our parents had and how they lived, well, we want to step it up a level. How we lived last decade, it's time to look for a newer car and a new house. Not only that, we want our car **better equipped** and our house **bigger and more impressive. Morally,** we want to be **better people**. Treat others civilly. Be kind to strangers. Pet the dog. Donate to a homeless shelter.

In Deuteronomy 28:11-13, God reveals his plan to **give you the best that life can offer you**. "And the Lord will make you **abound in prosperity**, in the fruit of your womb and in the fruit of your livestock and in the fruit of your ground, within the land that the Lord swore to your fathers to give you. The Lord will **open to you his good treasury**, the heavens, to give the rain to your land in its season and to bless all the work of your hands. And you shall lend to many nations, but you shall not borrow. And the Lord will **make you the head and not the tail**, and you shall only go up and not down, if you obey the commandments of the Lord your God, which I command you today, being careful to do them."

Note the highlighted portions. The boldface isn't in the original: these three phrases showcase what this passage says. God wants you to **abound in prosperity**. When God promises us a **bright future**, he will bring it about. We can place our trust in him. God promises to **open to you his good treasury**. The jobs you work will give you a **good return**. Your backing is God, and he will be there for you. God will **make you the head and not the tail**. Your life is **not on a downhill spiral**, not when you have God in your viewfinder. He is your leader, and he always moves forward.

God wants to improve your situation, both generationally and personally. To get God's best, we must **adhere to his condition** in the last sentence of this passage. **"... If you obey the commandments of the Lord your God ..."** When we do our part, God will do his, and we'll get the best that God has for us.

September 8 – God Is Able to Deliver You

WHAT'S THE NAME of the bulldozer that's crashing through your life right now? What's **taking over your happy days** and sending **clouds of confusion** into every perfect thought? Are you convinced that **not even God can fix your situation this time? Let's look at a time in the Bible when someone was in a worse position than is likely ever to happen to you.**

Daniel 3:16-18 sets the stage: "Shadrach, Meshach, and Abednego answered and said to the king, 'O Nebuchadnezzar, we have no need to answer you in this matter. If this be so, our God whom we serve is able to deliver us from the burning fiery furnace, and he will deliver us out of your hand, O king. But if not, be it known to you, O king, that we will not serve your gods or worship the golden image that you have set up.' "

Here's a little background for this story. Shadrach, Meshach, and Abednego were the best in the land. They served God faithfully. These three men had **done nothing wrong**. Then came King Nebuchadnezzar's bulldozer, crashing through their lives. Nebuchadnezzar's vow to cast them into the fiery furnace took over their happy days and clouded their skies with thoughts of, **"Why, God?**

What have we done wrong?"

Now pay attention to this part. Even in the confusion, the three men didn't forget the source of their salvation. God was the "fixer" for any situation, and they **kept their faith in him**. They told the king, "God will deliver us … **but if not, we will still worship him**."

What's your bulldozer? Your health? Financial calamity? Personal relationships? Regardless of how things turn out, God is able to deliver you. Don't let the devil tell you otherwise. God does not bring confusion, rather he is the source of your peace.

September 9 – 7 Comforts for Those Who Are Lonely

GOD DESIRES to banish your sadness. He wishes for you to **find comfort in him**. Here are **7 Comforts for Those Who Are Lonely**.

John 14:18 says: "I will not leave you as orphans; I will come to you."

Isaiah 58:9 says: "Then you shall call, and the Lord will answer; you shall cry, and he will say, 'Here I am.' "

Isaiah 43:4 says: "Because you are precious in my eyes, and honored, and I love you, I give men in return for you, peoples in exchange for your life."

2 Corinthians 6:18 says: "I will be a father to you, and you shall be sons and daughters to me, says the Lord Almighty."

Genesis 28:15 says: "Behold, I am with you and will keep you wherever you go, and will bring you back to this land. For I will not leave you until I have done what I have promised you."

Colossians 2:10 says: "You have been filled in him, who is the head of all rule and authority."

Psalm 40:17 says: "As for me, I am poor and needy, but the Lord takes thought for me. You are my help and my deliverer; do not delay, O my God!"

Here are some steps God wants you to take.

1. **Find somewhere to volunteer.** Perhaps teach a class on Sunday morning.

2. **Get involved in a group.** You need people that expect you to show up.

3. **Refuse to stay at home** no matter how bad you feel. Call someone. Meet for lunch, to walk in the park, or to take a turn about the mall.

4. **Let others into your life**. Don't shut them out. They will help you step out of your shadows and into the light of day.

It's your time to shine, and you can be successful through the help of God.

September 10 – Resetting Our Playlist

PORTABLE MUSIC is a treat we've come to enjoy. We pack our player in our pocket, and we can listen **wherever we go**.

Years back, we carried **a radio**. If we bumped the dial, we had to **readjust it to find our station once again**. Then came **portable tape players**. We could pop in our tape, plug in our headphones, and the music was ours. The best ones even allowed us to **fast forward to our favorite songs**. We soon moved to **CD players** we could attach to our belt. Skip protection kept our music **flawless and pure**.

Then the world changed. The **portable music player** allowed us to add our own songs, even to shuffle the order of the music. Best of all, it fit in our pocket, and we could **listen anywhere**. When music styles changed, our boy band **went out of favor**, or we matured into real music, we could **wipe our music player's memory** and **build a fresh playlist**.

Mark 1:15 says that's how it works **when we come to Christ**. "The time is fulfilled, and the kingdom of God is at hand; repent and believe in the gospel." Our old life says a good time is at the bar. We aren't living until we've had a couple of cold ones and a dance or two. God's playlist says **the Word is our standard of excellence**. Everything else must be wiped from our lives so we can **become like Christ. We can't hold on to what we once were when we come to Jesus. Our old habits, friends, and goals must be renewed in Christ**. We build a new playlist when we become a Christian, and we make sure God is in every song.

September 11 – 6 Surprises When You Confess Your Guilt

GIFTS ARE SPECIAL. They are surprises, exciting when we don't know what's inside. The paper is pretty, the ribbon is tied, and we quiver with excitement. Birthday or Christmas, we can **hardly wait to see the surprise**.

God loves giving his children gifts. He looks forward to our joy when we see what he has wrapped for us … **especially when we feel guilty and that we don't deserve his love and attention.** Here are **6 Surprises When You Confess Your Guilt**.

1 John 1:9 tells us **we are made clean**. "If we confess our sins, he is faithful and just to forgive us our sins and to cleanse us from all

unrighteousness."

Isaiah 55:7 promises us **God's pardon**. "Let the wicked forsake his way, and the unrighteous man his thoughts; let him return to the Lord, that he may have compassion on him, and to our God, for he will abundantly pardon."

2 Chronicles 30:9 assures us God will **welcome us in his presence**. "For if you return to the Lord, your brothers and your children will find compassion with their captors and return to this land. For the Lord your God is gracious and merciful and will not turn away his face from you, if you return to him."

Psalm 103:12 says our guilt is cast **farther than the horizon**. "As far as the east is from the west, so far does he remove our transgressions from us."

1 John 3:20 unwraps **God's understanding nature**, for he created us like him. "For whenever our heart condemns us, God is greater than our heart, and he knows everything."

Hebrews 8:12 guarantees our wrongdoing and guilt are forgotten. We are **brand new in God**. "For I will be merciful toward their iniquities, and I will remember their sins no more."

God has your gifts wrapped and ready. He waits for you to come before him.

God is our champion in all things. We become new in him.

September 12 – **Our Shepherd Arises**

A BRILLIANT SUNRISE is the best start to any day. It's life returning to a darkened sky, and **it lifts our spirit along with the rising sun.** Revelation 7:16-17 tells of the rising of the Son, of the Shepherd that will **one day preside over all creation**. "They shall hunger no more, neither thirst anymore;"

Our bodies will change from mortal bodies, subject to famine and drought, to **spiritual ones, never to suffer hunger or thirst again**. "… the sun shall not strike them …"

Sunburn, sunstroke, and dehydration **will be a thing of the past**. "… nor any scorching heat …"

Our feet will be protected in our travels **from the burning ground beneath us**. "… For the Lamb in the midst of the throne will be their shepherd …"

We are given a guide to **watch over us in danger, to provide for us, and to embrace us in our difficulties**. "… and he will guide them to springs of living water …"

Our happiness becomes real, as **the sweetest parts of life envelope us**. "… and God will wipe away every tear from their eyes."

All disappointments and cares are vanquished. Our human condition is changed into **one of exquisite tenderness and beauty**. The rising of God at the end of times is the sunrise that will change all creation. **The Son will rule with the Father, and those who have come to trust in him will stand at his side**.

Our Shepherd arises, and his name is Jesus.

September 13 – 2 Smart Things to Consider

PERCEPTION IS ninety percent of who we are. If people think we're courteous, we probably are. If our lawn is green and our car shiny, we are considered prosperous. We can only do those things if we have money to spare. **If we walk and talk like a church member, we must** be a Christian.

Yet it's possible to **say kind words to people we don't care for**, even as we cringe inside. That green lawn? Perhaps the water bill is **draining our budget** more than we can afford. And to think about our car … can anyone see how **close we are to having it repossessed?** Then there's **our church face**. Is it possible to wear it all week long?

Here's what this is about: We can appear one way, and the reality can be totally different … two sides of a coin, or a welcome sign that says on the reverse, Come Back and See Us. **We need to be as we appear to be**, honest in how we deal with others, and in **line with the reality of who we are**.

Here are **2 Smart Things to Consider** when trying to live like Christ.

Proverbs 25:23 tells us we water our relationships with **how we interact with people**. "The north wind brings forth rain, and a backbiting tongue, angry looks." We must use our words wisely if we want to draw people to the cross.

Psalm 34:13 tells us to let **honesty and consideration be our guide** for living with those around us. "Keep your tongue from evil and your lips from speaking deceit." Gossip? Banished to the cold. False versions of events? Wiped from our lips. We must treat people **as we want to be treated**.

Our actions are the mirrors of our hearts. What we are inside will come out in our words and the way we treat the people we meet.

203

Let's let the **grace of God reveal itself** in every moment of every day.

Jesus is the mirror we want to reflect unto the world.

September 14 – **6 Places God Needs You**

THERE IS SOME confusion about why God doesn't **step in and solve all our problems**. "You have the power, God," we cry. "Get to it. Wipe our troubles from the board so we can get on with life."

Yet picture a child throwing a tantrum in a toy store or at the park. We watch in amazement, and we understand exactly where the parent went wrong. **Assert your authority**, we think. **Make the child responsible for their actions. That'll ensure good behavior.**

Are you seeing it yet?

That's what God is doing with us. If we're never given the opportunity to deal with our life, we'll never **accept the responsibility** for our actions, and we'll **never mature** in him. God places us in situations that enable us to **develop our Christian witness** to the world. He wants us to be his **hand of grace** to those around us.

Here are **6 Places God Needs You**.

At Home. John 15:8 is your call to **bring your children up in the teachings of the Lord**. "By this my Father is glorified, that you bear much fruit and so prove to be my disciples."

Your Church. Philippians 1:9 says to **cultivate your spiritual family**. They provide a depth of love that comes nowhere else. "And it is my prayer that your love may abound more and more, with knowledge and all discernment."

Your Place of Work. Philippians 1:11 says upright living will **model Christ to your coworkers**. "[Be] filled with the fruit of righteousness that comes through Jesus Christ, to the glory and praise of God."

On Social Media. 2 Corinthians 3:18 calls for the standards of Christ to **be in each word we type** or image we post. "And we all, with unveiled face, beholding the glory of the Lord, are being transformed into the same image from one degree of glory to another. For this comes from the Lord who is the Spirit."

At the Gym. Psalm 138:8 says our physical house (our body) requires care, and **the Lord will honor our efforts**. "The Lord will fulfill his purpose for me; your steadfast love, O Lord, endures forever. Do not forsake the work of your hands."

In Your Car. Proverbs 4:18 promises that **our connection with Christ** will translate into better (and more considerate) driving habits. "But the path of the righteous is like the light of dawn, which shines brighter and brighter until full day."

God wants these places to be **points of success** for his children. Yet he knows we must grow in him. The Lord doesn't want us **throwing a tantrum when things get rough.** We become mighty warriors in Christ <u>when we mature in him</u>.

God wants you to be his example every place you go.

September 15 – 3 Worry Busters from Psalms

WRINGING YOUR hands again? Are your eyes **black from lack of sleep?** Do all the **bad possibilities keep you preoccupied**, preventing you from leading the life you really want to live? It's time to **break out of your worry zone**, to **cast off your worry shawl**, to crawl out from **beneath your cloud of worry** to find freedom under the sun. Or maybe that should say, **to find your freedom** *under the Son.* Here are *3 Worry Busters from Psalms* to start you on the way to a brighter tomorrow.

Worry Buster No. 1: Psalm 9:9-10 says you can **trust God when worry overtakes you.** "The Lord is a stronghold for the oppressed, a stronghold in times of trouble. And those who know your name put their trust in you, for you, O Lord, have not forsaken those who seek you."

Worry Buster No. 2: Psalm 32:7 tells you God will **deliver you when you become entangled** in worry. "You are a hiding place for me; you preserve me from trouble; you surround me with shouts of deliverance."

Worry Buster No. 3: Psalm 91:15 is your assurance God will **disperse the storm clouds**, and you'll bask in the warmth of the sun once more. "When he calls to me, I will answer him; I will be with him in trouble; I will rescue him and honor him."

Worry fixes nothing. No marriage problems have been resolved by worry. Worry hasn't **made a car payment**. Worry hasn't <u>resolved global warming</u> or kept the floodwaters from rising around us. You must depend on God for your peace. He watches over you. In the Lord, you can get a good night's rest, confident in his abiding care.

When God is your firm foundation, your worries will vanish like fog in the light of the morning sun.

September 16 – **The Last Tears You Will Ever Cry**

SADNESS DESERVES a boot in the backside. Sayōnara, bon voyage, **out the window you go**. Your place is in the trash. We're gonna dump you in the garbage can.

Isaiah 25:8 says God will forever **wipe away our tears**. "He will swallow up death forever. The Sovereign Lord will wipe away the tears from all faces; he will remove his people's disgrace from all the earth. The Lord has spoken."

Luke 6:21 promises us that **one day we will laugh**. "Blessed are you who hunger now, for you will be satisfied. Blessed are you who weep now, for you will laugh."

2 Timothy 1:3-4 assures us we will be **filled with joy**. "I thank God, whom I serve, as my ancestors did, with a clear conscience, as night and day I constantly remember you in my prayers. Recalling your tears, I long to see you, so that I may be filled with joy."

Psalm 116:7-9 says God **rescues us from our tears**. "Return to your rest, my soul, for the Lord has been good to you. For you, Lord, have delivered me from death, my eyes from tears, my feet from stumbling, that I may walk before the Lord in the land of the living."

Psalm 56:8 tells us God **stores away every tear.** "Record my misery; list my tears on your scroll— are they not in your record?"

Revelation 7:17 is our promise that God will **take away every tear**. "For the Lamb at the center of the throne will be their shepherd; he will lead them to springs of living water. And God will wipe away every tear from their eyes."

Revelation 21:4 guarantees that mourning, crying, and pain will be **forever banished to the furthest realm possible**. "He will wipe every tear from their eyes. There will be no more death or mourning or crying or pain, for the old order of things has passed away."

Whatever's broken your heart, God asks you to let it go. Find your strength in Jesus. Your future will be tear free. Your solace is in the Lord.

Jesus takes our sorrow, for he's the only one that can.

September 17 – **Looking Forward to Our Fantastic Future**

SCIENCE FICTION fans love to imagine what's next. Computer intelligence taken to the next level. What will it be like? Self-driving cars … will they even need us as backup operators? And our homes, spaceships all, **floating in the clouds on the merest tether of**

technology.

We want it to be fantastic, a trip to the stars, filled with dreams of long life, magic-like inventions, and more things to do than we can ever get done. **God's way ahead of us.** He's already **Looking Forward to Our Fantastic Future.** 1 Corinthians 2:9 says: "But, as it is written, 'What no eye has seen, nor ear heard, nor the heart of man imagined, what God has prepared for those who love him'—"

Computer intelligence? We can look forward to "God intelligence," **smart enough to create an entire universe.** Self-driving cars? We won't need cars where we're going. **We'll fly with the wings of angels.** Floating home? We will live along streets of gold, in a land anchored by the **bright and shining God of Creation**.

Science fiction fans aren't thinking big enough. *God says we can't even imagine how fantastic our future will be.* When we stick with God, we'll go places we could never dream.

September 18 – **Safety on the Rock**

IN THE MID-90s, Chevrolet had a successful ad for its line of trucks. *"Like a Rock."* Their trucks tackled crazy roads, had boulders dropped in the beds by cranes, and towed massive loads up impossible inclines. 30 seconds of advertising washed us with emotion, brought tears to our eyes, and *made us want to drive a Chevy.* The trucks were senselessly abused during the commercials, but that didn't break the appeal they carried for the American public.

That's what we need to portray as Christians, an appeal that will supersede the abuse that happens in everyone's life. Matthew 7:24-25 gives us Jesus' words: "Everyone then who hears these words of mine and does them will be like a wise man who built his house on the rock. And the rain fell, and the floods came, and the winds blew and beat on that house, but it did not fall, because it had been founded on the rock."

Three truths are in this passage: 1. When we follow Jesus' teachings, we *reveal the wisdom of good living* in everything we do. 2. Trouble might batter us, but God is our security. He is our *light in the darkness*. 3. Our foundation in Jesus will never shift. We rest in him, and he *wraps us in his love.*

Let's be a Chevrolet. *Like a Rock.* **Secure in Jesus.** Standing on the cornerstone, bound up in his love, and *forever trusting in him.* The world needs something they can trust. They need us to reveal the nature of God to them *through how we live in Christ.* Jesus is our place of safety, for he is the Rock on which we stand.

September 19 – **The Best Money God Can Give**

AH, TO BE RICH. Fine houses, one on the beach, and another in the mountains. Maybe we can have our food delivered … a chef! That's the ticket. We never have to cook again. Then we stop and consider the facts. How much money would that take? Where would we get it? **How hard would it be to keep it? What are we willing to trade to be rich?** Our time? Our morality? Our family? Truth, justice, and the American way?

There are people who **trade these things and more** just for the chance to have money, **money,** *money.* El Chapo. We've heard the name. Pablo Escobar. He had tons of dough and ran for his life. Then there's Griselda Blanco, a woman who painted Miami red, instigating as many as 250 murders to ensure her income stream.

Ecclesiastes 4:6 says: "Better is a handful of quietness than two hands full of toil and a striving after wind."

What is money worth to us? What are we willing to trade? **Our peace of mind?** Our evenings watching the sunset? **Our security in God and our family**? "Better is a handful of quietness …"

There's nothing wrong with money, and it can be very useful. We must keep its acquisition in perspective. **Money isn't everything.** *God, our family, and our integrity must take first place.* Our plan must be Christ. Everything else will come from him.

September 20 – **A Day for Your Pastor**

IT'S EASY TO SHOW up for Sunday service, chase the kids down after the benediction, and need a nap by the time lunch is finished. Today's a good day to remember your pastor, to take time from your sleepy afternoon, and **write him or her a note telling how much you appreciate the sermon and the time it took to prepare.** Your pastor is a servant of God, but God's servants need a pat on the back from time to time. 2 Thessalonians 1:3 says: "We ought always to give thanks to God for you, brothers, as is right, because your faith is growing abundantly, and the love of every one of you for one another is increasing."

When you tell your appreciation to your pastor, you will **provide encouragement,** a **lift to their spirit**, and motivation to **jump into next week's teaching with extra fervor.** Here are some other things you can do: 1. Provide a gift card to a good restaurant. 2. Offer to sit

208

with their kids so they can have a night out. 3. Send over a lawn service to do their yard.

They will appreciate the break, and **you will show the love of God to them through your actions**. Our leaders need our love as they serve us as our pastors.

September 21 – **A Lesson About Gossip**

WE LOVE tantalizing tales. The more juice in our story, the **better it tastes going down**. What did Misty do with Justin? Oh, my! Who would believe it? **This is too good not to share.** *Not so,* **says God.** If we share it, **we've become a gossip.** We're passing around information better left unsaid.

"But, but ..." we sputter. "It's going to get out, anyway. And it's true. You mean we can't ... maybe ... just hint at the truth?"

God says, **No! You are hurting those you talk about, and that's not my way.** Read in Proverbs 26:20-22 where God outlines how vital our choice of behavior is. "For lack of wood the fire goes out, and where there is no whisperer, quarreling ceases. As charcoal to hot embers and wood to fire, so is a quarrelsome man for kindling strife. The words of a whisperer are like delicious morsels; they go down into the inner parts of the body."

When we share our secretive information, we're **putting wood on the fire. We're making it worse.** God says we must stop. As long as we continue to whisper to those who will listen, **we prolong the hurt feelings and arguments**. We are the charcoal that stokes the embers and the wood the fuels the fire. We are **feeding the evil one's goals**, creating a morass of ill feeling that we should have left alone. God's lesson about gossip is **Leave It Alone! Quit saying it.** True or not, **refuse to listen and don't repeat it**. Easy enough, right? Gossip tastes good going down, but in the stomach, it becomes a bilious turmoil that **serves no one any good**.

God expects our best, both in our commitment to him and in how we treat the people around us.

September 22 – **What Sort of Fish Are You?**

THE SEAS ARE filled with fish. **Many are harmless to mankind and often beautiful. The giant manta ray is one of the brightest fishes in the sea and friendly toward divers.** They have been known to approach people for help in removing hooks and entangling lines, waiting patiently until they are free. At 3,600 pounds, these fish could do some damage, yet they are **generally benign to people** swimming nearby.

Then there is the unusual and deadly reef stonefish. What's disconcerting about the stonefish is how it can mimic its surroundings. It picks up the beautiful colors and stunning patterns of the reef, and **it can appear beautiful at first glance.** Get closer, though, and its venomous spines can **inject poison through your skin.** It's one of the deadliest fishes in the world and can be lethal to swimmers.

What sort of fish are you? Are you beneficial to be around or deadly when people get too close? Let's see what James 4:1-4 has to say about our choices. "What causes quarrels and what causes fights among you? Is it not this, that your passions are at war within you? You desire and do not have, so you murder. You covet and cannot obtain, so you fight and quarrel. You do not have, because you do not ask. You ask and do not receive, because you ask wrongly, to spend it on your passions. You adulterous people! Do you not know that friendship with the world is enmity with God? Therefore whoever wishes to be a friend of the world makes himself an enemy of God."

Sin is a wastrel, appealing from far off and deadly to the touch. It will **draw you in and squander your life.** Just one touch, and the venom of sin will steal away your future. Choose God. Wait patiently, and the Lord will **remove sin's hooks and entangling lines**, and **you will be free once more**.

Your best choice is God who cares for you gently and tenderly.

September 23 – **Jesus Explains Salvation**

SOME THINGS just don't make sense. Gravity. How's that work? Just because we're on the outside, we're being **pulled to the inside?** Huh? And another thing, how does the atmosphere not **float away into space?** Someone, an answer, please. Then there's magnetism. It's **invisible.** Is it magic? And radio waves. They're shaking up our speakers and our radio's not attached to wires **anywhere.**

That brings us to salvation. Just a few words, and a desire to change, and we become a **completely different person?** Nah. It can't be as simple as that. Jesus explains salvation in John 3:3-7. "Jesus answered him, 'Truly, truly, I say to you, unless one is born again he cannot see the kingdom of God.' Nicodemus said to him, 'How can a man be born when he is old? Can he enter a second time

210

into his mother's womb and be born?' Jesus answered, 'Truly, truly, I say to you, unless one is born of water and the Spirit, he cannot enter the kingdom of God. That which is born of the flesh is flesh, and that which is born of the Spirit is spirit. Do not marvel that I said to you, 'You must be born again.' "

Here's what makes this magnificent. Jesus compares salvation to something every person is familiar with, **birth.** Salvation has **nothing to do with a changed physical body.** This is a spirit thing, a thing of the **heart, mind, and emotions. We believe, and that changes us.** We become different, from our <u>desires</u> to our **plans** to our **attitudes.** The old man (what we once thought and desired) is washed away and the new man (our desire to become like Jesus) fills us inside. **We are reborn in Christ. Our salvation is made real through him.**

Salvation makes total sense. We can't see it, but the **results are perfectly obvious.** We behave differently on the outside because we are completely new inside. Salvation is life changing. Today is your day to try it on for size.

September 24 – **Our Great Uplifting**

THE DUMPS ARE no place to be. We want out, to be in the sunshine, and to have a smile on our face. God lifts us up from the shadowy places. We see this in the life of Jehoshaphat in 2 Chronicles 17:5. "Therefore the Lord established the kingdom in his hand. And all Judah brought tribute to Jehoshaphat, and he had great riches and honor." Let's break down this verse so we can know what to expect from the Lord.

Therefore the Lord established the kingdom ... This is God's doing. He's the one that will change things in our life. He will establish us when we draw close to him and commit our lives to his way.

... in his hand ... We can't expect to reside in the blessings of God if we insist on our own way. We must remain in the hand of the Almighty Father.

And all Judah brought tribute to Jehoshaphat ... When God honors us, those around us will sense our honor, and they will respond.

... and he had great riches and honor. This is the plan of God, for us to draw close to him and make him the center of all that we are. The shadows are banished from our life, and the sunshine is here

211

to stay.

Here's the verse summed up: It's about God. It's not about us. God loves to hand out honor. His riches are endless.

The dumps are banished forever! It's time to live in the light! Jesus is our path out of our troubled times! We are lifted high when we soar with the Master of creation, our great Jehovah God.

September 25 – 3 People Who Made a Difference for God

DOING THE RIGHT thing is a tricky business. Everyone has their own opinion, and we're asked to consider every viewpoint. At some point we must draw a line in the sand and say, "Enough! Today's the day I make a difference." Let's look at **3 People Who Made a Difference for God** in the Bible.

Our first person who made a difference for God was Gideon. No one expected Gideon to take on the mantle of hero. His clan was of little importance. Gideon doubted his own ability. Gideon started out as a nobody who had to be prompted into action by an angel of God.

Judges 6:12 tells us: "When the angel of the Lord appeared to Gideon, he said, 'The Lord is with you, mighty warrior.' "

Gideon made a difference by sending home the greatest part of his army and defeating one of Israel's major enemies, the Midianites, using guerilla warfare and a small, core band of spiritual brothers.

The second person who made a difference for God was Samson. We hear the stories of Samson's fall from grace, but Samson's potential for size and strength was heralded by an angel of God. This biblical hero was no peaceful negotiator. He wasn't a "gentle giant" who used his size to sway others to his cause. Samson was a loner and vanquished every enemy by his God-given strength. Samson regained God's favor after his fall, and in the final moments of his life, God granted him the opportunity to kill more of Israel's enemies than he had in every battle before.

Judges 16:30 says: "Then he pushed with all his might, and down came the temple on the rulers and all the people in it. Thus he killed many more when he died than while he lived."

Samson made a difference by repenting of his wrongdoing and turning once again to God.

Finally, let's look at Moses, the reluctant leader, our third person who made a difference for God. Moses is the only man on record who spoke to God face to face. Moses never sought fame. Rather, he avoided it, once running away to spend forty years herding sheep in the desert. God called on Moses to lead his people despite Moses' reticence.

Exodus 3:5 is Moses' call to holiness: " 'Do not come any closer,' God said. 'Take off your sandals, for the place where you are standing is holy ground.' "

Moses made a difference by taking on the mantle of responsibility when God called to him from the burning bush.

What has God called you to do? **What's the difference you can make in your world?** Now's your time. Now's your opportunity. God says to take his hand. He's ready to use you today.

September 26 – God's Turnabout Reward

IT'S NOT FUN for people to say bad things about us. The pain is a **knife to our heart**, a searing brand **burning into us**, crushed glass **under our feet**. Social media makes it worse. The whole world knows, and it can **never be returned to the anonymity of our electronic devices**.

We're angry. How can we get even? We want them to **feel the despair** that's clouding our horizon. We wish upon them the thunder of desperation and the battering winds of humiliation that have become ours.

God tells us to hold up. We can't go there. We need to sit on our hands and *let him take care of the situation*. He will, too. God has **plans in place for our protection**, and he will intervene. Matthew 5:11-12 tells us: "Blessed are you when others revile you and persecute you and utter all kinds of evil against you falsely on my account. Rejoice and be glad, for your reward is great in heaven, for so they persecuted the prophets who were before you."

Note the first three words in this passage: Blessed are you. **Blessed.** Not happy, not satisfied, **but blessed**. Our blessing comes on us when others revile us; when others persecute us; when they say evil things about us that aren't true. When we **don't retaliate in kind**, we are flooded with the blessing of God. The Father's goodwill flows across us, irrigating the **seeds of God's goodness** in everything we do.

We become mighty oaks in the kingdom of God when we **bear the attacks of the world** with the *saintly halo of our Christian testimony* **surrounding us every day**.

God rewards us for our trust in him. In every situation, our Father has our best interests at heart.

September 27 – **Your Future Is Yet to Come**

SO, LIFE HAS punched you in the face. Your childhood, it was a dysfunctional mess. Your rap sheet with the local police department is as long as Santa's Christmas list. You couldn't even make it as a parent, and the child support eats at your weekly paycheck.

God is molding you for a better tomorrow. With every hurt, every tear, you are **becoming what God needs you to be.** Clay is useless **until we reshape it.** Metal doesn't become a car **until we heat it.** We don't become God's treasured child until we **survive what life puts us through.**

Psalm 92:14 says your best is **just in front of you.** "They still bear fruit in old age; they are ever full of sap and green."

Hosea 14:5 says your sustenance **comes from the Lord above.** "I will be like the dew to Israel; he shall blossom like the lily; he shall take root like the trees of Lebanon."

2 Peter 1:8 assures you that your salvation is your **ticket to ample and plenty** in the service of Jesus our king. "For if these qualities are yours and are increasing, they keep you from being ineffective or unfruitful in the knowledge of our Lord Jesus Christ."

So, what's holding you back? Your childhood? It's **over and done with.** Don't let it define your future. Move on. Your trouble with the law? Don't let that become an **excuse for failure.** You are strong enough to move past it. Your failed family? God is the **renewer of relationships.** He is your **strength and your patient confidant.** His love will get you through.

You are being rebuilt for a better future. You will succeed because of what you've come through. Take Jesus' hand. It's time to step up to tomorrow.

September 28 – **You Are Important**

WHAT'S YOUR WORTH in this world? What difference can you make against the oncoming flood of wrongdoing and indifference? Where do you stand in the grand scheme of things? Does God have a purpose for you? Those are valid questions. It doesn't matter if you leave for work each morning in a glittering luxury car or bang your starter with a wrench to get the motor going. The big decider isn't whether you vacation in Vail or visit the local campground. God says you are important to him.

How can you verify that? What's your proof?

You are fashioned in the **image of the holy God** of all creation. You are his child, and God **cares for what he has created**. Genesis 1:26 reveals the tender hand of God and the authority he has imbued you with. "Then God said, 'Let us make man in our image, after our likeness. And let them have dominion over the fish of the sea and over the birds of the heavens and over the livestock and over all the earth and over every creeping thing that creeps on the earth.' "

That's nothing to sneer at. You are the **special gift of God** to the world and to those around you. You are filled with the **power of the Kingdom**, and your time to **make a difference** is now. **You are important.** You are vital to the people around you. Your circumstances are unique to you, and you are the **only one who can fulfill** the place God has for you. God is your stamp of approval when you find your place of authority in him.

September 29 – 3 Examples Jesus Sets for Us to Follow

WHAT'S YOUR STRUGGLE today in following Jesus? In a moment of weakness, did you **fudge the truth** to a traffic officer? Or did you say a **harsh word** to your spouse before leaving for work? Maybe it's something simpler. Your coworker irritated you, so you **revealed a secret** they told you in confidence.

Or, and this is an easy trap to fall into, you chanced on an old friend and stumbled into your **old patterns of poor behaviors**. Later, when remorse hits us, we bleed tears and wonder **why we struggle** with our Christian walk. How is this so difficult when we want to do the right thing?

Jesus is our guide that **points us along the correct path**. In Hebrews 12:1-3, we find **3 Examples Jesus Sets for Us to Follow**. "Therefore, since we are surrounded by so great a cloud of witnesses, let us also lay aside every weight, and sin which clings so closely, and let us run with endurance the race that is set before us, looking to Jesus, the founder and perfecter of our faith, who for the joy that was set before him endured the cross, despising the shame, and is seated at the right hand of the throne of God."

Example No. 1: Jesus endured the cross. What does this mean for us? We will reach moments of decision where we must choose between right and wrong. The best choice *isn't always the easy one*.

Example No. 2: Jesus despised the shame. To despise means to consider unimportant. The people around us won't always understand our choice for Christ. We must make the *right choice anyway*.

215

Example No. 3: Jesus is seated at the right hand of God.
Here's our motivation. We will one day be gifted with the supreme
prize, to *join Jesus in his reunion* with the Father. We will get what
we deserve.

While on earth we will struggle. We will **continue to face
difficult choices**. We must always choose Jesus. <u>His example is a
guiding light to help us find the way</u>. Jesus is the founder and perfecter of our faith, and we find our security in him.

September 30 – **God's Plan to Riches**

SO, YOU WANT to come to Jesus. You've listened to the televan-
gelists proclaim God's promises, and **you want a piece of the pie**.
You hope for money, a fine house, a sleek car, and lots of goodies to
impress your friends. You've even underlined the passages in the
Word that **reveal the good things** God has said you can have.
You're ready to **sign on the dotted line** just to have the good stuff.

You can't afford to overlook Proverbs 13:4. "The soul of the
sluggard craves and gets nothing, while the soul of the diligent is
richly supplied."

The Bible tells us it **rains on the just and the unjust**. Evil
people get rich, and many devout believers have little to their name.
**Does it make any sense that getting saved will automatically open
heaven's treasury to fill up your bank account with lots of cash?**
The verse tells you that the lazy person (the sluggard) wants and
expects a rich life, but **they don't work and so do without**. It's the
person who gets off the sofa and looks for a job (the diligent person)
who **gets the financial reward**. *Here's God's plan to riches:*

First, **get an education**. Second, **search for a job**. Third, continue your education so you can **get a better job**. Fourth, **spend
carefully**. Be wise in your purchases. Fifth, leave room in your
budget to be **generous with your paycheck**. Don't have it spent
before you receive it.

Here's the thing about **God's Plan to Riches**. If your every
thought is about spending the next dollar, you'll **never get there**.
The first hiccup along the way will toss you off into financial ruin.
<u>Being generous is vital</u>. It's a state of mind that says you don't need
to spend every dollar. You can live below your means and be con-
tent. God wants you to be successful. That's his plan. Now get off
the sofa and do it.

— October —

October 1 – **Becoming Our Best Self**

HOW DO WE become better people? Is there a self-help class we can attend, perhaps a university course teaching *The Best Me I Can Become?* Or is it something closer to home, a process of self-awareness, one where we pay attention to what we do each day and try to fix things we don't like? Do we need to change everything about us? Or are we pretty much okay, and the little changes we make are because God asks us to?

Here's a big change God sets before us if we want to become the best self we can be. Proverbs 22:22 says: "Do not rob the poor, because he is poor, or crush the afflicted at the gate."

We read this with relief. That's not us. We've not robbed or crushed anyone. But wait! **Do not rob the poor.** Have we driven by a panhandler at a signal light and thought, "Get a job and you won't have to beg"? **Do not crush the afflicted.** Do we move to the opposite side of the street to avoid the homeless person, dismissing them as a blight on the city streets?

Let's be the best person we can be. We'll become our best self when we become selfless in helping others in their need.

Jesus gave himself for us, and the poor and afflicted need us to be the hand of Jesus unto them.

October 2 – **7 Steps to Your Higher Calling**

THE LORD IS guiding you to perfection. Choosing to follow Jesus means you accept a higher calling. You have a duty to portray your best for him. It's not likely you'll get there until you trade your mortality for the Immortality of the Father, but you are encouraged to climb that ladder **one step at a time**.

Luke 6:35-38 gives *7 Steps to Your Higher Calling*. They are a guide to the perfection you endeavor to achieve. "But **love your enemies**, and **do good**, and **lend, expecting nothing in return**, and your reward will be great, and you will be sons of the Most High, for he is kind to the ungrateful and the evil. **Be merciful**, even as your Father is merciful. **Judge not**, and you will not be judged; **condemn not**, and you will not be condemned; **forgive**, and you will be forgiven; give, and it will be given to you. Good measure, pressed down, shaken together, running over, will be put into your lap. For with the measure you use it will be measured back to you."

The 1st Step to Your Higher Calling: *Love your enemies.* You must be concerned about their welfare and be willing to help them succeed.

The 2nd Step to Your Higher Calling: *Do good.* Find worthy causes. Commit your time and money to further their goals.

The 3rd Step to Your Higher Calling: *Lend, expecting nothing in return.* No contracts. No repayment schedules. It's more like a gift.

The 4th Step to Your Higher Calling: *Be merciful.* Even when someone does you wrong, forgive them anyway, just because you want to.

The 5th Step to Your Higher Calling: *Judge not.* Don't assume you see the entire picture. The reality might be eye-opening.

The 6th Step to Your Higher Calling: *Condemn not.* No public shaming, no gossip, none of it. You are not the judge and jury wrapped up in one.

The 7th Step to Your Higher Calling: *Forgive.* Truly, really, let it go. Wipe your grudge slate clean and start each day afresh.

Follow Jesus, and you will be up the ladder of perfection in no time.

October 3 – Rise Up, Rise Up!

LIFE IS ABOUT choices. What appeals to us? Do we want the green tea or the black tea? Then we are distracted by the herbal variety … or white … or yellow … or even fermented teas. **Then there are the flavored versions.** Soon we are pulling our hair … who can decide?

Living by God's standards is clearer cut. It's this way or that. **This choice or that one.** Do we lie or tell the truth? Keep the extra change or return it to the cashier? Yell at our children or count to three?

It's time for us to rise up and live to a higher standard. The time for walking in the muck is over. We can't put on that dirty smock one more time. **We must choose the power of the cross and become champions for God.**

2 Samuel 22:33 assures us God will be our support in our fight for the right. "This God is my strong refuge and has made my way blameless."

2 Chronicles 20:6 guarantees we will be undefeated in our

spiritual battles. "O Lord, God of our fathers, are you not God in heaven? You rule over all the kingdoms of the nations. In your hand are power and might, so that none is able to withstand you."

Matthew 22:29 encourages us not to underestimate God's power. "But Jesus answered them, 'You are wrong, because you know neither the Scriptures nor the power of God.' "

Hebrews 1:3 promises God's sustaining power will be ours through our relationship with Jesus. "He is the radiance of the glory of God and the exact imprint of his nature, and he upholds the universe by the word of his power. After making purification for sins, he sat down at the right hand of the Majesty on high."

2 Peter 1:3 reveals our ultimate armor from the Lord. "His divine power has granted to us all things that pertain to life and godliness, through the knowledge of him who called us to his own glory and excellence."

Now's our time. Rise up for Jesus. He is ready to lift us high before the world. There's no time like now to be the best God wants us to be.

October 4 – 4 Things About Faith

WE'RE FAMILIAR with the word faith. We use it all the time. **"I don't have any faith in that bicycle. The tires won't hold air." "Have faith in me. Have I ever let you down?"**

Yet what does faith *really mean?* Merriam-Webster tells us the first meaning of faith is an allegiance to a duty or a person. In other words, **loyalty.** Our second definition in Merriam-Webster focuses on applying our loyalty to God.

Now let's look at Hebrews 11:1, a familiar verse to many of us. "Now faith is the assurance of things hoped for, the conviction of things not seen." This verse isn't long, but it's packed with meaning. Let's look at four things we can take from this verse.

Our 1st Thing About Faith: *Assurance.* Our faith is a done deal. We don't have to worry about whether it will happen. Merriam-Webster says we are **certain in our mind.**

Our 2nd Thing About Faith: *Things hoped for.* God wants us to aspire to more than we are, more than we have. It's in our nature to desire to **move forward in life.**

Our 3rd Thing About Faith: *Conviction.* Our conviction comes about by belief. We choose one thing over another, to see something in doubt or to **accept it as truth.** It's our choice.

219

Our 4th Thing About Faith: *Things not seen.* That's the thing about faith. It's not visible. The results, however, are **as solid as the chair** in which we sit. Our conviction makes it real.

Let's **proclaim our allegiance** to God. Let's **establish our loyalty** to God as our brand. Let's **practice our assurance** in his promises. Let's **hold our conviction** to his Word in our hearts.

God is faithful to us, and his promises will come to pass.

October 5 – 2 Calls for Patience

THE WORLD TURNS quickly. We're hard pressed to **keep up with the hustle and bustle**. Our job requires **constantly updated skills**, the roads grow **ever more crowded**, and there's no time left to **spend with our kids**. We must "knock out" life, leaving us no room for error. **Or room for incompetent fools that get in our way**.

Are you keeping me from a promotion? **Banished!** Are you slowing me down on the way to work? **Get out of my lane!** You want me to come in for a parent-teacher conference? Arrgh! **Not today!**

God wants us to get out of the fast lane, to slow down, to **find room for people over our list of things** to get done. Hebrews 10:36 says: "For you have need of endurance, so that when you have done the will of God you may receive what is promised."

Romans 5:3-4 tells us: "Not only that, but we rejoice in our sufferings, knowing that suffering produces endurance, and endurance produces character, and character produces hope."

Doing the will of God must come before all the other "important" things in our life. When our job becomes stressful, maybe it's time for a **few days of vacation**. We can leave a half hour earlier for work, and we won't **stress over the cautious driver**. Making time for our children is **always the choice** we should take.

God says he is our hope. When we endure the problems of life with patience, the Father **counts it as experience**, and that brings us his **enduring presence every day**.

Our hope in God becomes real when we make time for him.

October 6 – When Trouble Comes from God

SOME PEOPLE TOUT God as a source of good things – **and only good things**. After all, he's all about love, so how could he be any other way? If bad things happen to us, we can only blame the **Angel of Light**, also known as **Lucifer** or **Satan**.

220

That red light, when you're late for work? **The work of the devil**. Getting sick on your vacation? It's the **hand of Satan** ruining your good time. God would never bring us problems or slap our hands. That's not his style. Look at the story of Job in the Bible. That's your proof. Lucifer did all the dirty work. **God's hands were clean.**

Yet, yet. God's Word says trouble **can and should** come from God.

What?!? Trouble should come from God? **How can you say that?** I don't. **The Bible does.** Read it in Hebrews 12:6-7. "For the Lord disciplines the one he loves, and chastises every son whom he receives. It is for discipline that you have to endure. God is treating you as sons. For what son is there whom his father does not discipline?"

If we're not enduring trouble from God, **we aren't walking in his will**. That's scripture, not a teaser to get you to read this teaching. It's like our earthly fathers. If they don't correct their children – **send them to the corner, take away their phone, refuse to let them attend the party** – they will release spoiled and entitled brats onto the world.

God is the **source of all that's good** in the world. He's also the **source of our correction** as Christians. That's how we mature in our walk with him. **That's how we grow to become more like Jesus.** Our lessons from God are there for our good, for he loves his children.

October 7 – 6 Reasons God Wants You Busy

WE SAY THE **early bird gets the worm**. Or, it takes **your feet** and not **your seat** to get things done. How about this one – you get ahead when you *get out of bed*. Functional ecology, the system of defining the role animals play in an ecosystem, says the early bird also has a greater number of offspring, perhaps due to **dining on extra worms each morning**.

What's your motivation for getting busy each day? Anthony Bourdain, chef and travel host, once said, "I have a lazy man inside who wants to lay in bed and watch cartoons all day. My whole life is outwitting that guy."

God's Word offers **6 Reasons God Wants You Busy**.

Reason No. 1: You can get rich **when you get busy**. "A slack hand causes poverty, but the hand of the diligent makes rich."

Proverbs 10:4

Reason No. 2: You will receive the **first selection of the best**. "It is the hard-working farmer who ought to have the first share of the crops." 2 Timothy 2:6

Reason No. 3: Lazing in bed will start you on a **slide toward poverty**. "Love not sleep, lest you come to poverty; open your eyes, and you will have plenty of bread." Proverbs 20:13

Reason No. 4: Your life will be easier when you **keep your hands busy**. "The way of a sluggard is like a hedge of thorns, but the path of the upright is a level highway." Proverbs 15:19

Reason No. 5: You will avoid **late payments and financial penalties**. "The hand of the diligent will rule, while the slothful will be put to forced labor." Proverbs 12:24

Reason No. 6: You will have enough to **share with the poor**. "Let the thief no longer steal, but rather let him labor, doing honest work with his own hands, so that he may have something to share with anyone in need." Ephesians 4:28

Go out and get your worm. Your feet will carry you forward. You will get ahead and **no one will be able to hold you back**. Now is the moment of your success. God says, "Go for it."

October 8 – 4 Ways to Turn Loose of Our Anger

IT'S NOT FAIR when people rile us, especially when we've **tried to do the right thing**. It backfires on us, we get caught blindsided, and we have **no idea what's going on**. Our first response is to lash out, to make them feel how much we've been hurt.

God says don't do it. He offers us a better choice, one that **doesn't burn bridges that we might not be able to repair**.

Matthew 5:44-45 gives **4 Ways to Turn Loose of Our Anger** when we've been offended. "But I say unto you, Love your enemies, bless them that curse you, do good to them that hate you, and pray for them which despitefully use you, and persecute you; that ye may be the children of your Father which is in heaven: for he makes his sun to rise on the evil and on the good, and sends rain on the just and on the unjust."

This passage is a "do this, get that" example of God's plan for us. If we work to turn loose of our anger – **forgive our offender, in essence** – God will recognize us as his children. That's a strong message of hope for those of us with bruised intentions. Here are God's **4 Ways to Turn Loose of Our Anger**:

222

No. 1 – Love your enemies. Do something nice for them. A cupcake on their desk. A card congratulating them for a successful presentation.

No. 2 – Bless them that curse you. Speak to them in a friendly manner, even as your anger tells you not to. Do it anyway. You can, you know.

No. 3 – Do good to them that hate you. Offer to help with a project. Invite them to lunch. Step up. Be more than nice.

No. 4 – Pray for them that despitefully use you. Ask God to give them good opportunities. Then turn them over to God.

What this does is **change us**. Our attitude toward our offender changes. In the process, our anger fades into the background, and one day, **it's no longer there**. God knows us. **He understands how to guide us.** When we follow his precepts, we become more like him than ever before. We are God's children when we live as he instructs us to live.

October 9 – It's a Temporary Thing

SOME THINGS ARE not meant to last. Like those henna tattoos. We can be wild and crazy, because we know it will **eventually fade away**. Want even less permanence? Get the lickey-kind, the sort of temporary tattoo you can lick and stick. Kids love them, and parents rarely mind. Stick the kid in the tub, and **the tattoo washes down the drain**. A real tattoo, the sort done in a tattoo parlor, has more staying power. Goof it up, and it's with you for the **rest of your life**. Tattoo removals are imperfect and leave scars that never disappear.

If we crave spiritual permanence, what are our options? Is it in a drug-infused "experience" or a sensual encounter? Or maybe self-fulfillment? We achieve enough in life, and we **"complete ourselves."** How about this passage from 1 John 2:16-17? "For all that is in the world—the desires of the flesh and the desires of the eyes and pride of life—is not from the Father but is from the world. And the world is passing away along with its desires, but whoever does the will of God abides forever."

We can now divide the world into **henna and ink**, into **temporary and permanent**. Let's make a list. **Temporary Things in the World:** Desires of the flesh. Desires of the eyes. Pride of life. **Permanent Things that Will Last Forever:** Those who do the will of the Father.

It's time to decide. Which do you want, to be that which washes off and runs down the drain, or to display God's permanence which cannot be removed? Life happens now. Let's make God a permanent part of who we are.

October 10 – Loving the Invisible

WHAT WE CAN touch is easy to love. Grandma's vase, the one we inherited and treasure. Each time we dust its patterned surface, we feel her presence over again. A puppy when it jumps in our lap and wants to snuggle. We're charmed. How can we not love that, to be warmed by a cuddly ball of fur that wants nothing more than our attention? How about a spouse? An arm, a hug, and a kind word can cause a surge of emotion that's undeniable. We're in love, now and forever.

Yet what happens when those things are gone? Does absence make the heart grow fonder, or do we lose touch with the things we no longer have at our side? 1 Peter 1:8 tells us the sincerest form of love: "Though you have not seen him, you love him. Though you do not now see him, you believe in him and rejoice with joy that is inexpressible and filled with glory."

We can't see God. We can know him by his creation, but he's out of our line of sight. That's why Christianity is called a faith-based religion. We believe **even though we haven't seen him.** You see, we **choose to believe.** That's how it works. We stand on faith that God is real, and we fall in love with him, even though we can't see him. We love the invisible as though it were visible. Faith makes it possible, and an all-enveloping relationship with the Father is the result.

God sees that we love him when our worship is filled with inexpressible joy and the glory of his presence.

October 11 – Picking Up Our Pace

WATCH A MILITARY exercise at basic training. The recruits seem to move as one, **from this spot to that**, from here to there. If anyone gets behind, **heaven help them**. They'll have a drill instructor behind them **yelling to pick up the pace**. You can't afford to fall behind when you're training for the battlefield.

Our Christian walk is a battlefield. We are **at war with evil and the devil**. The world's temptations will try to take us down, and we must **keep up with God or risk exposing ourselves to a dire situation**. 1 Corinthians 16:13 tells us: "Be watchful, stand firm in

224

the faith, act like men, be strong." **Paul's words are brief and to the point, emphasizing four important points in this verse.**

Point No. 1: We must be hyper-vigilant. The enemy will sneak up when we least expect.

Point No. 2: We must study the Bible so we know what it teaches. We can't go off track.

Point No. 3: We must live up to God's standard, exhibit exceptional fortitude, and refuse to back down.

Point No. 4: We must exercise our faith in little things so the big ones don't overwhelm us.

It's time to pick up our pace. **We have a battle to fight, and we can't do it alone.** Christ leads us in the fight, and we're protected when we march at his side.

October 12 – 5 Causes to Celebrate Rahab

THE STORY OF Jericho is a popular one in Biblical lore. Hollywood has glamorized the tale in film, with the Israelites marching around the city, and on the final day, **the walls crashing to the ground.**

Did they just crumble, did God bring an earthquake, or did a tornado batter the walls into dust? Perhaps we will never know, but we do know the heroine of the day: **Rahab, a woman with a dubious past.**

We have **5 Causes to Celebrate Rahab.**

First, Rahab took a risk and sheltered the men of God. Joshua 2:1 tells us: "And Joshua the son of Nun sent two men secretly from Shittim as spies, saying, 'Go, view the land, especially Jericho.' And they went and came into the house of a prostitute whose name was Rahab and lodged there."

Second, Rahab was rewarded along with her family for placing her faith in God. Joshua 6:25 relates: "But Rahab the prostitute and her father's household and all who belonged to her, Joshua saved alive. And she has lived in Israel to this day, because she hid the messengers whom Joshua sent to spy out Jericho."

Third, Rahab's example encourages us to be open to the move of God in our lives. Hebrews 11:31 reminds us: "By faith Rahab the prostitute did not perish with those who were disobedient, because she had given a friendly welcome to the spies."

Fourth, Rahab links the Old Testament with the New in the lineage of Jesus. Matthew 1:5 lists for us: "And Salmon the father of

Boaz by Rahab, and Boaz the father of Obed by Ruth, and Obed the father of Jesse."

Fifth, Rahab lived out her faith when she performed the Lord's duty. James 2:25 sets our standard: "And in the same way was not also Rahab the prostitute justified by works when she received the messengers and sent them out by another way?"

Our past doesn't matter. **We must focus on where God wants to take us. Let's take a risk for God.** Who knows the path he wants to lead us down?

We become a pivot pin in God's plan when we let him use us as he will.

October 13 – 6 Blessings God Wants You to Have

WE SING THAT old song telling us to **"count our blessings, to name them one by one,"** and we get all excited. Then we start to count, and we have trouble coming up with more than one or two, maybe three **if we think about it** for a while. All we can come up with are the **troubles and problems** that have infected our week. We feel forgotten by God, and we grow tired of asking for help that doesn't seem to be coming our way.

God says to stop feeling sorry for ourselves. He's already set up the blessings, and he's ready to **let them come our way**. We have **one requirement** God puts on us to get our blessings flowing through his pipeline and on their way to us. Let's look at Deuteronomy 28:2-6 to read God's requirement and the *6 Blessings God Wants You to Have*. "And all these blessings shall come upon you and overtake you, if you obey the voice of the Lord your God. Blessed shall you be in the city, and blessed shall you be in the field. Blessed shall be the fruit of your womb and the fruit of your ground and the fruit of your cattle, the increase of your herds and the young of your flock. Blessed shall be your basket and your kneading bowl. Blessed shall you be when you come in, and blessed shall you be when you go out."

God's Requirement: "Obey the voice of the Lord your God." The Bible is our guideline, the written voice of God. We must do what it says.

Blessing No. 1: "Blessed shall you be in the city." You will be looked up to by the people you interact with daily.

Blessing No. 2: "Blessed shall you be in the field." When you venture into unfamiliar situations, God's protection will surround you.

Blessing No. 3: "Blessed shall be the fruit of your womb and the fruit of your ground and the fruit of your cattle, the increase of your herds and the young of your flock." Your children, your work, and your financial investments will be successful.

Blessing No. 4: "Blessed shall be your basket and your kneading bowl." The people you interact with will overflow with good things.

Blessing No. 5: "Blessed shall you be when you come in." God will bring your plans for a better life to a good conclusion.

Blessing No. 6: "Blessed shall you be when you go out." God will spill blessings out of your life onto those around you.

Our blessings are already lined up for our benefit. We can initiate them today. Our part is to **read the Bible** and **do what it says**. God is waiting on us. It's our turn to step up and be blessed by him.

October 14 – 4 Benefits from Walking with God

WE ARE ON the lookout for things that benefit us. **Exercise** … it renews our energy and burns up those cupcake calories. **A car with a high MPG** … we can drive farther for less money, and we all love that. **Insulated windows** … to keep our utilities low. **A home close to our job** … who likes to commute? Not us.

So, what benefits do we get from dedicating our life to Christ? Riches? Will God do that for us, **plump our bank accounts and provide us with houses and cars?** How about relationships? A spouse and children, ones who love us and will **cater to our every whim?** Fame … how can we not want that? Our name will be **known across the world.** Isaiah 43:1-2 is specific about the **4 Benefits we receive from Walking with God**. "But now thus says the Lord, he who created you, O Jacob, he who formed you, O Israel: 'Fear not, for I have redeemed you; I have called you by name, you are mine. When you pass through the waters, I will be with you; and through the rivers, they shall not overwhelm you; when you walk through fire you shall not be burned, and the flame shall not consume you.' "

Benefit No. 1 – God will be with us through the waters. These are the daily stresses we endure. They surround us and are part of our lives. God is always with us.

Benefit No. 2 – The rivers will not overwhelm us. Unexpected events can become a wave of distress. God will lift us up, and we will still be there when the wave passes us by.

Benefit No. 3 – The fire will not burn us. Fire represents the dangers that will try to consume us. Failed relationships, illness, financial ruin. God is our protection.

Benefit No. 4 – The flames shall not consume us. Our fourth benefit extends into the future. No thing that comes against us today, tomorrow, or at any time will prevail against the shielding grace of our Father in heaven.

We are God's children. **He created us and called us by name.** *His protection is ours.* Our trust in God is our stalwart staff. He is our strength in our walk with him.

October 15 – 6 Reasons You Are the Best Dressed in the Room

GOD DOES NOT want you to do without. In his Word, he tells you over and over that **he will take care of your needs**. His biblical guidelines point to **abundance, wealth, and prosperity**. God gives you ways to achieve each of these. God says **you do not have to live the life of a poor person.** You can be emboldened to have the God of all creation **providing for your every need**. Here are **6 Reasons You Are the Best Dressed in the Room**:

Joel 2:26 says you will **eat well and be generously provided for**. "You shall eat in plenty and be satisfied, and praise the name of the Lord your God, who has dealt wondrously with you. And my people shall never again be put to shame."

Psalm 147:14 says you will live a satisfying life **filled with the finest the world has to offer**. "He makes peace in your borders; he fills you with the finest of the wheat."

Psalm 111:5 says God will never fail to **live up to his promises to provide for your needs**. "He provides food for those who fear him; he remembers his covenant forever."

Proverbs 13:25 says **every provision you need will come from God.** "The righteous has enough to satisfy his appetite, but the belly of the wicked suffers want."

Psalm 132:15 says even if you're poor, God will **be your hand of blessing.** "I will abundantly bless her provisions; I will satisfy her poor with bread."

Matthew 6:31-32 says you are God's special concern, and **he will not leave you in need**. "Therefore do not be anxious, saying, 'What shall we eat?' or 'What shall we drink?' or 'What shall we wear?' For the Gentiles seek after all these things, and your heavenly

Father knows that you need them all."

Look for God's opportunity. Give the Lord the chance to pull you out of your difficulties. **Let Jesus connect you with success, and you will shine with his love**. You will eclipse those around you when you excel in the Love of Christ.

October 16 – **Our Hand of Compassion**

WE'VE SEEN the pictures of starving children on the streets. Please send money! **You can save this hungry child today**. Only $5 a month will provide two nutritious meals each day. There's no question that's an agenda we can all take seriously. We can board that bandwagon, and **people's lives will be better**.

What about, however, the **family down the street** that's facing a hard time? Or our cousin fighting addiction and **unable to hold down a job?** Or our child's classmate that wears **worn-out clothing** and doesn't have classroom supplies? Does the $5 child (as good as that program is) **relieve us of our responsibility** to those closer to home?

Proverbs 19:17 tells us: "Whoever is generous to the poor lends to the Lord, and he will repay him for his deed."

Handing $5 to the homeless man on the corner is not wasted cash. Not by a long shot. Rather, it's **an investment**. An investment? How's that? **We gave it away.** True, but our action isn't invisible. **God is watching.** He knows what we've done, and **his heart swells with joy** for our generosity. Then God sees our need and he **repays us generously** for what we've given away. Your donation to the homeless shelter? **God will renew your business.** Your time spent with inner-city youth? **God will lift you up in your family.** Your Wednesday evenings delivering meals to the poor? **God will fill your pantry to overflowing.**

It's right there in the Word. God says **he will repay** you your deed. How else do we say it? Do unto others as you would have them do unto you. For us that means what we do for others, **God will generously repay** unto us. When we offer compassion, God's blessing flows back onto us.

October 17 – **Jesus for the Long Haul**

TO BE IN SOMETHING for the long haul means to commit to the cause. Having a child is a 20-year challenge. Even longer when we take in college and emotional support after they leave home. We've

229

gotta **commit to the long haul** if we want our children to be the best they can be.

Investing in the stock market isn't for the faint of heart. Warren Buffet, investment genius, bought Dexter Shoes in 1993, losing $3.5 billion on the deal. Still, Buffet has made billions in the investment market. He's **in it for the long haul**, not for quick money.

Now for our spiritual connection. **Are we in it for the long haul?** Or do we turn and run when one bad thing happens to us? John 11:25-26 reveals Jesus speaking to Martha. Lazarus has died, and Martha struggles to believe. "Jesus said to her, 'I am the resurrection and the life. Whoever believes in me, though he die, yet shall he live, and everyone who lives and believes in me shall never die. Do you believe this?' "

What in your life has fallen apart so badly that **you feel it's permanently dead?** Your marriage? You feel there is no rescue. Your finances? You are broker than a shattered china plate. Your health? The doctor says there's nothing else to be done.

Jesus says, "Hold on. Read my lips. I said it already, it's in the Bible, and it's still true. I am the resurrection and the life." Then Jesus holds up his hand and says, **"Do you believe this?"**

You should have chills up your spine by now. **That's Jesus talking. He's offering you his power in whatever situation you are in.** When you accept salvation, **Jesus is committed to you for the long haul**. Turn to him. Trust him. He wants to be your resurrection and your life.

There is no death in Jesus, for he is our life and our salvation.

October 18 – A Reason to Be Kind to Strangers

FOR WHOM ARE we responsible? Who takes priority in our lives? Our family? Our coworkers? The people we worship with at church?

Do we owe anything to the stranger we may never meet again? Hebrews 13:2 says we do. "Do not neglect to show hospitality to strangers, for thereby some have entertained angels unawares."

Everyone deserves our kindness. The wait staff at the restaurant. The gas station attendant. The punk-haired youth beside us on the subway. **It's about balance. What you do comes back to you.**

2 Corinthians 8:13-14 reveals kindness in perfect balance. "For I do not mean that others should be eased and you burdened, but that as a matter of fairness your abundance at the present time should

supply their need, so that their abundance may supply your need, that there may be fairness."

We give out to others, and in turn, they **give back unto us**. Romans 12:13 describes God's plan to keep our needs in balance. "Contribute to the needs of the saints and seek to show hospitality."

That sounds simple enough, but **the Word goes further**. We're given a plan. Matthew 25:35-36 gives us **six ways to show kindness to strangers**. "For I was hungry and you gave me food, I was thirsty and you gave me drink, I was a stranger and you welcomed me, I was naked and you clothed me, I was sick and you visited me, I was in prison and you came to me."

Let's make a list so God's instructions are easy to follow.
1. **Donate to a food bank.**
2. **Drop off bottled water at a battered women's shelter.**
3. **Invite your teen's friends to sleepovers at your house.**
4. **Offer your spare clothing to a homeless shelter.**
5. **Join the hospital visitation team at your church.**
6. **Locate the nearest prison. Correspond with inmates in an encouraging way.**

God is counting on you. Hurting people need your time. You are emulating Christ when you <u>live as he would have you live</u>.

Jesus draws us out of our churches so we can minister for him.

October 19 – **Looking Forward to God's Promises**

WE'RE TOLD to trust in God. Then the fridge goes south, and we **scramble for funds** to get it up and running. Or our church needs more room, but there's no money to expand. The building fund barely grows, and **a loan is a long stretch** for the financially beleaguered congregation.

Where are God's promises then?

War, and poverty. We pray that **God's peace spreads across the world**, and we get another **car bombing in London** or Tel Aviv or in Detroit. The Federal Building in Oklahoma City. **Where was God then?** Sandy Hook or Littleton … is God **even paying attention?**

Or do we have skewed expectations of God? Maybe those things are not in his "bag of tricks." Isaiah 30:18 gives us an **update on how God sees things**. "Therefore the Lord waits to be gracious to you, and therefore he exalts himself to show mercy to you. For the Lord is a God of justice; blessed are all those who wait for him."

God is **still on his throne**. He is the ruler that **controls all of**

creation. He respects the laws he has instituted.

God doesn't shift the sun and moon simply because it might suit us. Some things happen because of circumstances or because people have made decisions one way or the other. God's promises are to **be gracious to us and to show us mercy**. If we wait on the Lord, everything he has promised will be done. *The urgency is ours, not God's*. Our duty is to give him space to perform his perfect will.

God shows us mercy when we live in his will.

October 20 – The Treasure in the Well

IN 2016, AN INDIAN man whose wife was denied access to his village's common well took matters into his own hands. After a prayer to his local deity, he began to dig. For forty days, he worked at his regular job as a laborer, plus spent **an additional six hours** digging his new well. The village laughed at him, and even his wife told him he was insane. He persisted, however, and after forty days, **water gushed from the bottom of the well. The man had found his treasure.**

How persistent are we in unearthing the blessings of God? How long do we cling to our hope in Christ before we wail in despair that we've been abandoned? Here are five treasures from the Word we can release when we begin to dig in God's well.

Treasure No. 1: *We become purified in Christ.* 1 John 3:3 tells us: "And everyone who thus hopes in him purifies himself as he is pure."

Treasure No. 2: *Death loses its grip of fear over us.* Proverbs 14:32 says: "The wicked is overthrown through his evildoing, but the righteous finds refuge in his death."

Treasure No. 3: *Christ offers us the hope of joining him in eternal glory.* Colossians 1:27 promises: "To them God chose to make known how great among the Gentiles are the riches of the glory of this mystery, which is Christ in you, the hope of glory."

Treasure No. 4: *We are filled with courage and imbued with a strong heart.* Psalm 31:24 says: "Be strong, and let your heart take courage, all you who wait for the Lord!"

Treasure No. 5: *We are assured of the resurrection of Christ from the dead.* 1 Peter 1:3 gives us confidence: "Blessed be the God and Father of our Lord Jesus Christ! According to his great mercy, he has caused us to be born again to a living hope through the resurrection of Jesus Christ from the dead."

What has the devil denied you? What do you feel shut out of? What walls surround you, finances encumber you, relationships founder **even as you strive to walk closer to Jesus? Dig in God's well.** *Read the Bible.* Spend time in prayer. Your forty days are coming to an end, and <u>you will find your hope in God</u>. Never give up or surrender your dreams in God. He is your champion.

October 21 – **Our Main Man**

WHAT DOES IT mean to be a "main man" in today's world? What credentials do we need to flash, degrees to display, or organizations to join? *A church deacon, will that do it?* We can gather with the other leaders of the church and **make the decisions** that determine the body's success (or sometimes failure). *Or maybe choir leader fits the bill.* We are at center stage, **orchestrating the mood of the service**, from the introductory chorus to the rousing finale as the attendees exit the door. *Have you considered the lowly Sunday school teacher?* They mold our children's minds, teaching them **exactly what the Christian experience** is all about. (Not so lowly after all.)

Really, none of these fit the bill.

"**What!?!**" Your amazement bleeds down your face. "**These are the most important people in the church.**" Let's see what John 3:16 has to say. "For God so loved the world, that he gave his only Son, that whoever believes in him should not perish but have eternal life."

Read it like it says it. God gave his only Son … his **only Son**. How many of us would do that? And why? For God's benefit? **Nope.** For the benefit of his Son? **Not even warm.** Our Master's sacrifice was for the church deacon, the choir leader, and the (not so) lowly Sunday school teacher. **Jesus came to earth for the unbeliever, the believer, the in-between, and anyone else who walks the world.**

So, who's the main man? **Who's got it going on?** Who's the one we should cheer? **Jesus, Jesus, you're our man.** *You can save us if anyone can.* Seriously, Jesus is the **center of everything**. He came, not because he had to but because **he wanted to**. *He loved us, and in exchange, he died for us.* Hats off to Jesus. He's the best there is.

October 22 – **The Good Thing in Our Years**

OBSOLESCENCE IS America's mantra. Make it **new for the new season**. It's the only way to sell. If it looks or feels like yesterday, who'll be interested? Who wants to wear **last year's styles**, drive **last year's car**, or live in a house that **looks like the last decade?**

Recently a YouTuber showcased a car brought into his shop to be repaired, a black Porsche 911 only a couple of years old and in pristine shape ... except for a slight dimple in the back bumper. The gleaming beauty was in for an upgrade. The owner wanted the rear of his car **upgraded to the newest look**, with new taillights, new rear grilles, and the latest style of bumper. Most people wouldn't know the difference, but to the car's owner, it was **all the difference in the world**. His car had become obsolete, and he wanted an upgrade, even if just in his own eyes.

God says we are never obsolete. Getting older is getting better. Even in our gray hair, we have *a vital role to play*. Titus 2:1-5 tells us how we continue to fit into God's plan as we mature. "But as for you, teach what accords with sound doctrine. Older men are to be sober-minded, dignified, self-controlled, sound in faith, in love, and in steadfastness. Older women likewise are to be reverent in behavior, not slanderers or slaves to much wine. They are to teach what is good, and so train the young women to love their husbands and children, to be self-controlled, pure, working at home, kind, and submissive to their own husbands, that the word of God may not be reviled."

That's a long passage, so **let's break it into manageable segments**.

Men are to be: Sober-minded. Dignified. Self-controlled. Sound in faith and love. Steadfast. **Women are to be:** Reverent. Not slanderers. Not slaves to much wine. Teaching what is good. Training young women to a better standard

It sounds like **our work isn't done**. In fact, **our job in the kingdom of God is just begun. We can't afford to sink into self-pity or hide away in our retirement just yet.** Let's be after the work of the Lord. Now that we know what God expects of us, let's get to it.

October 23 – Breaking Out of the Mold

MAKING PLASTER ITEMS is a repetitive process. We pour the slip in the mold, let it harden, then we pull apart the mold. We can scrub the mold with water and a brush and prepare it for another casting, one just like the first. **Here's the conundrum we face.** If we have a flaw in our mold, every piece we form will have **that identical flaw**. It's inherent in the design. We can try to polish it out after the casting is complete, but we will not get identical results. **The flaw will always be a rough spot in the plaster's design**.

God says it's time to break out of our mold of self-interest and worldly living. It's our opportunity to **become someone new**. We don't have to be like the old man we once were. 2 Corinthians 5:17 is an exciting verse. "Therefore, if anyone is in Christ, he is a new creation. The old has passed away; behold, the new has come."

When we allow God to pour us into the Christ mold, we **become just like him**. We begin to live like Jesus. Our mannerisms. Our treatment of the people around us. Our concern for our fellow man.

There's talk today of the refugees gathering at the First World's borders around the globe. What did Jesus do when 5,000 refugees approached him? He fed each one. **That's what we become when we come out of the Jesus mold.** That's the Christian example the **needy and hurting need to see**. That's us when we are broken and remade into the beauty that is Jesus our Lord. Let's break out of the world's mold. Let's let Jesus shape us into something new and wonderful.

October 24 – **4 Ways to Sharpen Our Image**

RESPECT IS EARNED. We get it by **what we do**. We volunteer at a homeless shelter, and we get a nod in the newspaper. We tack **another degree** onto our name, and people's estimation of us **jumps a notch**. We get married, have children, and move to an exclusive neighborhood ... it all affects the image we present to the world.

How do we sharpen our image before God? Can we **volunteer enough, get enough degrees**, or **marry into God's respect?** If those don't work, what will?

Here are *4 Ways to Sharpen Our Image* before God from the book of Deuteronomy.

Our 1st Way to Sharpen Our Image: Deuteronomy 6:3 says we must **study the Bible** to understand God's expectations. "Hear therefore, O Israel, and be careful to do them, that it may go well with you, and that you may multiply greatly, as the Lord, the God of your fathers, has promised you, in a land flowing with milk and honey."

Our 2nd Way to Sharpen Our Image: Deuteronomy 7:12 says it's vital to **remember what God's told us** in the past. "And because you listen to these rules and keep and do them, the Lord your God will keep with you the covenant and the steadfast love that he swore to your fathers."

Our 3rd Way to Sharpen Our Image: Deuteronomy 29:9 says if we **follow what we discover** in the Bible, we will find success in our endeavors. "Therefore keep the words of this covenant and do them, that you may prosper in all that you do."

Our 4th Way to Sharpen Our Image: Deuteronomy 5:29 says **our descendants will benefit** from our respect for God's laws. "Oh that they had such a heart as this always, to fear me and to keep all my commandments, that it might go well with them and with their descendants forever!"

Do you want to **move up a notch** on God's respect meter? It's easy. He's given us the instructions. *We call it the Bible*. **It is the written Word of the Holy God.**

We become closer to God when we adhere to his Word.

October 25 – 3 Style Tips from God

ARE YOU A grumpy cat in the morning? Your claws come out when someone talks to you before you have your coffee. Can't they see you **aren't awake yet?**

Your detractors say, Put a smile on your face, Grumpy Cat. Let the sunshine in, and you say, **That's not my style.**

Or how about this one? Your finances are in a tumble, and you're not sure how you're going to pay the bills. Keithie needs new shoes, and the oil pump in the car is on the blink. You're overcome with worry.

Your pastor says, Turn it over to God. Worry's not your friend, and you reply, **That's not my style.**

We feel the need to be in control. Give me the alarm clock. I'll set it to get up when I want, or I'll figure out the finances. Just give me time to worry over it a while.

God says we need a new attitude. We need to model his standards in everything we do. We need to **find our style in him.**

Our 1st Style Tip from God: Psalm 4:7 says we find more happiness when we style ourselves after God **than in riches and fine living**. "You have put more joy in my heart than they have when their grain and wine abound."

Our 2nd Style Tip from God: Psalm 126:5-6 says **God is our turnaround**. Our new style is on its way. "Those who sow in tears shall reap with shouts of joy! He who goes out weeping, bearing the seed for sowing, shall come home with shouts of joy, bringing his sheaves with him."

Our 3rd Style Tip from God: Psalm 16:11 says we are living **in the epitome of style** when we walk with Jesus. "You make known to me the path of life; in your presence there is fullness of joy; at your right hand are pleasures forevermore."

We learn God's style when we turn our life over to him. He is our standard. No grumpy cats allowed. Worry is on yesterday's calendar. **We must stretch higher to become like him.**

When we live like Jesus, we are today's trendsetter.

October 26 – The Flavor of Christ

MANY FOODS ARE made to be mixed. Stir this in with that, and one food will take on the flavor of another. Pepper. Salt. Cinnamon. Nutmeg. Each adds a special sensation we recognize in a moment.

What flavor is revealed when people spend time with us? The flavor of Jesus, or that of the world? Matthew 5:39-41 tells us how to take on the taste of Jesus. "But I say to you, Do not resist the one who is evil. But if anyone slaps you on the right cheek, turn to him the other also. And if anyone would sue you and take your tunic, let him have your cloak as well. And if anyone forces you to go one mile, go with him two miles."

Turn to him the other cheek. That's kindness, not striking back in anger.

Let him have your cloak as well. God wants us to be generous no matter who it is.

Go with him two miles. We are to persevere in helping others, no matter what it requires of us.

We're tasting like Jesus already. We're taking on the aroma of Christ. Soon we'll be permeated with the flavor of Jesus, and people will recognize him in us as soon as they get near.

When we act like Jesus, we start to become more like him.

October 27 – Anchoring in God

HAVE YOU EVER been out in a small boat? It's fun. You're right there on the water, close enough to touch. All you need to do is reach, and you can wet your fingers in the cool, clear wake.

It's when the skies darken and the wind increases that we realize how small our boat really is. **Emotional trauma** builds on the horizon. The **wind of change** batters the sides of our craft. And the shore begins to look **farther and farther away**. Now we are frightened. What will we do if we lose our job? Is that noise from under the hood **our engine going bad? I can't be sick, God. I can't afford to take off work.**

When our ship is in a storm, and it can't get back to shore, the solution is to *drop the anchor and trust in its ability to hold secure.* **That's what God wants us to do.** Nahum 1:7 tells us: "The Lord is good, a stronghold in the day of trouble; he knows those who take refuge in him."

God is our Coast Guard cutter **on the way to our rescue.** He is the dispatcher on the radio with us, giving us advice on **how to make our way home.** He is the lighthouse that **shines through the storm,** giving us directions on how to weather the wind and rain until skies are clear once more. This verse, small though it is, reveals **three exciting facets of our Lord.**

No. 1 – The Lord is Good. God cares for our welfare. He desires good things for us.

No. 2 – God is our stronghold in the day of trouble. Life can batter us, but it can't defeat us. The Lord surrounds us on every side.

No. 3 – God knows those who take refuge in him. God's eye is on us. We are not invisible to him – **not even when we are being pummeled by the storms of life.**

Let's anchor in God. He's the rock that never lets go.

October 28 – Getting What We Expect

PLANNING IS A good thing. An impromptu wedding is likely to exclude loved ones, be held in a less-than-desirable venue, and showcase wedding photos that **reveal our lack of preparation.** Our kiddos … how many lives have shifted gears because we didn't plan for baby number one or two – **or for that late-in-life tyke we were told we couldn't conceive?** Retirement, we want our money to last. **We must start saving decades before we make our transition from the work-a-day world.** It's the same with taking a vacation, choosing the best college, or taking care of our insurance needs. If we're operating by the "seat of our pants," **we will always be scrambling to catch up to where we should be.**

Proverbs 12:15 says to **open our eyes to reality.** "The way of a fool is right in his own eyes, but a wise man listens to advice."

Here's the thing about advice. It comes **before** the event. Afterwards it becomes hindsight, and while hindsight may be 20/20, it's **useless in changing what has already occurred.** Hindsight says, "If only I had known …" and "It's not my fault …" or "I did the best I could ..." Sometimes those statements are true ... and sometimes we must admit that **we've fallen down on the job**.

It's up to us to change, starting now. Let's seek advice from the experts. We can no longer barrel ahead doing what we want just because it feels good. **Seat-of-the-pants living will not improve our situation or lift us out of our struggles.**

Here are some sources of advice to change your life. *Your parents.* They have experience they can share with you. *Your pastor*, an expert in spiritual advice. *Successful people.* They have a track record you can trust. *Your local library.* Your librarian can suggest the right books. *The Word of God.* Your spiritual improvement can start today.

If you plan on success, seek advice. You will become prepared to achieve the success you expect. The Word is your source for spiritual growth. Take time to read it today.

October 29 – **Walking in God's Favor**

SOME PEOPLE SAY life takes us where it wants us to go. We're at the mercy of fate. **We have no choice in the big picture.** The swell of life's ocean carries us where it will.

God says differently. He says we can **walk in his goodness**, take a **stroll through his garden**, and feel **solid ground beneath our feet**. God wants us to take off our shoes and **let the warmth of his presence soak into our soles**.

Hebrews 10:23 says **he is faithful**. "Let us hold fast the confession of our hope without wavering, for he who promised is faithful."

2 Timothy 2:13 assures us **he will be there for us** in our darkest times. "If we are faithless, he remains faithful—"

2 Peter 3:9 is our promise he will **never turn his face from us**. "The Lord is not slow to fulfill his promise as some count slowness, but is patient toward you, not wishing that any should perish, but that all should reach repentance."

1 Kings 8:56 offers us **rest in him**. "Blessed be the Lord who has given rest to his people Israel, according to all that he promised. Not one word has failed of all his good promise, which he spoke by Moses his servant."

Isaiah 25:1 tells us to **give him praise** for his blessings. "O Lord, you are my God; I will exalt you; I will praise your name, for you have done wonderful things, plans formed of old, faithful and sure."

Psalm 9:10 says **all we need to do is seek him**. "And those who

239

know your name put their trust in you, for you, O Lord, have not forsaken those who seek you."

It's time to step out with God. **Take his hand.** Enjoy the bountiful benefits of his companionship. Walking with God is a delight forevermore.

October 30 – **What to Do with Your Words**

WORDS CARRY power. They can **repair relationships** or **slice someone's heart** to the core.

A good speaker can navigate the pitfalls of pending legislation and **keep government on its course**, and a bad one can fail at every junction along the way.

Closer to home, **whispered words of gossip are our downfall**. The news is so juicy, and everyone wants to know. Of course, we must tell.

God says to stop with the gossip. Shut it down. Keep it to yourself, even if you know it's true. It doesn't need said.

Here are **six reasons to let gossip die before it leaves your tongue**.

Leviticus 19:16 says **God doesn't permit it**. "You shall not go around as a slanderer among your people, and you shall not stand up against the life of your neighbor: I am the Lord."

Proverbs 18:8 says **gossip is a poison** that destroys us from the inside. "The words of a whisperer are like delicious morsels; they go down into the inner parts of the body."

Proverbs 20:19 says **we are to avoid gossipers**. "Whoever goes about slandering reveals secrets; therefore do not associate with a simple babbler."

Proverbs 11:13 says we are **faithful when we conceal** harmful secrets. "Whoever goes about slandering reveals secrets, but he who is trustworthy in spirit keeps a thing covered."

Proverbs 16:28 says **gossip drives friends apart**. "A dishonest man spreads strife, and a whisperer separates close friends."

Psalm 52:2 says **our tongues can be deadly** when we speak carelessly. "Your tongue plots destruction, like a sharp razor, you worker of deceit."

We are in control of our words. Sometimes we need to simply close our mouths, no matter how difficult it seems. **Turn your head**. Hang up the phone. Take a drink. **Bite into your sandwich. Walk out of the room. Say, "No, thanks."** Your words are more powerful

240

than you know. Use them carefully. God expects kindness. It starts with what we say.

October 31 – **Life in Christ**

LIFE AND DEATH. Polar opposites, right? That's how we speak of them. **This is a life or death situation.** We mean it's "do or die." Break the bank. This or that. There's no in-between. Polar opposites. Yet, we speak of the worst situations in life as a "living death." What does that mean? Take this example. A spouse dies, and we are heart-broken. Someone asks how we are, and we exclaim in our grief, "I wish I had died instead. This is a living death." What we mean is **we are emotionally devastated**. We are empty inside and can **no longer see any good thing** before us.

    Life and death. Not a polar opposite in this case.

    Spiritually, we can be caught up in the same conundrum. We walk, we talk, but we are **spiritually dead** inside. We have no spiritual connection with the heavenly Father, and we can see **no spiritual future beyond what we can touch**. John 8:51 says: "Truly, truly, I say to you, if anyone keeps my word, he will never see death."

    What does this verse mean? That we will **never physically expire** and be placed in a grave? Even Jesus faced that, as did every one of the Apostles, and we're pretty certain they kept the word of the Lord. **What death will we not see?**

    *The living death, the walking and the talking with **no spiritual connection** to the Almighty God above.*

    What word must we keep to remain spiritually alive? We must treat every person **as we would wish to be treated** and **model our behavior after the example of Christ**.

    We have life in Christ when we are spiritually connected with our Lord.

November 1 – **Keeping a Record of Us**

WHO CARES about yesterday? It's over and done, and we **can't move backwards**. Shouldn't we all get a fresh start each morning? Several years back, a grandmother raising a rowdy grandson kept her even keel during a repeated bout of disruptive behavior. "How do you do it?" a friend asked. "He never learns, and you still love him." The grandmother replied, "Every day is brand new. I wipe the slate clean every night."

That helped that grandmother work with her grandson, but the reality is our past doesn't disappear **just because we want a new beginning**. We must deal with the dregs of our behavior. They will trail us through life, and they will **leap out to bite us** when we least expect them. Romans 14:12 says it like this: "So then each of us will give an account of himself to God."

Everything we've done will come up on that great computer in the sky. God will click on **Search,** and the system will locate **every deed we've been involved in**, whether for good or ill. Our only free pass will come in the **acceptance of Jesus** as our Savior and Lord. God will scan down the deeds we've done, he'll come to our **moment of salvation**, and everything before that will be **chucked into the Trash**. Until then, it's important to keep a record of how we behave, what we do, how we treat others, and whether we are **living by the standards** given us in the Bible.

Keeping a record of us helps us know where we stand when it's time to stand before our King. Jesus is our standard. He is our example of how to live.

November 2 – **Shaping Up to God's Standard**

WHAT DOES it mean to shape up? Merriam-Webster gives us two definitions. 1. We can work to improve ourselves. Study, exercise, even immerse ourselves in the rules of etiquette and propriety that surround us. **We learn to become what people expect of us**. 2. We can do the same to things or people around us. Paint our house, encourage our children in school, or invite people to church. **We want others to become what we expect of them**.

When we turn **shape up** into a noun, it gets a hyphen and takes on a whole new concept. **A shape-up** means to **hire people for a day's work**.

Are we shaping up to God's standard? Are we lined up, ready to **do his work**, impatiently waiting for God's instruction for the **next great thing** we get to do for him?

Colossians 3:8 says this is our chance to **get rid of the wickedness of our youth**. "But now you must put them all away: anger, wrath, malice, slander, and obscene talk from your mouth."

Proverbs 27:4 tells us envy is to be **tossed by the wayside**. "Wrath is cruel, anger is overwhelming, but who can stand before jealousy?"

Romans 12:19-21 says to **jump into good** if we want to defeat evil. "Beloved, never avenge yourselves, but leave it to the wrath of God, for it is written, 'Vengeance is mine, I will repay, says the Lord.' To the contrary, 'if your enemy is hungry, feed him; if he is thirsty, give him something to drink; for by so doing you will heap burning coals on his head.' Do not be overcome by evil, but overcome evil with good."

Ephesians 4:31-32 assures us **our job is kindness**. It's forgiveness that gets God's job completed. "Let all bitterness and wrath and anger and clamor and slander be put away from you, along with all malice. Be kind to one another, tenderhearted, forgiving one another, as God in Christ forgave you."

Our **shape-up** requires us to **shape up**. To do today's job for God, we must **improve ourselves until we meet his expectations**. Only then can we stand tall as the workers God needs us to be.

Our reflection of Jesus is our qualification for God's employ.

November 3 – **God's Wall of Protection**

LIVING ON THE coast is wonderful … **except when a hurricane blows in**. During the rest of the year, we enjoy warm sand, pleasant temperatures, and bright sun. We roam the roads with our car's canvas top open to the sky, and we wonder why **anyone would live anywhere else**.

Then the dark clouds build on the horizon. We know what's coming. We have plenty of warning. We wait for the evacuation notice. Then we're gone, **not sure if our home will be there when we return**.

That's just like our Christian experience. We come to Jesus and are ready to explode over the world with his goodness. We are refreshed in him, and we are confident **nothing will darken our days ever again**. Then the dark clouds of **financial hardship** appear. The rain of **fractured relationships** spatters our windows. The pounding hail of a **life gone awry** thunders around us.

God says to hold tight to him. He is our rescue. He will build a wall of protection around us. The clouds and rain can come, but we **will not be destroyed**. Psalm 37:28 tells us: "For the Lord loves justice; he will not forsake his saints. They are preserved forever, but the children of the wicked shall be cut off."

God gives us two assurances in this verse.

Assurance No. 1: God will not forsake his saints. In our darkest hour, God is at our side. He hasn't abandoned us. He is our constant companion.

Assurance No. 2: God's saints are preserved forever. The human condition is to face repeated challenges. That won't change. Yet we will not be defeated. We are saved forever from the attack of the evil one.

God's wall of protection is his assurance of his love to us. We can **trust him in the storm**. He will keep us **secure in every situation**. When we face fear, God kicks the fear out the door.

November 4 – 2 Calls to Indulge Righteousness

RIGHTEOUSNESS. Merriam-Webster has something special to say about this word: 1. We do things by a divine standard. 2. We exercise a moral prerogative. 3. We remain free from guilt over bad choices.

Merriam-Webster goes on to give the changes we experience: 1. We become better, justified by our good decisions. 2. We begin to expect more of other people, that they should meet our standard.

Where does this place us as Christians? How do we achieve what the world accepts as the height of human calling? Romans 8:12-13 says our **higher calling is a spiritual one**. We can't live by a divine or moral set of rules in our flesh alone. "So then, brothers, we are debtors, not to the flesh, to live according to the flesh. For if you live according to the flesh you will die, but if by the Spirit you put to death the deeds of the body, you will live."

Titus 2:11-12 tells us **salvation is our pivot point**, the moment that swings us from self-indulgence to self-denial and success in Jesus. "For the grace of God has appeared, bringing salvation for all people, training us to renounce ungodliness and worldly passions, and to live self-controlled, upright, and godly lives in the present age."

Righteousness is something we can all have. The important thing to keep hold of is that we can't get there on our own. Salvation is the key. Jesus is our helper, and in him, we are better than we were.

November 5 – 3 Reasons Worry Is for the Birds

WHAT'S GOT your thoughts tied up? What keeps you awake at night, consumes your sanity, and **threatens to keep you from rest and relaxation?** What is it that's so big to you that everything else pales in comparison?

God says he is your redemption in every situation. Psalm 46:1-3 gives **3 Reasons Worry Is for the Birds**: "God is our refuge and strength, a very present help in trouble. Therefore we will not fear though the earth gives way, though the mountains be moved into the heart of the sea, though its waters roar and foam, though the mountains tremble at its swelling."

The 1st Reason Worry Is for the Birds: God is our refuge. **The 2nd Reason Worry Is for the Birds:** God is our strength. **The 3rd Reason Worry Is for the Birds:** God is a very present help in trouble.

We love to call out those assurances when we are looking up just to find the bottom of life's well. **Let's see what this verse really means.** Earthquakes can shatter every security we know, and still, **God is our refuge.** Mountains can crumble under the assault of time, but **God remains our strength.** Oceans of troubles can batter us at every turn, but **we will not be washed away. We stand on the mountain of God.** We are connected to the greatest lighthouse on the planet, the maker of the winds and the waves, and there is *no harm that can come to us.*

Our dwelling place in God is higher than the nests of eagles and more firmly entrenched than the foundations of the earth. Let's say it again. **God is our refuge.** He is our strength. **He is a very present help in the time of our trouble.** It's not worth your time to worry. God has your life under his control.

November 6 – God's Time Machine

H.G. WELLES was one of the first. His time machine is iconic, a story of a man who wishes to **manipulate the days and months** and reorder them to his desires.

Other writers and filmmakers have tackled the prospect of time travel in different ways. Can we physically **move our bodies from one point in time** to another? How much damage will we do if we **change something** in the past? Is the future already set, or are our futures **as infinite as the pages** on the calendar?

Dr. Who in the British television series travels in a magic telephone box (a Tardis) to the beginning of time and to the end of the world. It's like it's all already happened, **every moment in history and the future**.

A Sound of Thunder is a movie based on the butterfly effect. One small butterfly is killed in the distant past, and the entire future is changed because of it.

How is time travel presented in the Bible? Isaiah 65:24 tells us: "Before they call I will answer; while they are yet speaking I will hear."

Does this really say what it sounds like? **Before they call**, God has already answered. That sounds like time travel. Bending the calendar to our will. Knowing what will happen before it takes place. This verse also says that he hears **while they are yet speaking. That sounds like God knows their words before they even say them.**

Several years ago, Michael J. Fox starred in a movie series titled **Back to the Future.** One of the characters in the movie said, "Where we're going, we don't need roads."

That's God. He travels where he will. Time is of no concern to him. God is our time machine, and when we travel with him, our future is assured.

November 7 – **4 Measures of God's Love**

WE KNOW the verse telling how much God loved us. We can probably quote **most if not all** of John 3:16 by heart. That's heady stuff. To give your child, the heir to all you've worked for and accumulated, to **offer a better life** to other people … who would do that? The answer, of course, takes us back to John 3:16. **God loves us just that much.** Here are four more verses that give us a measure of how much we are **loved and adored by the almighty Father** above.

Psalm 146:8 says he **loves the righteousness** he sees in the upright believer. "The Lord opens the eyes of the blind. The Lord lifts up those who are bowed down; the Lord loves the righteous."

Proverbs 15:9 tells us **his heart is moved** when we do our best to uphold the standards of the Bible. "The way of the wicked is an abomination to the Lord, but he loves him who pursues righteousness."

Isaiah 62:5 describes his love with the **intensity of a newly married couple** on their wedding day. "For as a young man marries a young woman, so shall your sons marry you, and as the bridegroom rejoices over the bride, so shall your God rejoice over you."

1 John 4:10 reminds us he loves us enough to **give up his most treasured possession** to ensure our future betterment. "In this is love, not that we have loved God but that he loved us and sent his Son to be the propitiation for our sins."

What's holding us back? We have a God who loves us **at any cost**. *We should run to him*. God's arms are open wide waiting for our embrace.

November 8 – Taking God in Stride

THE WORD tells us God loves us. We all know the verse in the Book of John that tells us God loves us so much that he gave his Son **to be a sacrifice for our sins**. Why then do we often feel God is **wagging his finger at us** and telling us that we're bad, bad, bad?

We must learn to take God in our stride. Think of our own children. When they misbehave, we place them in time out, take away their phones, or **cut off their allowance**. We wag our finger (figuratively) and let them know **we disapprove**. We haven't stopped loving them, and they understand that. There's a problem that needs corrected, and we are **working toward that end**.

That's our relationship with God. Hebrews 12:10-11 tells us **God's love is bringing about good for us**. "For they disciplined us for a short time as it seemed best to them, but [God] disciplines us for our good, that we may share his holiness. For the moment all discipline seems painful rather than pleasant, but later it yields the peaceful fruit of righteousness to those who have been trained by it."

Do our children say, "Goodie! Dad has taken away my phone."? Do we really think our kids love Mom sending them to time out? God is not the bad guy here. Neither are we. We are created in his image, he understands us, and he works to bring us to perfection in him. Just like the children we call our own. Salvation is just the beginning. Becoming like Jesus is the plan.

November 9 – 4 Traditions for Honesty

A SOCIAL MEDIA site recently posted that tradition is just **peer**

pressure from dead people. The statement was clearly a joke, but there's a degree of truth in the words.

Peer pressure has taken on a negative connotation, but it's not always bad. Social standards from our equals **(our peers)** can support better hygiene, improved schools, and higher social integrity. Take honesty. Traditions of honesty are discovering what worked for our ancestors **(mom, dad, gramps, and so on)** and applying that to our daily lives. We do much of it naturally. If our parents regularly kept a rainy-day fund, we're **likely to do the same**. Returning extra change? Yes, that comes from our **parents and grandparents**, also.

Let's look at *4 Traditions for Honesty* from the Bible.

Tradition No. 1: Leviticus 25:14 says we must be fair in our business dealings. We **can't take advantage** using scrupulous business practices. "And if you make a sale to your neighbor or buy from your neighbor, you shall not wrong one another."

Tradition No. 2: Psalm 37:21 says **defaulting on our obligations** is bad for us and for those around us. "The wicked borrows but does not pay back, but the righteous is generous and gives."

Tradition No. 3: Leviticus 25:17 says to **respect others** as deserving of God's blessings. "You shall not wrong one another, but you shall fear your God, for I am the Lord your God."

Tradition No. 4: Colossians 3:9-10 says the **truth is never overrated**. We must be the person inside that others see on the outside. "Do not lie to one another, seeing that you have put off the old self with its practices and have put on the new self, which is being renewed in knowledge after the image of its creator."

We learn from the past. Our traditions instruct us to a better today. Our future is bright when we remember those who've come before us. History is our guide. We don't want to get lost along the way.

November 10 – Sending Satan into the Cold

SOME PEOPLE can't be trusted. They promise us a good time, and **as long as we're paying**, they come through. Then the money runs out, and they **move on without us**. Or Internet phishing schemes. The offer looks **too good to be true** (and it probably is). Our only smart choice is to **send it to the recycle bin**.

The devil tried his moves on Jesus. He found him at **his lonely time, his weak spot**, and **pitched an offer** the Son of God couldn't possibly refuse. Read about it in Luke 4:6-8. "And the devil said

248

unto him, All this power will I give thee, … to whomsoever I will I give it. If thou therefore wilt worship me, all shall be thine. And Jesus answered and said unto him, Get thee behind me, Satan: for it is written, Thou shalt worship the Lord thy God, and him only shalt thou serve."

Good answer, Jesus. That's a kick in the teeth for the old sour-puss. You bonked him in the head with the **Word of God**, bumped him into the cold without a second glance.

We must follow Jesus' example. When our old party friends come a-calling, "Get thee behind me, for I'm a new creation." When New Agers try to prove the Bible is wrong, "Get thee behind me, for the Word of God is truth to me." When we are lonely, kick false love in the teeth. When the devil finds our weak spot, bonk him on the head with the truth found in the Bible.

The world will offer us easy solutions that will feel good in the moment, but our job is to **turn to Christ** and **kick Satan into the cold** without a second glance.

Christ resisted temptation, and he expects us to do the same.

November 11 – **Our Outline for Following Jesus**

AN OUTLINE is an organizational tool. It's not the complete book or the entire report. The outline is our **guideline**, and we **fill in the details** as we make progress. James 1:21-25 gives us *Our Outline for Following Jesus*.

Verse 21 tells us we must step **back from wrongdoing** and spend time **studying the Word**. "Therefore put away all filthiness and rampant wickedness and receive with meekness the implanted word, which is able to save your souls."

Verse 22 says we must **live by what the Bible says**. It's not enough to **listen to the pastor on Sunday** and do what we want the rest of the week. "But be doers of the word, and not hearers only, deceiving yourselves."

Verses 23-24 says if we fail to read the Bible and **do what it says**, we've **become blinded** to how we appear to others. "For if anyone is a hearer of the word and not a doer, he is like a man who looks intently at his natural face in a mirror. For he looks at himself and goes away and at once forgets what he was like."

Verse 25 is our guarantee of God's **blessing over everything** we do when we **live out what we learn** in the Word of God. "But the one who looks into the perfect law, the law of liberty, and perseveres, being no hearer who forgets but a doer who acts, he will be blessed in his doing."

These are the four steps, the four layers to our Christian outline. The details in between are the lives we live. Yet, this gets us started. **This is our guideline.** If we come back to it when we find ourselves off track, we will build our successful Christian story **one chapter at a time**. God has a plan. He wants us to follow him.

November 12 – 5 Ways to Please God

HOW DO WE please others? **It depends on who they are.** What might please our boss may have little impact on our spouse. Our 4-year-old requires something **completely different** from us than our teenager. Our dog is likely pleased with a **tussle around the ears** and a **walk in the park**. A treat and a game of fetch help, too.

We can find **5 Ways to Please God** in James 4:7-8. "Submit yourselves therefore to God. Resist the devil, and he will flee from you. Draw near to God, and he will draw near to you. Cleanse your hands, you sinners, and purify your hearts, you double-minded."

Let's turn our 5 ways into a list for easy remembrance. 1. Submit to God. 2. Resist the devil. 3. Draw near to God. 4. Cleanse our hands. 5. Purify our hearts.

Now, let's restate each one for relevance in our modern world.
- Read the Bible. Do what it says.
- Refuse to fall into wrongdoing. Make good choices each day.
- Find time for prayer. Consider God throughout the day.
- Stop doing things you know don't fit within Godly principles.
- Our intents and desires, not just our outward actions, must be patterned after the life of Christ.

There. Now all you need to do is **get out there and live it**. If your life hasn't changed since accepting salvation, ask yourself why. Then pull out your list of 5 Ways to Please God and give it another try. God's instructions are perfectly clear. Do what the Father says, and our Lord will be pleased with us.

November 13 – 3 Guidelines for Becoming God's Champion

WHAT'S THE COST of reaching the top of your game? For an Olympic athlete, there are **financial sacrifices**, hours in training, and the **stress of competing** against the best in the world. In the medical field, you'll face **a decade of higher education**, long hours in the dead of night, and **excruciating moral responsibility**.

What's the cost of becoming a top-notch Christian? What does God require of us to become a champion for the Lord? Luke 12:33 gives us *3 Guidelines for Becoming God's Champion.* "Sell your possessions, and give to the needy. Provide yourselves with moneybags that do not grow old, with a treasure in the heavens that does not fail, where no thief approaches and no moth destroys."

Our 1st Guideline: We must *sell our possessions.* That's a hard one for modern-day Americans. We have so much stuff, and it all feels vitally important to us. When our stuff is more important than God, it's time for it to go.

Our 2nd Guideline: *Give to the needy.* What!?! Don't they have two legs? Can't they do something to improve their own situation? Why should it be up to me? It's our care and concern for others that lifts us above the world.

Our 3rd Guideline: Our moneybags that don't grow old *aren't moneybags at all.* This guideline says some things are more important than money. Service to our fellow man. Consideration for others. A life lived in dedication to advancing the cause of Christ. True Christianity isn't what we get out of it but what we can do for others.

How's your workout going? Are your champion muscles gaining strength? Are you **chasing God's knowledge**, spending **time in the Word**, and shouldering the **moral responsibility** Christ has made ours? God wants you for his champion. Now's the time for you to make your move.

November 14 – **An Amazing Leap of Faith**

TRUSTING GOD is a practiced skill. It's like the high-dive board at the pool. We jump off the side of the pool at first, **maybe six inches**. That seems easy enough, but for a beginner, it can be very frightening. Then there's the low board. Our heart pounds, we're not sure how to bounce correctly, and **what if we hit our head on the way in?**

It grows easier, and slowly we work our way to the tallest platform. We look over the edge, **our stomach flips**, and we <u>try not to look frightened or dizzy</u>. **We are, though.** Then we remember standing at the pool's edge, and we imagine jumping off the low board … and we *feel our confidence return.*

That's how we learn to trust in God. Matthew 8:2-3 tells the

251

story of the leper who came to Jesus. "And behold, a leper came to him and knelt before him, saying, 'Lord, if you will, you can make me clean.' And Jesus stretched out his hand and touched him, saying, 'I will; be clean.' And immediately his leprosy was cleansed."

We don't have recorded the leper at the side of the pool. Perhaps he heard the story of someone healed, and his **faith was pricked**. He may have seen the crowds **gathering to celebrate the Master**, and he imagined himself on the low board, wondering if his germinating faith would betray him. Then he worked his way closer to Jesus, looked on as the **miracles of the Lord swirled about him**, and he tried not to let the crowd see his fear of failure. Then, **in a surge of confidence**, the leper knelt before Jesus and asked, "Lord, if you will."

The leper took a giant leap of faith, and he **received what he asked for of Jesus**. That's what God wants from us. When we practice our faith in the little things, we'll be able to **step out boldly in the big ones**.

Faith flows from God, but the first step comes from us.

November 15 – **God's Cooling Touch**

GOT A FEVER? **A damp cloth will help you feel better.** Have you run a hard race? **A splash of water will refresh your skin.** Is the sun bearing down on you? How about that air conditioner? **It feels good, doesn't it?**

When things begin to heat up, we look for ways to **ease the situation**. What about when things heat up in our finances? In our relationships? On our job? How about with the neighbor next door that harasses us constantly? We are hot under the collar because they won't leave us alone.

How can we cool down from that? Proverbs 3:25-26 gives us a cooling touch from God. "Do not be afraid of sudden terror or of the ruin of the wicked, when it comes, for the Lord will be your confidence and will keep your foot from being caught." When bad things happen around us, God says **he has our back** in two ways.

First, he will be our confidence. We are to take heart in the promises of God. We are to stand on his Word, take charge of our trepidation, and forge ahead into the Lord's work. We can't let our faith in the Father be shaken by what's happening around us.

Second, he will keep our feet from being caught. The mess in the world won't stain us. Their financial disasters? Bah, God's got it

252

covered. Are they being caught up in missteps and bad judgment calls? That's on their record, not ours.

God says we are to exude confidence, for we will move on past the circumstance tripping up others. When worry comes our way, God's cooling touch will reassure us that we will excel in God, for he is with us all the way.

We have no fear of failure when our faith is in God.

November 16 – Take No Thought of Your Troubles

WHAT'S GOT you down? Your kids? Are they acting out again? **Or is it your job?** Your boss has cut your hours, and you **don't know how you'll make it up?** Or maybe your car … or your washing machine needs repair … **how are you going to afford that?**

God, aren't you listening? Your children need help down here.

God smiles in his gracious goodness, and he puts his arm around us and whispers to us, **"Don't worry on these things. I know about every situation you are facing."**

Matthew 6:31-32 says: "Therefore do not be anxious, saying, 'What shall we eat?' or 'What shall we drink?' or 'What shall we wear?' For the Gentiles seek after all these things, and your heavenly Father knows that you need them all."

This passage covers three promises from God.

1. "What shall we eat?" God owns the wheat and the corn and every good provision. **He will not skimp on you.** 2. "What shall we drink?" Every river and water source are God's. **He offers you the living water.** 3. "What shall we wear?" Every plant and animal that produces clothing is God's gift to us. **He desires that no one goes without.**

These are things we all deal with. Maintaining the things that keep us functioning. **Putting food on the table.** Keeping our kids clothed. We can't ignore them. God is telling us that these are not to consume our thoughts. They will work themselves out. They will. *Just give God a chance.* He knows our needs and will meet every one. God wants our trust, for he desires to take care of us.

November 17 – 10 Ways We Overcome the World

LIFE IS A battle. Sometimes it seems to the death. How can we be *successful in Christ* when we can't even get out of bed in the morning? Romans 8:38-39 gives us **10 Ways We Overcome the World.** "For I am sure that neither death nor life, nor angels nor rulers, nor things present nor things to come, nor powers, nor height nor depth, nor anything else in all creation, will be able to separate us from the love of God in Christ Jesus our Lord."

Death has no power over us. *We will rise to live with him.*

Life cannot beat us down. *We have the power of God in our strong right arm.*

Angels are not our masters. *Even they are subservient to God.*

Rulers cannot dictate to us. *Our spiritual destiny flows from heaven.*

Our **present circumstances** are of no consequence. *God has defeated the trials we face.*

Nothing in the **future** can harm us. *We walk in the footsteps of Jesus.*

Karma doesn't affect us. *Our days are mapped out by the holy Father.*

Neither the **heights** of success nor the **depths** of failure tell who we are in Christ. *We have a conquering Lord who rescues us in all situations.*

Nothing, nothing, nothing in creation can drive a wedge in between us and our Lord who came to offer us salvation on the cross. Jesus didn't come so that we could live a life of defeat, not spiritually, not physically, not economically, and *not in our relationships with others*. Through Christ, we have overcome the world. Let's live like it today.

November 18 – **God's Promise of a Long Life**

GOD'S PROMISES come with conditions. I know we don't like to hear that. We want his cornucopia to open in the sky and **pour out good things on us**. A new car? **It floats down on a parachute, payment free**. A charming spouse? **Landing at our side as we speak**. Fat bank accounts? It's like a paint gun, **filling our balance sheet with green, green, green**.

Why should we have to do anything? **Doesn't God love us?**

That's hardly the point. **We must accept the responsibility God puts on us.** We have a part to play **if we want God's promises to manifest in our life. Here are four promises God makes to us of a long life.**

Isaiah 46:4 says our Lord is our keeper **even to our twilight years**. "Even to your old age I am he, and to gray hairs I will carry you. I have made, and I will bear; I will carry and will save."

254

Job 12:12-13 tells us God gives us wisdom **as we advance in years**. "Wisdom is with the aged, and understanding in length of days. With God are wisdom and might; he has counsel and understanding."

Proverbs 20:29 assures us age carries its own beauty and **is a treasure**. "The glory of young men is their strength, but the splendor of old men is their gray hair."

Deuteronomy 6:2 promises that if we keep God's laws, **he will add to our days**, giving us a long life. "That you may fear the Lord your God, you and your son and your son's son, by keeping all his statutes and his commandments, which I command you, all the days of your life, and that your days may be long."

How do we know what God expects of us? It's in our instruction manual. It's **in the Bible**, in black and white, there for us to study anytime and anyplace.

When we work for God's promises, he comes through every time.

November 19 – **Our Hope Comes Through God**

THE WORLD shatters our illusions. Train bombings. School shootings. **People who kick their dogs without justification. What are we coming to?** Then we read of melting glaciers, disappearing sea ice, and we have **repeated heat waves that cover half the globe**. Thousands die, and we wonder if *this is the way the world ends*.

God says to keep our hope in him. No matter what transpires, what we read in the newspaper or see on the television, **God still sits on the throne of heaven**. Psalm 42:11 shouts his glory. "Why are you cast down, O my soul, and why are you in turmoil within me? Hope in God; for I shall again praise him, my salvation and my God."

Train bombings are horrific. Why would anyone do that? Even so, **God is mighty, and he reigns forever**. School shootings. Despicable. Yet even through the horror, **the love of the Father is undiminished**. Those who mistreat the less powerful are misfits that don't fit in God's plan. Still, **we can find solace in our God**.

Our changing world? Will the end come through climate change? That story is unwritten. What we do know is that **God controls tomorrow**, and we are *held securely in his hand*. This verse tells us to have hope in God. Quit worrying about the news. Stuff will happen. Bad things will continue, but **we mustn't become**

despondent. God is our victory, and in him, we will see a brighter tomorrow.

November 20 – **Your Brand-New Day**

WIPE THE SLATE clean. That's what we're to do with old hurts and failures. **They are in the past.** We are to cast them off and begin afresh, even should we stumble again. It's how we move from the darkness of depression and despair **into the fresh light of another day.**

Let's read about the first time that light banished the darkness in Genesis 1:1-6. "In the beginning, God created the heavens and the earth. The earth was without form and void, and darkness was over the face of the deep. And the Spirit of God was hovering over the face of the waters. And God said, 'Let there be light,' and there was light. And God saw that the light was good. And God separated the light from the darkness. God called the light Day, and the darkness he called Night. And there was evening and there was morning, the first day."

It's important to see how strongly this connects to our human condition and our despair at our old hurts and muck-ups. God hovered over a dark world without form. There was nothing redeeming about the earth. It was a useless failure of a place. **God saw more.** He knew the possibilities that existed in his rough and unformed creation. God changed everything with his words, **"Let there be *light.* "**

He does the same in our lives. He changes everything with a word, **bringing new purpose and direction into our darkness**. God knew light and darkness couldn't co-exist, and he separated them. We need to take that and separate ourselves from our failures and look forward to our success in God.

Today is your brand-new day. God says you are no longer who you used to be. He has instilled the light of Christ into you, and **you will shine brighter than ever before**. When God is your guide, the darkness is banished in the light of your journey with Jesus.

November 21 – **Three Steps to Our Release in Jesus**

PENANCE. It's a punishment for what we've done. Taking it on the chin. **Paying our dues.** Name it what you will, we're stepping up and **accepting the responsibility for our actions**. Especially our bad ones.

256

God says that's unnecessary. We don't need to beat ourselves up. **We have a forgiving Father in heaven who came up with a better plan:** *Jesus.* John 3:18 tells us: "Whoever believes in him is not condemned, but whoever does not believe is condemned already, because he has not believed in the name of the only Son of God."

The **dividing line between freedom and penance** is our faith in Jesus.

Ask yourself this: Who is not condemned? Who no longer has to take it on the chin? Who can toss the dues for our wicked deeds out the window and have a fresh start? **Whosoever believes in Jesus.** It's a simple thing, an easy move. Easy-smeasy, we might say. We have **Three Steps to Our Release in Jesus**.

1. *Believe.* We must believe that Jesus is truly the Son of God who lived and was raised from the dead.

2. *Accept.* We must give Jesus control over the course of our life. We choose to model our actions after his.

3. *Receive.* We must let the power of Jesus flow through us so that we become the hand of God to everyone around us.

God's not standing in the sky ready to beat us over the head. We can choose a higher path. **We can decide to walk hand-in-hand with Jesus from this point on**. We choose the course of our life, and our best choice is Jesus.

November 22 – You Are God's Favored Child

SO WHAT, if life's not going your way? You are **God's favored child**, even when you struggle with life. A tornado crashed through your living room? Hail battered your car? **It doesn't matter.** You are **God's favored child** even in the storm.

You ask for proof? Let's look to the story of Noah for proof that **you are God's favored child.** Genesis 6:5-8 reveals how you can be God's favored child even in a challenged life. "The Lord saw that the wickedness of man was great in the earth, and that every intention of the thoughts of his heart was only evil continually. And the Lord regretted that he had made man on the earth, and it grieved him to his heart. So the Lord said, 'I will blot out man whom I have created from the face of the land, man and animals and creeping things and birds of the heavens, for I am sorry that I have made them.' But Noah found favor in the eyes of the Lord."

Things weren't going well in Noah's world. **Even so, Noah was God's favored child.** Men were wicked and doing terrible things to

257

each other. **Noah was still God's favored child.** God desired to wipe every creature and thing from the earth, and yet, **Noah remained God's favored child.**

Here's what we must take from Noah's story. Being God's favored child didn't give Noah a life of ease and high standing among his neighbors. God didn't gift him with the biggest house in the subdivision or the slickest car. Instead, God said to Noah, "You are my favored child, so I want you to spend 100 years doing backbreaking work building me a useless boat, even though it's never rained before."

Is that how we feel sometimes? We're God's children, and we get all the dirty jobs? You can take heart that **at the end of your troubles you will find success.** Noah saved his family, and the world began anew, all because Noah was God's favored child. **You will survive the storms of life while comforted by God's presence along the way because *you are God's favored child.***

God becomes our joy as we set to work for him.

November 23 – **4 Opportunities for Wisdom**

WE ALL KNOW the highly educated uncle who can tell us anything about anything but **can't make a good decision** to save his life. Or the recent divorcee with a college degree who remarries on the rebound to someone **worse than the original.**

Then there's the people who invest money **without doing their homework**, yet they don't understand why all the money is lost like water in a sieve. It seems the train's left the station, and they weren't on board.

Wisdom is different than learning. Anyone can open a book or join an online study group. To look at two choices in a situation and select the correct one, well, that's something we only get from **making a few mistakes** along the way. Here are *4 Opportunities for Wisdom* to help jumpstart your journey to a better future.

James 1:5 tells us to **look to God for wisdom.** "If any of you lacks wisdom, let him ask God, who gives generously to all without reproach, and it will be given him."

Isaiah 2:3 promises God will instruct us in **how to make good choices.** "… That he may teach us his ways and that we may walk in his paths."

Psalm 32:8 is our assurance **God's hand will guide us** in making the right choices. "I will instruct you and teach you in the way you should go; I will counsel you with my eye upon you."

Ecclesiastes 2:26 says our wisdom is **accompanied by knowledge and joy**. "For to the one who pleases him God has given wisdom and knowledge and joy …"

C'mon now, let's jump on the wisdom train. It's leaving the station. God is the conductor, and you are welcome aboard.

November 24 – Focusing on What Matters

SNAP A PHOTO with your phone, and the camera inside will take an acceptable picture. You'll **occasionally get a good one**, while from time to time you can expect to **delete your image and retry the shot**. Some of the most interesting snaps you can take are when you move the phone **right up next to something** small and force the lens to **choose the center of focus**.

See, it can't focus on everything. **It's impossible.** The object is too close. **Something will be out of focus, and *that's what makes the picture extraordinary*.** The item in focus will jump out of the image, **impossibly beautiful,** and people will ooh and ahh over your skills.

2 Chronicles 15:2 gives us a marker for our focus. "… The Lord is with you while you are with him. If you seek him, he will be found by you, but if you forsake him, he will forsake you."

What is your life lens focused on? From a distance, the picture might look pretty good, but just like with your phone, when we get close, **only one thing will remain sharp and clear**. What's important to us will jump out, and everything else will be out of focus.

Is your focus God **or time spent at the lake?** Your family **or your business associates?** Your church **or a new investment opportunity?** Anyone who looks closely enough will be able to tell. You can't hide it.

A brilliant photographer puts the most important things in the center of his shot. We are brilliant when we put God in the center of our lives. Get close to God, and everything else will fade into the background.

November 25 – The Jesus Job Description

WHEN WE APPLY for a job, it's helpful to know what's expected of us. It's called **our Job Description**. It's what we will be doing if we're hired. Maybe we don't want to keep the coffee pot filled. If it's in **our job description**, we'd better be prepared to **fill the coffee pot**

if we choose to accept the job.

The hardest jobs are those with no job description. We can be asked to do anything, and if we're on our own, we must create our own schedule, whatever that may be. Who knows if we're even following company policy? Things become a mess and deteriorate from there.

What job description do we have as Christians? What's our role for Christ? Where do we fit in the Master's plans for establishing the work of Jesus on this earth? Perhaps Jesus' job description will help us understand.

Matthew 1:21 puts **salvation in his job description**. "She will bear a son, and you shall call his name Jesus, for he will save his people from their sins."

Acts 13:38 says he was required to **spread the message of forgiveness**. "Let it be known to you therefore, brothers, that through this man forgiveness of sins is proclaimed to you."

Galatians 1:4 tells us he will **deliver us from the bad things** surrounding us. "Who gave himself for our sins to deliver us from the present evil age, according to the will of our God and Father."

1 John 2:1-2 touts him as an Atlas, **bearing our sins to the throne** of the Father in Heaven. "My little children, I am writing these things to you so that you may not sin. But if anyone does sin, we have an advocate with the Father, Jesus Christ the righteous. He is the propitiation for our sins, and not for ours only but also for the sins of the whole world."

Which of these job descriptions are we expected to take on? The Word says we are to be like Christ in Ephesian 5:1-2. How can we be like him if we don't **assume his responsibilities** from his time on the earth?

Our job is to be like Jesus in every way, fashion, and form.

November 26 – Stepping Onto Air

A HOT AIR BALLOON ride can be invigorating, with the beauty of the earth spread below us … **so long as we have a competent pilot onboard.** No one wants to be rudderless. To be cast adrift is frightening. Yet, what happens when the guywires are severed, and we float free from our mooring, with no one to guide us? **How will we find our way home? Can we escape our desperate situation?** Where's our rock, our firm foundation, to be found when there's nothing real around us?

Is our faith in Christ a tangible rescue line? Is God even there? Here are five verses to support you in your quandary, to lift you closer to the Savior, and to **be your firm footing** when you step out in faith to follow the Master.

John 3:16 tells of **Jesus' total commitment to us**. "For God so loved the world, that he gave his only Son, that whoever believes in him should not perish but have eternal life."

Acts 10:43 says he is **true to his word**. "To him all the prophets bear witness that everyone who believes in him receives forgiveness of sins through his name."

Romans 9:33 is our assurance of **Christ's eternal nature**. "Behold, I am laying in Zion a stone of stumbling, and a rock of offense; and whoever believes in him will not be put to shame."

John 1:12 promises **no one is excluded**. "But to all who did receive him, who believed in his name, he gave the right to become children of God."

Mark 9:23 tells us **how simple our rescue is**. "And Jesus said to him, … All things are possible for one who believes."

We don't have to worry about our situation. When we step outside our disaster, Jesus is **our steppingstone, our foundation, and our emotional and spiritual support**. He's there for us, and **we can place our faith in him**.

Jesus will never fail us. We are secure in him.

November 27 – The Worth of Our Soul

THE VALUE of things is in what we will trade for them. In the summer of 2019, the newest mid-engine Corvette debuted on the world stage with a **promised price tag of under $60,000**. That's **far above the price most people can afford** for a car but well below the price of **other sports cars with comparable stats**. A week later, Chevrolet reported its proposed first year run for the 2020 Vette **was already pre-ordered**. The last redesign in 2014 **produced 35,000 cars** during its first build year.

Ford's GT is a sports car that lands squarely in the super-car lineup. It's priced **over $500,000**. Yet Ford has already increased its production numbers, and that's just for cars **already designated for specific buyers**. The public won't have an opportunity to purchase until well in the future.

How valuable are we? **What's our worth?** What are we willing to trade to **move ourselves into the next level?** Matthew 16:24-26 tells **three things it will cost us if we truly want to follow Jesus**. "Then Jesus told his disciples, 'If anyone would come after me, let him deny himself and take up his cross and follow me. For whoever would save his life will lose it, but whoever loses his life for my sake will find it. For what will it profit a man if he gains the whole world and forfeits his soul? Or what shall a man give in return for his soul?' " To bring this into sharp relief, let's lay out the price Jesus gives us.

Our 1st Cost: **We must deny ourselves.** Jesus is saying we can't come first. Our wants and desires can't take precedence over the promptings of the Holy Spirit. *Our 2nd Cost:* **We must take up the cross of Jesus.** What did Jesus accept as the price of his divinity while he walked among us? He was taunted, ridiculed, and misunderstood, yet he continually shared the message of salvation. *Our 3rd Cost:* **We are to follow Christ.** We are to model our lives after his. Be kind. Go out of our way to help others. Refuse to retaliate. Treat others as we would wish to be treated.

That's it. ***That's the price we pay for our soul***. One, two, three, Jesus summed it up. Jesus is our example. Our lives must emulate his.

November 28 – **2 Words in Our Trouble**

HAS THE MORTGAGE company sent you a late notice **again?** Is your pantry filled with empty shelves? Is your best shirt **threadbare at the elbows?** Has every job interview this week been a dud?

Trouble stalks us every day. We can't avoid it. **Even those of us who appear successful from the outside struggle with things that can bring us down.** The Bible gives us **2 Words in Our Trouble** to get us to the other side.

Psalm 138:7 tells us: "Though I walk in the midst of trouble, you preserve my life; you stretch out your hand against the wrath of my enemies, and your right hand delivers me."

Psalm 18:2 says: "The Lord is my rock and my fortress and my deliverer, my God, my rock, in whom I take refuge, my shield, and the horn of my salvation, my stronghold."

Being alive means we will have things go wrong. Several years ago, after the death of Aaron Spelling (one of the wealthiest men in the entertainment field), his wife inherited his estate. She lived alone in Spelling Manor, a 56,000 square foot home on nearly 5 acres. She put it on the market, telling woes of the upkeep. At the time, multiple air conditioning units were on the blink, and she was having to arrange repairment for the lot. That seems small change when your pantry is empty, true, but **having money doesn't mean we lead a trouble-free life. Without God, even great wealth can lead us astray.** Jeffrey Epstein went from underpaid private school teacher to billionaire financier, and he spent the final months of his life under a dark cloud of misbehavior and criminal activity.

Whatever we have, we can **find our trust in God**. He is our strength, our strong right arm, and our tower of safety. He is better than wealth and more treasured than gold. God is our source of life, and our assurance flows from his throne.

November 29 – No More Fear of Death

A VIDEO SURFACED on the Internet recently. A puppy is afraid to descend a set of stairs. His owner gets down on all fours and shows the puppy how to place its paws on one step at a time and find a place of safety before moving to the next step. The puppy has to be rescued a few times from tumbling, but with patience and examples, the man builds the puppy's confidence. By the time they reach the bottom of the stairs, the puppy no longer needs the man at its side. **It runs joyfully down the final steps**.

That's us and Jesus. We're afraid of the future. It seems too daunting to imagine, and we think we'll come to a bad end. Yet Jesus says, **"Look. I've been there. I returned. You can cross over, and I'll be waiting for you on the other side."** Let's read of it in Hebrews 2:14-15: "Since therefore the children share in flesh and blood, he himself likewise partook of the same things, that through death he might destroy the one who has the power of death, that is, the devil, and deliver all those who through fear of death were subject to lifelong slavery."

Read this part again: **"... that through death he might destroy the one who has the power of death ..."** That's something to shout about. *Jesus died on the cross to destroy the one who has the power of death*. Who might that be? Read it and shout: **"... that is, the devil ..."**

The fear of death had us enslaved. **Jesus set us free**. We are the puppy. We lived in fear for a time, but no longer. When death approaches, we've reached the final few steps to glory, and it's time for us to **leap forward and run into the Master's arms**. The staircase of life is our duty and reaching the end is our goal. Let's rejoice

263

in the days we are given without the fear of death at the end. Jesus is our Lord, and he has already traversed the great divide.

November 30 – **Rooted in the Lord**

GARDENS ARE teaching paradises. The lessons we learn from planting and reaping are far-reaching, yet they are as **immediate as the soil under our fingernails**. It doesn't matter if our garden encompasses a dozen acres or if it's two clay pots on our apartment balcony. The lessons are the same.

What we plant first disappears into the soil. It's gone, invisible, as if wasted. Even so, we must still attend to it or it's lost forever. We must **till, water, fertilize as if it's already green and growing**. If we throw up our hands and say, "What's the use in this? I don't see any results," we've given up too soon.

It's exciting when **the seedling breaks the soil**, but that's just the beginning. We must **foster its growth**, water just enough to wet the soil, and not over fertilize. It's easy to lose our new plant at this stage. **It can be months before we reap our harvest.** Whether flowers, nuts, or fruit, *our results come only after the plant matures*.

James 5:7-8 tells us: "Be patient, therefore, brothers, until the coming of the Lord. See how the farmer waits for the precious fruit of the earth, being patient about it, until it receives the early and the late rains. You also, be patient. Establish your hearts, for the coming of the Lord is at hand."

God understands planting and harvest. He sees that same process in us. We don't become a Christian one day and a mighty warrior the next. *We must be allowed the opportunity to mature in him.* **God's promises to us are the same.** Our answer is brought about through the natural processes of **planting, nurturing, and maturing**.

Let's remain rooted in the Lord. Our harvest is on the way.

— December —

December 1 – Our Satisfaction Is Found in God

WHAT DOES IT take to make us happy? That question sets our mind to running. We imagine a large home, perhaps with a gourmet kitchen and an inviting pool. We need a car that fits our new status, and travel? Absolutely. We want to see everything – in the best of accommodations, of course. And if we pull up to a stoplight in our status car, and the one at our side is even better, suddenly **ours loses much of its charm** …

God says to chill. *Quit sucking on our envy candy.* That doesn't reflect how he wishes us to live. Deuteronomy 5:21 gives us clear instructions: "And you shall not covet your neighbor's wife. And you shall not desire your neighbor's house, his field, or his male servant, or his female servant, his ox, or his donkey, or anything that is your neighbor's."

Yes, this verse means exactly what it says. Ownership is ownership. What's not ours **is not ours**, and we can't take it, **not even in our thoughts**. **The intent behind this verse, however, is a deep well of meaning.** If our satisfaction in life is in our elite home, our shiny automobile, and the exotic places we've been, we're *missing God's mark*.

Our satisfaction must be found in God.

Here are **three things to think about**: Which means more to you, prayer time in the morning **or getting in your early morning jog?** How do you spend your vacation time, on a mission trip or **fishing at the lake?** When the offering plate comes around, do you think first of funding the church or whether you have enough left for **an afternoon at the mall?**

"Do not covet" sounds much the same in God's ears as "be satisfied in me." Let's turn loose of the world and hold tightly to Jesus our Lord.

December 2 – The Enemy Is Defeated

SO, THE CAT got your tongue? You feel you can't **speak your faith?** The world is hovering over you, and <u>the dark clouds threaten to overwhelm you?</u>

Stop thinking that way! God is your salvation. <u>He is your</u>

rescue. He has defeated the enemy, and you are a victor in him. What do you think the cross was all about? Did Jesus lose the battle with the evil one? **Absolutely not!**

Here are four verses to **lift your spirits**, to get you **supercharged**, and to **reestablish your overcoming life** through Christ your Savior.

Deuteronomy 28:7 says: "The Lord will cause your enemies who rise against you to be defeated before you. They shall come out against you one way and flee before you seven ways."

Psalm 27:5-6 tells us: "For he will hide me in his shelter in the day of trouble; he will conceal me under the cover of his tent; he will lift me high upon a rock. And now my head shall be lifted up above my enemies all around me, and I will offer in his tent sacrifices with shouts of joy; I will sing and make melody to the Lord."

Luke 18:17 promises: "Truly, I say to you, whoever does not receive the kingdom of God like a child shall not enter it."

Isaiah 54:17 assures us: "No weapon that is fashioned against you shall succeed, and you shall refute every tongue that rises against you in judgment. This is the heritage of the servants of the Lord and their vindication from me, declares the Lord."

It's time for you to **act like the warrior you are**. Jesus is your champion. God is your shield. The Word is your sword. The Holy Spirit has you covered on every side. **Defeat isn't in your vocabulary when you march forward with Jesus at your side.**

Lift a cheer of victory, for in the Lord, it's already yours.

December 3 – In the Heart of the Sea

SEVERAL YEARS AGO, a man was seen on the side of the road next to his wrecked station wagon. Clearly the old car had seen better days before it crashed and died. The man sat on the curb and laughed every time he looked at his car.

Surely, **he had good insurance**, you might say. He would soon have a nicer car, and his life would start an **uphill trend to better days**. "I don't carry insurance," the man said, "**not to repair my car**. I've never been able to afford it." The crowd asked why he was laughing. His reply? To keep from crying because his life was so bad.

God has a strong arm, and his mighty power can reach out to save us no matter how bad things get. **We needn't fear the bad things that come our way when we place our trust in him.** Psalm

46:1-2 tells us: "God is our refuge and strength, a very present help in trouble. Therefore we will not fear though the earth gives way, though the mountains be moved into the heart of the sea."

This passage tells us **God is a present help**. Not a future help or a shine in someone's eye. He's here **now, today, in the moment** we need him. We may experience a car wreck, or our investments might go sour. It doesn't matter. Our salvation doesn't **rest on things or money**. Reread that verse. **Though the earth be removed … though the mountains be carried into the midst of the sea**. You can't get any more catastrophic than that, and still, **God is with us, our refuge in trouble**, *our strength when we are weak*, and our light in the midst of the storm.

God cares for us. The worst the world can do is as a gnat to our magnificent God.

December 4 – 4 Helps When You Are Angry

WE PICTURE the perfect Christian as soft-spoken and always willing to turn the other cheek. That's our goal, yes, but it's **not how we're hardwired**. Our propensity for anger is a **survival mechanism**. It ramps up our bodily systems, floods us with adrenalin, and magnifies our "fight or flight" ability.

We can be bolder, punch harder, and run farther when our flash of anger emboldens us.

So, what are the benefits of **not** getting angry? How does a cool head help us out? What better decisions can we make when we can **set our anger aside** and function in a **calm and benevolent** manner? *Is it even possible to set our anger aside?*

Here are *4 Helps When You Are Angry:*

Help No. 1: Proverbs 15:1 says we can help other people **keep their calm** when we control our anger. "A soft answer turns away wrath, but a harsh word stirs up anger."

Help No. 2: Colossians 3:21 tells us we will **encourage our children** when our anger remains on the back burner. "Fathers, do not provoke your children, lest they become discouraged."

Help No. 3: Ephesians 4:26 assures us we can feel anger and **remain in control** of our responses. "Be angry and do not sin; do not let the sun go down on your anger."

Help No. 4: Matthew 5:22 says we **keep ourselves safe** when we dodge unjustified hard feelings. "But I say to you that everyone who is angry with his brother will be liable to judgment; whoever insults his brother will be liable to the council; and whoever says, 'You fool!' will be liable to the hell of fire."

We may be hardwired for anger, but **that doesn't dictate how we behave**. God also enables us with **good judgment and self-control**.

To choose Christ means to walk a better path. When we turn the other cheek, we become more like Jesus.

December 5 – **The Mystery of Forever**

THERE IS NO afterlife. **Have you heard that one before?** Lots of people think it. Martin Hughes, writing on Breaker Barrier, his blog, says he wishes there was a heaven after death. **The Bible says his wish has been granted.** Let's look at 1 Corinthians 15:51-54.

Verse 51 tells us the afterlife is **nothing like our life on earth. We will be changed into a new creature.** "Behold! I tell you a mystery. We shall not all sleep, but we shall all be changed."

Verse 52 assures us **we will be imperishable. We will live on and on in our new and perfect form.** "In a moment, in the twinkling of an eye, at the last trumpet. For the trumpet will sound, and the dead will be raised imperishable, and we shall be changed."

Verse 53 says the event of **death is simply the start** of our transition to **our journey to forever**. "For this perishable body must put on the imperishable, and this mortal body must put on immortality."

Verse 54 assures us **death isn't the end. It's only the beginning.** "When the perishable puts on the imperishable, and the mortal puts on immortality, then shall come to pass the saying that is written: 'Death is swallowed up in victory.' "

So, come on, Martin Hughes, join in the throng that will **soon be rejoicing before the King. We will lift our hands and shout.** We hope to see you there. Our journey to forever is already mapped out in God's atlas. <u>We call it the Bible, and our path is plain to see.</u>

There are no mysteries when we trust in the Word of God.

December 6 – **Our Fine Suit of Clay**

CLOTHING MAKES the man. Or the woman. Even children fall into this axiom. As well as athletes, explorers, and religious leaders. **What we wear affects how the world views us.** If we dress as a success, those around us will see us in a positive light, and they will react to us accordingly. If we need a loan, the banker will find it easier to approve our funds. Shop for a car, and we will gain the salesman's respect.

There's one small point of conflict with wearing fancy clothes. We must make sure they are not polished with pride.

When automakers design a new car, one step is to form a clay model. They shape it, shaving off extra and adding where necessary. They cover it with a beautiful finish, and to walk around it, it looks like the real thing. Scratch the surface, however, and the truth comes out. The car is no more than a creation of clay and useless for driving around town.

Pride does that to us. We think we are beautiful, dolled up in the finest attire. Just underneath we are clay, formed by our own hand, and not much good for anything at all. Let's read Job's cry to God in Job 40:12. "Look on everyone who is proud and bring him low and tread down the wicked where they stand."

We must dress in humility and longsuffering. Concern for those less fortunate than ourselves must be our dress code. Let's leave pride in the closet. It's no more than a suit of clay, with the appearance of excellence, but with no usefulness to be found. God is our source of success, and in him, we are dressed well, indeed.

December 7 – 3 Proofs of Our Trust in God

VISIT THE POUND someday. Check out the abandoned dogs. They don't trust anyone. The people who've loved them have cast them aside, and they only have steel and concrete walls for companionship. Adopt one, and you must build a relationship. It takes time. They must learn to trust you. You hold out your hand. Are you going to strike them? Will the food bowl be refilled … ever? Is your exit to work the last time they will see you?

How do you tell when your new pet has shifted from doubt into trust? Asking for a tummy rub? Not gobbling food? Asking to go outside in the middle of the night?

Psalm 37:3-5 gives us three ways God will know we've learned to put our trust in him.

Verse 3 says we must see God as our source for our daily requirements. "Trust in the Lord, and do good; dwell in the land and befriend faithfulness." When we do, God will provide all our needs.

Verse 4 says to find our pleasure in God rather than the world. "Delight yourself in the Lord, and he will give you the desires of your heart." When we do, God will *give us the extra things* we desire.

Verse 5 says to **live by God's standards** and not man's. "Commit your way to the Lord; trust in him, and he will act." When we do, our prayers **will become manifested** before us.

We are that abandoned pup. God has adopted us, but we must learn to trust him. He understands that it's not easy. God is patient. When we finally come around, he will find his joy in our complete trust in him.

God means us good. He's waiting to shower his love on us.

December 8 – **Three Times a . . . Christian?**

SEVERAL YEARS AGO, singer Lionel Richie crooned a sultry ballad that included the words, "Once, twice, three times a lady." The Shadows, Isaac Hayes, and Johnny Mathis performed the song in the 1980s, but the original version was released by the Commodores in 1978, with Richie singing lead, topping the charts for two weeks that August. The song also reached the top of the charts in Canada, the U.K., Ireland, Australia and New Zealand. **Richie's inspiration for the song was his mother**, when his father toasted her as **"a great lady, a great mother, and a great friend."**

Can people say that about us as Christians, that we exemplify the Lord in multiple ways? If the people we work with, ride the subway with, or see at church were asked, **could they come up with three things about us that define our walk with Jesus?** *Would we qualify to be three times a Christian?*

Matthew 25:35-36 says: "For I was hungry and you gave me food, I was thirsty and you gave me drink, I was a stranger and you welcomed me, I was naked and you clothed me, I was sick and you visited me, I was in prison and you came to me."

Which of these things is Jesus saying about us? As many as three … or four … or even five? **Let's make a list of ways we can be Christ-like to those around us.**

- Work at a food bank once a month.
- Volunteer to deliver meals in your community.
- Donate unused clothes to a shelter.
- Read to disadvantaged children at the local library.
- Spend an afternoon encouraging people at a hospice center.
- Join a prison ministry and show up regularly.

You can do this. Start with one. Master that and **see what else you can do**. Jesus will be your strength. Your reward will be *the joy you bring to those you help*.

The world needs Jesus, and they find him in us. Let's start showing Christ's love today.

December 9 – 6 Ways God Is the Best

GOOD, **BETTER**, *BEST*. That's a shopping mantra. **How much to you want to spend?** Your cash outlay determines the quality of the product you receive. Go for the cheap, and you get a poor product. Sometimes we must **invest a lot** to take home the best.

How much is God worth in your life? How much are you willing to pay? Maybe Sunday morning for a **good experience?** How about an hour of prayer **to get something better?** Or are you willing to go "all in" to get **the best experience from God** available?

Here's what we get when we sacrifice other things to live a life closely connected to the Father.

1 Samuel 15:29 reminds us **God is more than human**. "And also the Glory of Israel will not lie or have regret, for he is not a man, that he should have regret."

Psalm 119:160 illustrates his nature of **truth and righteousness**. "The sum of your word is truth, and every one of your righteous rules endures forever."

2 Corinthians 1:20 is our **call to worship** him. "For all the promises of God find their Yes in him. That is why it is through him that we utter our Amen to God for his glory."

Psalm 119:89-90 says the cosmos **cries out in God's favor**. "Forever, O Lord, your word is firmly fixed in the heavens. Your faithfulness endures to all generations; you have established the earth, and it stands fast."

Deuteronomy 7:9 places God **above every problem** we have. "Know therefore that the Lord your God is God, the faithful God who keeps covenant and steadfast love with those who love him and keep his commandments, to a thousand generations."

Psalm 89:34 gives us the promise that God will do **everything he has promised** us in his Word. "I will not violate my covenant or alter the word that went forth from my lips."

Is your wallet open? Your calendar available? Are you willing to **volunteer**, spend time **in the Word**, and dedicate yourself **to**

prayer? When you sacrifice to God, he is the best reward you can receive.

December 10 – 4 Times Joseph Stepped Up

THE BIBLICAL portrait of Joseph, the husband of Mary, seems to portray a man who is hardly there at all. He's there for a few verses in Matthew, returns for a short encore, and leaves the scene **as far as we can tell**.

Yet, we know there is more to Joseph's life than **playing the earthly father of Jesus**. Jesus grew up with **four brothers and two sisters**. Joseph faced the challenge of keeping his gang fed, clothed, and housed as they matured into adulthood. He probably negotiated a few of his sons' fisticuffs along the way, as well as ardent suitors for his daughters.

Much of that is supposition, but we have recorded **4 Times Joseph Stepped Up** in his duty as Mary's husband.

The 1st Time Joseph Stepped Up: Joseph refused to humiliate Mary when she became pregnant without his involvement. Matthew 1:19 says "he had in mind to divorce her quietly."

The 2nd Time Joseph Stepped Up: Joseph listened to another side of Mary's story. Matthew 1:20 says "an angel of the Lord appeared to him in a dream."

The 3rd Time Joseph Stepped Up: Joseph reconsidered his stand and took Mary for his wife. Matthew 1:24 says "he did what the angel of the Lord commanded."

The 4th Time Joseph Stepped Up: Joseph waited until after Jesus was born to ensure there was no question about his divinity. Matthew 1:24 says that "he did not consummate their marriage until she gave birth to a son."

The Bible may not give us much about Joseph, but that doesn't mean he played a small part in the life of Jesus. Joseph stepped up, and Jesus was vaulted into the annals of history as the greatest initiator of change ever born.

When we follow God, our role might well change the world.

December 11 – 4 Proverbs to Improve Your Standing with God

IT'S THE SANTA CLAUS thing. "You better be good, you better not cry. You better not pout, I'm telling you why …" We want on **Santa's good side** so we can **get the best presents**. See, Santa brings everyone gifts, but we only get the good ones if we're on our most excellent, Santa-inspired behavior. No one wants a lump of coal in their stocking when Christmas morning rolls around.

So, how do we get on God's good side? What does **being good** mean to God? **How do we "buck up" our attitude?** What does God **want?** Here are **4 Proverbs to Improve Your Standing with God.**

Our 1st Proverb: Proverbs 22:4 tells us that to put God's plans before ours and to accept his authority without question returns the blessing of a good life. "The reward for humility and fear of the Lord is riches and honor and life."

Our 2nd Proverb: Proverbs 3:34 says give our fellow travelers the benefit of the doubt. Don't criticize their behaviors when we don't know their situations. "Toward the scorners he is scornful, but to the humble he gives favor."

Our 3rd Proverb: Proverbs 15:33 requires us to show respect for God's position of power. We are wise when we give all credit and honor unto God. "The fear of the Lord is instruction in wisdom, and humility comes before honor."

Our 4th Proverb: Proverbs 29:23 insists we kick pride and arrogance out the window. Honor will find us as a reward for our humility. "One's pride will bring him low, but he who is lowly in spirit will obtain honor."

Our Christmas song tells us exactly what Santa requires from us. The Bible lays out God's expectations equally clearly. **When we** *follow God's rules***, he lifts us up to dwell with him.**

God's agenda is the only one that brings good results.

December 12 – **In Anticipation of the Savior**

IT'S NO SMALL thing to say **Jesus changed the world**. His presence, first as a small child and later as a martyr upon the cross, **impacted the world's view of religion** and **how we are to conduct ourselves** in relation to God and other people. Matthew 1:12 reveals the words that *opened the possibility of a Savior* to minister to a hurting and needy people. "She will bear a son, and you shall call his name Jesus, for he will save his people from their sins."

Mary wasn't the only one to **receive the word of an impending Savior**. Luke 2:8-9 tells us: "And in the same region there were shepherds out in the field, keeping watch over their flock by night. And an angel of the Lord appeared to them, and the glory of the Lord shone around them, and they were filled with great fear."

Matthew 2:1-2 gives us three additional worshippers who **felt**

the drawing spirit of an upcoming heavenly visitation. "Now after Jesus was born in Bethlehem of Judea in the days of Herod the king, behold, wise men from the east came to Jerusalem, saying, 'Where is he who has been born king of the Jews? For we saw his star when it rose and have come to worship him.' "

John 1:29 reveals Jesus in his magnificent purpose, the Son of God come to **cleanse the world of wrongdoing** and its consequences. "The next day he saw Jesus coming toward him, and said, 'Behold, the Lamb of God, who takes away the sin of the world!' "

We've seen the posters proclaiming that **Jesus Is the Reason for the Season**, and that's true. More importantly, **Jesus is the reason we can stand in purity and without shame before the Lord in heaven**. Christ is our redeemer, our salvation, and the uplifter of our days. When we **anticipate his presence** each day, we look forward to **the best heaven has to offer**. As David Jeremiah, Christian author and pastor says, **"All the Christmas presents in the world are worth nothing without the presence of Christ."**

Our life is found in Christ, and our days are better when lived in his glory.

December 13 – God's Heart Revealed

SOME PEOPLE say we can't see God. That's right. They tell us we have **no way to tell the intents** of an invisible being that doesn't bother making his presence known on the earth. They go so far as to say that God **doesn't concern himself with humanity**. We were created and sent on our way to figure out things as we go.

That's nonsense! If we want to know what God is like and how he operates, we need only **turn to the most iconic verse** in the Bible. John 3:16 tells us: "For God so loved the world, that he gave his only Son, that whoever believes in him should not perish but have eternal life."

We do well to celebrate Christ's birth with trees, ornaments, fine food, and many parties, but there's much more going on here. This verse reveals God in 4 distinct revelations.

Revelation No. 1: *God so loved the world.* We are God's creation. He treasures us as part of his divine plan. He *has not forgotten us*, not for one instant.

Revelation No. 2: *He gave his only Son.* There's nothing God would not trade for us, *even his most treasured possession*, Jesus. We are truly important to God.

Revelation No. 3: *Whoever believes should not perish.* God is not vengeful. He **doesn't desire anyone to suffer**. He offers us his outstretched hand, hoping we will come unto him.

Revelation No. 4: *We can have eternal life.* God desires our presence forever. He wants to spend time with us. He **looks forward to us joining him**, and his anticipation is undisguised.

Who are the people who call out God as a fist of anger ready to smite the wrongdoer? **Their claims are unfounded and without justification!** God desires to redeem those who have wandered from his will. The words of **Pope Paul VI give the undeniable connection** between God and man. **"We consider Christmas as the encounter, the great encounter, the historical encounter, the decisive encounter, between God and mankind. He who has faith knows this truly; let him rejoice."** Our call is to spread the Good News, yes, at Christmas, but at **every time of the year**.

Christ is the message. We are his ambassadors. Today is our day.

December 14 – A Christmas Revelation for the Entire Year

WE LOVE TO unpack Christmas sometime during fall. Traditionally, we mark Thanksgiving as the day to break out our decorations. The more excited we are, the earlier we string the lights on our tree. Some people even forgo Halloween to get in **yet a few more weeks** of Christmas cheer in their homes. That old song, **"Deck the Halls ..."** truly rings for them.

We are often equally quick to **pack up the holiday** come the end of December. We box up Christmas, pack it into the attic, and **get back to the business of living** for another year. **There's one thing we can't afford to pack away.** It's a vital part of the Christmas season, and it needs to be practiced **even after the tree disappears** from our living room.

Romans 12:10 sums up the Christmas message: "Love one another with brotherly affection. Outdo one another in showing honor."

Here are some ways we can carry our Christmas love with us after the lights are wound up, the ornaments are packed away, and we step into yet another year.

Matthew 2:10 says to **express joy at the good news of Christ**. "When they saw the star, they rejoiced exceedingly with great joy."

2 Corinthians 9:15 tells us to **put thankfulness high on our list**. "Thanks be to God for his inexpressible gift!"

275

Luke 1:37 says to **raise our expectations** when we ask anything of God. "For nothing will be impossible with God."

Mother Teresa said it in the most elegant way: "It is Christmas every time you let God love others through you ... yes, it is Christmas every time you smile at your brother and offer him your hand."

Let's let Christmas be evident in our actions every day of the year. *It can when we show love, care, and concern in each situation that comes our way.*

December 15 – **Our True Name in God**

THE CHRISTMAS SEASON is a time for new beginnings. If we believe the Hallmark Channel, we need to reevaluate who we've become and the people who populate our lives and make sure we haven't veered from our core values.

We need to ensure the **name and the image** we've created for ourselves is **the way we want to be known** from here on out. Our friends and associates might call us Shawn, Beatrice, or Lucy, but how do they see us? **Who are we really in their eyes?**

The holiday season is about looking in our mirror and discovering how others see us. That's our real name: **friend, companion, or dependable worker**.

We become better when we are honest about who we are.

Matthew 1:23 gives the **true name of Jesus**. "Behold, the virgin shall conceive and bear a son, and they shall call his name Immanuel which means, God with us." We've seen the manger scenes and attended more Christmas plays than we can recount. We might even have a baby Jesus perched under our tree or on the mantle. "How sweet," we remark, when we see the iconic Christmas image in advertisements or store windows. **It's so cute our heart melts.** Here's the thing. **Jesus is not that baby's real name.**

Wha—!?! Of course, it is! Where is this teaching going?

Let's look at that verse again. **They shall call his name Immanuel which means, God with us.** That little baby in the manger? He is **God With Us.** That's his name. We can call him Jesus, Christ, or Lord, but it all means the same thing. Jesus arrived in that manger, and **God was with humanity** ... in the flesh ... and in real time.

Ann Voskamp, Christian author, says this: "So God throws open the door of this world—and enters as a baby. As the most vulnerable imaginable. Because He wants unimaginable intimacy with you. What religion ever had a god that wanted such intimacy with us that He came with such vulnerability to us? What God ever came so tender we could touch Him? So fragile that we could break Him? So vulnerable that His bare, beating heart could be hurt? Only the One who loves you to death."

We are to be like Jesus. When we model ourselves after him, **we become the presence of God to those who interact with us**. We want people to say about us, **God is with us**. That's what being a Christian means. We get a new name, and it's the name of the Savior. When we take our Christian walk to heart, we become more and more like Christ.

December 16 – Are You Listening for God?

HOW'S YOUR Christmas season going? By that, how busy are you? **What's got your time tied up in knots?** Do you have parties planned every weekend, maybe a school play with your kids? Perhaps you are under pressure to get the house decorated. There's no way you can leave that undone.

Here's the thing it's easy to overlook: The holiday is all about Jesus. We know that iconic tagline: **Jesus Is the Reason for the Season**. The question is whether we practice it.

Let's see what **Max Lucado, Christian teacher and author**, has to say about Christmas and listening for God: "Off to one side sits a group of shepherds. They sit silently on the floor, perhaps perplexed, perhaps in awe, no doubt in amazement. Their night watch had been interrupted by an explosion of light from heaven and a symphony of angels. God goes to those who have time to hear him—and so on this cloudless night he went to simple shepherds."

One sentence from this passage jumps out. *God goes to those who have time to hear him.* John 16:33 reflects this truth at us. "I have said these things to you, that in me you may have peace. In the world you will have tribulation. But take heart; I have overcome the world."

Jesus is **talking to us today**. He's telling us **we can have his peace**. Note what this verse doesn't say. Jesus doesn't promise to remove our troubles. He promises us **peace as we endure them**. How can he offer us peace? What qualifies him to settle our souls and even out our bumpy ride through life? Those words are there also. **Jesus has overcome the world by his sinless life and**

sacrificial death on the cross.

When we listen for Jesus, he will whisper his words of encouragement in our ear.

December 17 – **A Christmas Blessing**

CHRISTMAS CARDS are wonderful sources of inspiration. We feel the **warmth and reassurance of familial love** with each one we read. Open that glitter-painted red-and-green card, and the words inside **might sound something like this:** "May you feel God's presence in the candles, that softly spread their glow at Christmas, and may you experience the wonder of His abiding love, as He guides you, through each day of the coming year. May God's Blessings be with you. At Christmas and New Year!"

Here's how **Christian recording artist Amy Grant** says it:

"Faith is salted and peppered through everything at Christmas. And I love at least one night by the Christmas tree to sing and feel the quiet holiness of that time that's set apart to celebrate love, friendship, and God's gift of the Christ child."

Corrie Ten Boom, Holocaust survivor, tells us:

"Who can add to Christmas? The perfect motive is that God so loved the world. The perfect gift is that He gave His only Son. The only requirement is to believe in Him. The reward of faith is that you shall have everlasting life."

John 1:4-5 says:

"In him was life, and the life was the light of men. The light shines in the darkness, and the darkness has not overcome it."

Lucinda Franks is a Pulitzer Prize-winning journalist. Her turn of words gives us a picture of that night so long ago that crystalizes the beauty of God-come-to-earth in the embodiment of Jesus:

"Christmas in Bethlehem. The ancient dream: a cold, clear night made brilliant by a glorious star, the smell of incense, shepherds and wise men falling to their knees in adoration of the sweet baby, the incarnation of perfect love."

The incarnation of perfect love. That's Jesus. That's the *Reason for the Season.* That's **Christmastime**. Let's make Christmas last all year long. It's the love of the season that carries us through, and it's Jesus who revealed how to truly love one another.

We are the love of Christ when we offer hope to the world around us.

December 18 – 4 Reasons to Be Happy at Christmas

THE MOVIES portray happy Christmas scenes. Snow falls, children make snow angels, and **we sing carols around the fire**. Advertisers want us to picture the joy their products will provide when given as Christmas gifts. A car bedecked with a giant ribbon, that new computer, or **a simple cup of coffee steaming against a Christmassy backdrop**. The reality is that Christmas can be stressful. Family flareups, too many visitors, and **worrying about paying the bills** can pummel our joy. The Bible gives us **4 Reasons to Be Happy at Christmas**.

Proverbs 17:22 says it will **cure our ills**. "A joyful heart is good medicine ..."

James 1:17 assures us we will receive the **gift of happiness**. "Every good gift and every perfect gift is from above, coming down from the Father of lights, with whom there is no variation or shadow due to change."

Isaiah 11:1 tells us we are the **fruit of Christ's labors**. "There shall come forth a shoot from the stump of Jesse, and a branch from his roots shall bear fruit."

John 1:5 says we have **received new life** through the Son of God. "The light shines in the darkness, and the darkness has not overcome it."

Robert Flatt is known for his inspirational quotes. Here's a favorite: "The giving of gifts is not something man invented. God started the giving spree when He gave a gift beyond words, the unspeakable gift of His Son."

We can choose to let our holiday season be governed by forces outside our control, or *we can choose to enjoy a happy Christmas*. **God started the gifts. Let's continue the tradition.** When we share our happiness, we'll have more left over than we started with.

December 19 – Christmas Card from Jesus

BROWSE THE holiday rack at the greeting card counter. Mother's Day, birthdays, Thanksgiving ... ah, **there's the Christmas cards**. They are bright and colorful, among the best on the rack. Rudolph, Santa, a snowfall, even a **glitter-painted Christmas scene**. Then look, that one lights up when you open it, **a color-spattered tree with presents underneath**.

What would our Christmas card from Jesus look like? What would the Master write inside? What would he say to us during the holiday festivities that **surround the celebration of his birth?** It might read something like this: "Faith makes all things possible; Hope makes all things work; Love makes all things beautiful; May you have all the three for this Christmas. Merry Christmas."

The Reverend Richard J. Fairchild of the United Church of Canada says it like this: "May the hope, the peace, the joy, and the love represented by the birth in Bethlehem this night fill our lives and become part of all that we say and do."

Romans 15:13 says it this way: "May the God of hope fill you with all joy and peace in believing, so that by the power of the Holy Spirit you may abound in hope."

Christmas *isn't just the cards*, no matter how beautiful. It isn't the gifts or the tree, although the traditions we have certainly **carry on that first Christmas gift** when God gave us his Son. Christmas is about **finding faith in Jesus**, about the **hope that comes from our trust** in him, and the **love we learn to share** with everyone we meet. Christmas is about becoming more like Christ. It's our once-a-year reminder that we have been given something **bigger than ourselves**, and we can **become better than we were**.

Let's consider the words of C.S. Lewis, renowned author: "Once in our world, a stable had something in it that was bigger than our whole world."

The love of Jesus is bigger than we can imagine. There's no end to it. When we share the love of Christ, **there's more than enough to go around**. Christmas is about love. Let's practice it today.

December 20 – **The Good of Christmas**

WHAT'S GOOD about Christmas?

Everything, you say. It's all *perfect, wonderful, and joyous.* Setting up the tree! *How fun!* Cooking for a month! *Exciting!* Midnight gift-wrapping sessions! *Joy!* Clearing the after-Christmas debris! *Oh, boy!* Paying the bills! *Yea!*

Once again, *what's good about Christmas?* Psalm 117 says *lots.* "Praise the Lord, all nations! Extol him, all peoples! For great is his steadfast love toward us, and the faithfulness of the Lord endures forever. Praise the Lord!"

John 1:9-10 tells us we have *received the true light.* "The true light, which gives light to everyone, was coming into the world. He was in the world, and the world was made through him, yet the world did not know him."

Galatians 4:4-5 says we have *access to God's Son*. "But when the fullness of time had come, God sent forth his Son, born of woman, born under the law, to redeem those who were under the law, so that we might receive adoption as sons."

Isaiah 9:6 is our gift of *an honored companion*. "For to us a child is born, to us a son is given; and the government shall be upon his shoulder, and his name shall be called Wonderful Counselor, Mighty God, Everlasting Father, Prince of Peace."

Acts 5:31 guarantees us *forgiveness of sin*. "God exalted him at his right hand as Leader and Savior, to give repentance to Israel and forgiveness of sins."

You were right. ***Everything is good about Christmas.*** Here's our new list: God's steadfast Love. The Light of Truth. The Gift of God's Son. A Companion greater than all companions. New Life in the Father through Jesus his Son.

To understand Christmas from God's perspective, *we are loved, we are loved, **we are loved***. When we rejoice in Christmas, let's keep Jesus at the center of the holiday.

December 21 – You Have Found Favor with God

DOES GOD APPROVE of us? That's a valid question, but there's *an even deeper one* we must consider. How can we know? What device can we use to *measure whether God places us* in the acceptable zone? Guesswork isn't acceptable, not when the outcome of our life's choices makes such a difference once we cross death's threshold from this life to the next.

Why can't God just *tell us when we do something* right? You know, words *spoken aloud*, in the air, directly into our ear?

Sometimes he does.

Luke 1:30-31 begins the Christmas story even *before the conception of Jesus*. "And the angel said to her, 'Do not be afraid, Mary, for you have found favor with God. And behold, you will conceive in your womb and bear a son, and you shall call his name Jesus.' "

Martin Luther, German monk and principle figure in the Reformation, *echoes the words of Luke*. "Good news from heaven the angels bring, Glad tidings to the earth they sing: To us this day a child is given, To crown us with the joy of heaven."

John R. Rice, Baptist evangelist, *says it like this:* "You can never

281

truly enjoy Christmas until you can look up into the Father's face and tell Him you have received His Christmas gift."

We are God's creation, his children, and the *heirs of all he has*. His approval came in the birth of Christ. **God loves us.** Totally. ***Without reserve.*** It's time for us to choose to love him in return. That's the reminder that is Christmas. God sacrificed his Son, sending him to earth to live in human form, so that *we would know his eternal love*. ***What greater favor could God show than that?***

Jesus is our model. Living better through him is our goal.

December 22 – **And Then … There Was Jesus**

WHAT WOULD OUR lives be like without Jesus in the world? That's right. If Christmas were a *dream in an unknown eye*, no more than *wishful thinking* about what might have been, how would the world be different? *Where would the holes in our morality be?* What would happen to loving others as much as we love ourselves? Would the world tremble and shake with the disasters about to overtake it? **Thanks be to God that didn't happen.** We don't have to wonder where we would be.

John 1:14 gives us the *glorious start of all that was good* two thousand years ago. "And the Word became flesh and dwelt among us, and we have seen his glory, glory as of the only Son from the Father, full of grace and truth."

This Christmas, as we gather around our light-bedecked tree and prepare to open our brightly wrapped packages, let's pause and express our thanks for *three awe-inspiringly wonderful things Jesus' birth* allows us to experience.

Awe-Inspiring Experience No. 1: God became flesh, appearing in a *real and tangible way* to humanity.

Awe-Inspiring Experience No. 2: God lived among humanity *in the person of Jesus*, truly experiencing the trauma of what it is to be human.

Awe-Inspiring Experience No. 3: God through Jesus *let his glory shine* despite the mind-breaking muck of the human condition.

Charles Spurgeon, renowned Baptist minister, said: "And when the Lord Jesus has become your peace, remember, there is another thing: good will towards men. Do not try to keep Christmas without good will towards men."

When you decide to follow Christ, *your life will make a dramatic change.*

And then … there was Jesus.

You become a new person in him, and you *see and treat others with the concern* Jesus showed during his time on the earth.

Christmas is about Jesus, our example how to live for the good of everyone around us, not only us.

December 23 – **Stepping Into God's Future**

WHAT NEXT, God, we want to know. That's what we ask when we feel God's prompting evaporate. *You know what I mean.* We feel God's direction to give a huge check in the missionary offering, then the next week the *water pump on the car* goes out.

Then the *fridge starts spitting out ice* when we're not around.

And we find *a water leak in the yard* … just bubbling, bubbling, bubbling.

What next, God? It becomes our cry of frustration. *We gave a sizable check, and now this? God!* **Are you up there?**

Let's look to the shepherds when Jesus was born.

Luke 2:15 reveals a familiar situation. "When the angels went away from them into heaven, the shepherds said to one another, 'Let us go over to Bethlehem and see this thing that has happened, which the Lord has made known to us.' "

Here's what we can take from this verse:

Revelation No. 1: The shepherds, men of no note or importance, were visited by celestial beings of divine royalty. Think how they must have felt in that moment, how special, how connected to God.

Revelation No. 2: Then they were abandoned. The angels went away, leaving the shepherds in the dark, surrounded by smelly, bleating sheep. The shepherds surely smelled about the same.

Revelation No. 3: The shepherds didn't sit around and moan about it. They said, "Let's get up and do something." And they did.

When bad things seem to happen to us, we're not abandoned by God. He's waiting on us to *get up and do something*. That's right. Call the repairman. Take a part-time job. Ask for help. **Whatever fits your situation, just do something.** You'll be stepping into the future God has prepared for you.

A favorite greeting from a long-ago Christmas card says: "May your Christmas be filled with joy and gratitude because of all that Christ has given you."

When Christ is in our heart, we'll live in God's will and find joy in every part of our day.

December 24 – **Christmas Wisdom**

AH, CHRISTMAS EVE. *The night before Christmas when all through the house, not a creature was stirring ...* Oops, wrong story. That one's about a fat man in a red suit about to come down the chimney. Let's talk about a *baby boy about to be born into a rough-and-tumble manger* in the back room of an inn. Before we do, let's spend some time with a woman who, through the wisdom of God, became *one of the mightiest forces for good* on planet earth.

Mother Teresa, in her gentle and quiet voice, said: "At this Christmas when Christ comes, will He find a warm heart? Mark the season of Advent by loving and serving the others with God's own love and concern."

Ah, such sweet holiday sentiment. What a nice thing to say for Christmas. Then, a week later it's January 1, we shift into high gear, and Christmas is forgotten. *God says that's not how it works.* Mother Teresa echoes God's voice. Here's what's important about Mother Teresa's Christmas benediction:

1. We must have a warm heart. That's means we have *concern for others, emotionally, financially, and socially.*

2. We show that concern by volunteering in Christian charities that *help the poor and destitute.*

3. We show the love of Christ with smiles, hugs, and our pocketbook *even after Christmas is boxed up* and set on a shelf.

When we take on this level of love, we begin to *change the world*. It's like Ralph W. Sockman, senior pastor of Christ Church in New York City, once said: "The hinge of history is on the door of a Bethlehem stable."

Let's end with the proclamation found in Luke 2:14: "Glory to God in the highest, and on earth peace among those with whom he is pleased!"

God is great and greatly to be praised.

December 25 – **The Joy of Christmas Day**

WE HAVE A holiday song we sometimes sing. It starts like this: *Oh, the weather outside is frightful, but the fire is so delightful ...* Those words translate to more than *cold* and *snow* and the *warmth of a fire*. Certainly, we're singing about those quantifiable things, but the *essence we pull from them* is so much more. *It's family, companionship, and feeling like we're a part of something greater than we are.*

Here's a greeting card benediction that *warms the heart:* "May your heart be lifted in praise this Christmas for the wonderful gift of Jesus and the joy He brings to our lives. Have a wonderful Christmas and a blessed New Year!" *That's today.* **Christmas.** Our praise is lifted for Jesus. Certainly, we enjoy the smiles on our children's faces and the excited rush of opening presents to discover what's inside, but the core thread tying it together is the *birth of the Savior.*

Let's not forget Luke 2:16: "And they went with haste and found Mary and Joseph, and the baby lying in a manger." Without that *first gift from God,* that of *Jesus in a manger,* we **wouldn't have all the rest**.

W.J. Cameron, journalist and often-quoted author, said: "There has been only one Christmas – the rest are anniversaries."

If you showed up for your parent's anniversary party, ate cake, enjoyed the dancing, and even exchanged presents with your siblings *yet never acknowledged your parents in the same room* … well … we'd just *never do that.* **Never.** Not in a million years.

Christmas is about Jesus. Let's join in the festivities and not forget that *Jesus is in the room.* **The party is all about him.**

Jesus is THE REASON for the SEASON. Merry Christmas!

December 26 – 3 Means to Overcome the After-Christmas Blahs

COMING UP SHORT after Christmas? Are you emotionally empty, *your tank drained dry?* Have the holiday festivities taken everything from you, and there's just nothing left? Your enthusiasm has fallen in the gutter, your smile is barely painted on, and *why, oh why did I spend so much money!* Ouch! You've got the after-Christmas blahs. **God says to shake it off!** He has a better thing for you. You can move forward into the blessings of God if you *choose to do what he says.* Joshua 1:8 tells you three things you can do to *climb out of your holiday slump.* "This Book of the Law shall not depart from your mouth, but you shall meditate on it day and night, so that you may be careful to do according to all that is written in it. For then you will make your way prosperous, and then you will have good success." You can start up the ladder to better days. You can put your face into the sunlight.

You can begin today.

The First Rung on Our Ladder to Better Things: Plan a convenient Bible reading time. Be consistent. Earlier in the day is better so

285

you can think about what it says throughout the day.

The Second Rung on Our Ladder to Better Things: Practice what you read. Be kind to others. Share the message of Christ. Live like Jesus would want you to live.

The Third Rung on Our Ladder to Better Things: Step into God's prosperity. You will be showered with success when you read the Bible and do what it says.

Don't be blue. Refuse to let Christmas bills get you down. *Step away from situations that throttle your joy in life.* Your smile can be real. Your time with Jesus will lift your spirit. ***Your success in God will have you walking in the sunshine every day of the week.***

Our triumph over the blahs comes through Jesus when we place our trust in him.

December 27 – God's Reward for Honesty

WHAT'S SO GREAT about being honest? Take politics, for example. You already know what I mean. Who can be a good politician **if they have to tell the truth all the time?** Then there's the doctor. Tell a patient the bad news, or sugarcoat it? That's right. **You'll die tomorrow, sorry, now you get to pay your bill. Ouch!** We want to soften the message, make it better, especially if we're talking to a 4-year-old. Or a business associate. Or just about anyone we like and care about.

Wait right there! God says we **can't afford to create our own storyline**. The truth is never something to cast aside. Once we start down that slippery slope, it becomes a wild ride to the bottom, and the crash landing is a momentous disaster. Isaiah 33:15-16 gives us **six actions that show honesty and four rewards God gives us**.

Honesty Action No. 1: "He who **walks righteously** …" We must obey God's rules in all situations.

Honesty Action No. 2: "And **speaks uprightly** …" We must tell the truth in kindness and with empathy.

Honesty Action No. 3: "Who **despises the gain of oppress-sions** …" We must consider the motivation and not just the result.

Honesty Action No. 4: "Who **shakes his hands, lest they hold a bribe** …" We must not associate with wicked people.

Honesty Action No. 5: "Who **stops his ears from hearing of bloodshed** …" We must not focus on worldly events that bring us to despair.

Honesty Action No. 6: "And **shuts his eyes from looking on**

286

evil ..." We must avoid sordid tales or situations.

Let's get excited, because here's the good part. **Our honesty brings on God's reward. Here's what we receive when we lift ourselves to God's standard**.

Honesty Reward No. 1: "He will **dwell on the heights** ..." We will rise above our worldly problems.

Honesty Reward No. 2: "His place of defense will be **the fortresses of rocks** ..." God's mighty hand will defeat those who oppose us.

Honesty Reward No. 3: "His **bread will be given him** ..." God will meet our physical needs.

Honesty Reward No. 4: "His **water will be sure**." Our emotional and spiritual welfare are secure in God's hands.

There's everything great about being honest. From how we live to how we interact with others, God notices, and he rewards our faithfulness to his standards. Honesty combined with kindness makes for a more excellent life.

December 28 – Putting On Our Robe of Righteousness

CHOOSING WHAT to wear each day is a choice. We all get to make it. For business, perhaps a suit. Jeans to work in the yard, and a swimsuit for a day at the beach. To wear the wrong thing sends a message that **we don't have it together**. We are not on par with the "best" people. We have yet to **"figure out"** what society's expectations are.

Flip-flops with a business suit? **Not okay**. Sunglasses in church? **Toss them away**. Fancy-dress shoes to mow the lawn? **What were you thinking?** Yet Christians do this all the time. We dress for success in Jesus and listen to an off-color joke. Or we shortchange the waiter. Or we *cut someone off in traffic*.

It's not the same, you say. **Not true.** Our clothes are how we present ourselves to the world. If a teacher shows up in a speckled painter's jumper, where's the professionalism? If a farmer wears designer jewelry and fashionable wingtips, how will he portray his skill in the field? If a Christian stops for a drink at the bar, **what does the world read into our commitment to Jesus?**

Here are five passages from Psalms that tell us how we can put on our robe of righteousness.

Psalm 84:11 tells us: "For the Lord God is a sun and shield; the Lord bestows favor and honor. No good thing does he withhold from

287

those who walk uprightly."

Psalm 34:10 says: "The young lions suffer want and hunger; but those who seek the Lord lack no good thing."

Psalm 58:11 reminds us: "Mankind will say, 'Surely there is a reward for the righteous; surely there is a God who judges on earth.'"

Psalm 5:12 promises: "For you bless the righteous, O Lord; you cover him with favor as with a shield."

Psalm 23:6 offers us focus: "Surely goodness and mercy shall follow me all the days of my life, and I shall dwell in the house of the Lord forever."

To sum it up:

- We must live by God's standards.
- We must study the Word.
- We must slice all wrongdoing from our day.
- We must depend on God for our strength.
- We must trust in God to bless us in all things.

God wants us to be consistent, to be **true to his rulebook**, to follow the precepts **set out in the Bible**. It's not hard. As Harold Herring of the Debt Free Army says, **"Read the Bible. Do what it says."**

We are dressed in Christ when we follow the Word.

December 29 – 2 Guidelines about Truthfulness

WE CAN TALK about truthfulness, about saying what's there, **telling it like it is**, in other words, being plain and upfront. "State your case," we demand, and we expect it to **be the truth**.

On the other hand, we can discuss lies, people who dissemble, backtrack, and try to **lay it on thick**. If we can make our own reality, then life is better all around.

There's a reason courtroom rules require someone to **tell the truth, the whole truth, and nothing but the truth**. Colossians 3:9-10 says: "Do not lie to one another, seeing that you have put off the old self with its practices and have put on the new self, which is being renewed in knowledge after the image of its creator."

This passage is as bold as it gets. We are told in no uncertain terms **how we are to live as Christians**. *Stop lying.* Even the little stuff. **Cut it out.** *It doesn't work for the Christian.* Even the little white ones that we think keep from hurting other's feelings. **Don't say them.** As the courts say, the whole truth and nothing but the truth.

It's tough. Our society says differently. Don't tell Wanda she wasn't invited because her husband left her. Say instead that the invitation must have been lost in the mail. **Wrong, wrong, wrong.** Here's what God's Word says: "Seeing that you have put off the old self with its practices …"

White lies might have seemed okay before we came to Christ, but they **can't be excused now**. **Don't do it.** Here are our *2 Guidelines about Truthfulness* from the Word of God.

Guideline No. 1: Lies are not okay at any time.

Guideline No. 2: They are still not okay at any time.

There. That sums it up. Let's tell the truth, the whole truth, and nothing but the truth. We are to live Jesus' example in everything we say and do.

December 30 – 7 Signs God Has You Under His Protection

SIGNS ARE universal. Some are handwritten, a note on the fridge that says to take out the trash. Others dictate our speed on the freeway, which direction to turn, or whether we have a fast food option in the next town. Browse a hardware store, and you'll find signs you can purchase for all occasions. Here are **7 signs that God has you under his protection**.

Enter Here. Proverbs 18:10 says God **holds the door for you**. Just come inside. "The name of the Lord is a strong tower; the righteous man runs into it and is safe."

Exit. Psalm 34:7 says you have **a way of escape** when you trust in God. "The angel of the Lord encamps around those who fear him, and delivers them."

This Area Under Video Surveillance. 2 Chronicles 16:9 says **nothing good escapes God's attention**. "For the eyes of the Lord run to and fro throughout the whole earth, to give strong support to those whose heart is blameless toward him. You have done foolishly in this, for from now on you will have wars."

Safe Zone. Psalm 121:7-8 says you are **under God's protection**, and nothing can hurt you there. "The Lord will keep you from all evil; he will keep your life. The Lord will keep your going out and your coming in from this time forth and forevermore."

Quiet Zone. Proverbs 3:24 says the hubbub of the world **can't disturb your rest** in Jesus. "If you lie down, you will not be afraid; when you lie down, your sleep will be sweet."

Beware of Dog. 1 Peter 3:13 says that you have a guardian willing to **protect you from danger**. "Now who is there to harm you if you are zealous for what is good?"

Welcome Home. Deuteronomy 33:12 says you have a dwelling place in the Lord, a **respite from your situation**, and a protecting arm around you. "… The beloved of the Lord dwells in safety. The High God surrounds him all day long, and dwells between his shoulders."

The next time you see a sign, **make a connection to God**. Let it renew your faith in **God's love and concern for your wellbeing**. God loves you. Every sign you see tells you so.

December 31 – **9 Guarantees of God's Peace**

LIFE CAN SOMETIMES feel like riding a roller coaster without brakes or being in a clothes dryer with the heat on high. Our first mistake is to forget that on the other side of the storm, the **sun is still shining**. God doesn't disappear just because we're going through a bit of trouble. Here are **9 Guarantees of God's Peace** no matter how desperate we might feel.

Colossians 3:15 says: "And let the peace of Christ rule in your hearts, to which indeed you were called in one body. And be thankful."

Psalm 85:8 says: "Let me hear what God the Lord will speak, for he will speak peace to his people, to his saints; but let them not turn back to folly."

Philippians 4:7 says: "And the peace of God, which surpasses all understanding, will guard your hearts and your minds in Christ Jesus."

Isaiah 32:17 says: "And the effect of righteousness will be peace, and the result of righteousness, quietness and trust forever."

Luke 7:50 says: "And he said to the woman, 'Your faith has saved you; go in peace.' "

Psalm 37:37 says: "Mark the blameless and behold the upright, for there is a future for the man of peace."

Isaiah 57:19 says: " '… Peace, peace, to the far and to the near,' says the Lord, 'and I will heal him.' "

2 Thessalonians 3:16 says: "Now may the Lord of peace himself give you peace at all times in every way. The Lord be with you all."

John 14:27 says: "Peace I leave with you; my peace I give to you. Not as the world gives do I give to you. Let not your hearts be troubled, neither let them be afraid."

Our internal peace isn't dependent on our circumstances. Our peace is determined by **our trust in God to be with us** in every situation. Hold God's hand. He's the peacemaker in the storm.

January 1 – **8 Road Signs to Guide Your Way**

TRAVELING BY THE SEAT of our pants is a foolhardy venture. Every corner, every intersection, every opportunity to veer to one side or the other is a fresh misdirection waiting to happen. Our rescue comes in following the highway signs along the way. We look for street names, highway designations, even directions to the airport or a favorite restaurant. Each time we're reassured we are on the right track.

Let's look at 8 road signs God has placed in his Word.

One Way. Isaiah 30:21 says we will find our way when we listen to God's voice. "And your ears shall hear a word behind you, saying, 'This is the way, walk in it,' when you turn to the right or when you turn to the left."

No U Turn. Psalm 48:14 says no other road will carry us home. "… This is God, our God forever and ever. He will guide us forever."

Pedestrian Crossing. Proverbs 16:9 says we can step out only with God's help. "The heart of man plans his way, but the Lord establishes his steps."

Men at Work. Psalm 37:23 says to stay alert. Our fellow Christians are our priority. "The steps of a man are established by the Lord, when he delights in his way;"

Speed Limit 5. Isaiah 28:26 says we need to pay attention to God's teachable moments "For he is rightly instructed; his God teaches him."

Falling Rocks. Proverbs 11:5 says our choices will help us avoid danger. "The righteousness of the blameless keeps his way straight, but the wicked falls by his own wickedness."

Keep Right. Proverbs 3:6 says there is a right way to live in the eyes of God. "In all your ways acknowledge him, and he will make straight your paths."

Deer Crossing. Isaiah 42:16 says there are unexpected obstacles we can't predict. "And I will lead the blind in a way that they do not know, in paths that they have not known I will guide them. I will turn the darkness before them into light, the rough places into level

291

ground. These are the things I do, and I do not forsake them."

Whether we use a map, turn on our GPS, or simply look for the signs at the side of the road, we will get there safer when we pay attention. The same is true of our Christian walk. When we follow God's road signs, our success in him is assured.

When God says now, it's our time to move forward.

www.ingramcontent.com/pod-product-compliance
Lightning Source LLC
Chambersburg PA
CBHW051816090426
42736CB00011B/1506